THE WATERGATE GIRL

THE WATERGATE GIRL

My Fight for Truth and Justice
Against a Criminal President

JILL WINE-BANKS

HENRY HOLT AND COMPANY

NEW YORK

Henry Holt and Company
Publishers since 1866
120 Broadway
New York, New York 10271
www.henryholt.com

Henry Holt® and 🏢® are registered trademarks of Macmillan
Publishing Group, LLC.

Library of Congress Cataloging-in-Publication Data

Names: Wine-Banks, Jill, author.
Title: The Watergate girl : my fight for truth and justice against a
    criminal president / Jill Wine-Banks.
Description: First edition. | New York : Henry Holt and Company,
    2020. | Includes bibliographical references and index.
Identifiers: LCCN 2019048190 (print) | LCCN 2019048191 (ebook) |
    ISBN 9781250244321 (hardcover) | ISBN 9781250244314 (ebook)
Subjects: LCSH: Wine-Banks, Jill. | Lawyers—United States—
    Biography. | Watergate Affair, 1972–1974. | Nixon, Richard M.
    (Richard Milhous), 1913–1994—Impeachment. | United States—
    Politics and government—1969–1974.
Classification: LCC KF373.W512 A3 2020 (print) | LCC KF373.W512
    (ebook) | DDC 973.924092 [B]—dc23
LC record available at https://lccn.loc.gov/2019048190
LC ebook record available at https://lccn.loc.gov/2019048191

Our books may be purchased in bulk for promotional,
educational, or business use. Please contact your local
bookseller or the Macmillan Corporate and Premium Sales
Department at (800) 221-7945, extension 5442, or by email at
MacmillanSpecialMarkets@macmillan.com.

First Edition 2020

Designed by Meryl Sussman Levavi

Printed in the United States of America

1   3   5   7   9   10   8   6   4   2

For my husband, Michael Banks,
who brings laughter, adventure, joy, passion,
and love into my life every day

CONTENTS

Prologue   1

1. Joining the Team   7

2. Archie and the Gang   14

3. The Watergate Boy   26

4. Nine Conversations   39

5. Saturday Night Fever   50

6. The Morning After   62

7. Secretary of Morale   78

8. The Lady Lawyer   87

9. Kurt   97

10. The Days of Wine and Rose   107

11. Two Ladies Arguing   121

12. To Indict or Not   134

13. The Road Map   145

14. Indictment   156

15. Exit the King   172

16. The Trial   184

17. After Watergate   202

18. No Fear of Flying   212

Epilogue   225

A Note on Sources   239

Acknowledgments   241

Index   247

THE WATERGATE GIRL

PROLOGUE

Washington, DC
November 27, 1973

I didn't think I was nervous, but I could barely breathe.

President Richard Nixon's secretary Rose Mary Woods was on the stand in US District Court demonstrating how she accidentally erased eighteen and a half minutes from a key White House tape in the Watergate case—wiping out a conversation between the embattled president and one of his top aides just three days after the suspicious break-in at the Democratic National Committee headquarters.

The clunky Uher Universal tape recorder and headphones from Rose's White House office sat on the ledge of the witness box. A pedal that let her stop and start the machine with her foot rested on the floor. The bright, high-ceilinged courtroom, its wood-paneled walls burnished with years of crime and punishment, overflowed with lawyers, journalists, and spectators. From the bench, Judge John J. Sirica regarded me with a knowing expression. I felt he saw right through me. My face flushed, broadcasting my youth and vulnerability.

The previous day, Rose had testified that she was in the middle of transcribing the tape from June 20, 1972, when the phone rang at the far end of her desk, and she answered the call while keeping her foot on the pedal. *That*, she said, must have erased the president's recorded conversation, replacing it with a steady hum.

I asked her to demonstrate. She pushed the Start button on her machine and placed her sturdy black pump on the pedal. The crowd fell silent as the blank demonstration tape began to whir.

"What did you do after the phone rang?" I asked her, trying to keep my voice level.

Rose glared at me. At fifty-five, she was nearly twice my age, petite but fierce, dressed that day in a color-blocked turquoise, chartreuse, and orange sheath topped with a strand of pearls. A gold cross glinted from a ring on her right hand. "I had to take those off first," she said in a hostile tone, delicately pointing to the headphones resting on the ledge. With that slight movement of her fingers, her foot lifted from the pedal.

The tape stopped cold.

Even if she'd mistakenly pushed Record instead of Stop, releasing the foot pedal when she answered the phone would have halted the tape and there would be no eighteen-and-a-half-minute gap.

Rose had lied, and I had caught her.

The crowd gasped and a tsunami of journalists rushed from the courtroom, headed for the bank of pay phones in the hall.

"But I did it that way in my office. It worked there," Rose stammered.

"Then maybe we should continue the demonstration in your office," I proposed. Amazingly, neither her lawyer nor those representing President Nixon objected to this suggestion.

In the five and a half months leading up to this day, I'd been working sixteen-hour stints as one of three trial lawyers—and the only woman—on the Watergate special prosecutor's obstruction of justice and cover-up task force. We were investigating whether Nixon and his closest aides had obstructed the investigation of the June 17, 1972, break-in at the headquarters of the Democratic National Committee in the elegant Watergate complex in DC's Foggy Bottom neighborhood. Five burglars, the man who recruited them, and the mastermind had been caught, and their connection to the White House and Nixon's Committee to Re-elect the President had been made clear by the sleuthing of the *Washington Post*'s Bob Woodward and Carl Bernstein, by Judge Sirica's persistent questioning during the burglary trial, and by the US Senate probe of the scandal that had been underway since May.

Rose's testimony was the culmination of an astonishing battle in the courts. Just four months earlier, we and the nation learned that Nixon had secretly taped every conversation in the Oval Office and his ancillary office in the nearby Executive Office Building. We immediately subpoenaed nine tapes that we believed, on the basis of White House calendars and visitor logs, as well as grand jury testimony, included discussion of the Watergate break-in. Nixon stonewalled turning over the tapes until October, when public outrage forced him to acquiesce. A week after agreeing to give us the tapes, however, his lawyers stunned us with a claim that two were missing. A wary Judge Sirica ordered a public hearing that ended with an order for Nixon to deliver the seven tapes that he acknowledged having in his possession. Soon afterward, before we received any of the tapes, Nixon's lawyers revealed a problem in a third tape, the one from June 20 that recorded a conversation between the president and his chief of staff, H. R. Haldeman, three days after the break-in. For eighteen minutes and thirty seconds of that conversation, the tape simply buzzed and clicked.

Unlocking the mystery of that gap was the reason for Rose Mary Woods's testimony today. The White House said there was no innocent explanation and that only Rose could answer for the gap.

After court adjourned, I took a taxi to 1600 Pennsylvania Avenue to see Rose demonstrate her testimony one more time, without a court reporter and with only the White House photographer to record it. In Rose's office, I was astounded to see a large crowd, including a gaggle of lawyers, the wife of one of Rose's lawyers, and a friend of Rose's from New York who was identified simply as "Miss Val." The White House photographer snapped Rose as she contorted her body to reach the phone at one end of her desk while holding down the foot pedal of her tape recorder at the other end with her left foot. It was a tortuous position that would have been impossible to maintain for one minute, let alone for eighteen. Forever afterward it would be derisively known as the Rose Mary Stretch.

If there were any doubts that Rose had lied earlier in court, the pictures laid them to rest. And yet I felt sorry for her. When the image of her ridiculous stretch was spread across America's front pages and mocked in editorial cartoons in the following days, Rose became the butt of a national joke. I saw something of myself in the president's trim, copper-haired secretary, in the way we'd both had to survive in a world of men who'd often bullied and belittled us.

I felt sympathy for her, too, because the president had abandoned her. He let her be blamed for the eighteen-and-a-half-minute gap.

My picture also was in the papers the next morning, smiling in my miniskirt and tall boots as I hailed a taxi outside the White House after Rose's demonstration. But the flush of success caught by the photographers vanished when I arrived home late that night. As soon as I left the garage behind my brick town house on 20th Street NW, I saw the back door ajar. A cold fear spread through my body, but, as is typical for me, I didn't hesitate to walk into a potentially dangerous situation. I entered the kitchen, picked up the phone, and called the police. As soon as they arrived, I searched the house. Some canceled checks were missing from the antique desk in the basement, as was a safety deposit key that I kept in an unlocked metal box. Upstairs, a new green velvet pantsuit I'd laid out on the bed had vanished, along with a few inexpensive baubles from my dresser. In a panic now, I ran to the attic, where I had stashed copies of documents from the Watergate investigation in a brown cardboard box, a hedge against our office being shut down. The documents were exactly where I'd left them. Relieved, I spoke to the police.

After their initial search, one of the responding officers asked if he could use our phone to call the DC Mobile Crime Lab to dust for fingerprints. When he hung up, he casually mentioned that he thought there was some strange resistance on the line in my kitchen. "It's as if the phone has been tapped," he said. The next day, an FBI agent confirmed the cop's suspicion, but told me that the tap had been removed. Apparently there had been a previous break-in I was completely unaware of! Nothing had been taken from my house the first time, however. The entire episode was a frightening echo of the Watergate break-in. And though I knew it had to be a different group of criminals—the Watergate burglars were in prison—I couldn't shake the feeling that I, too, was a victim of White House dirty tricks.

What were the burglars seeking from my phone? Evidence from the special prosecutor's investigation? If so, they were out of luck. I was seldom home, and when I was, I was careful never to discuss confidential Watergate matters on the phone. But that hardly eased my mind.

I had other secrets, deeply personal ones, that I was desperate to keep.

JOINING THE TEAM

It was nine in the morning on Friday, May 25, 1973, the start of Memorial Day weekend, with the sun blazing through my bedroom windows and the sky beyond a bright, cloudless blue. In deference to the heat and a long-planned weekend trip, I put on a cotton miniskirt in a lilac floral print, a matching scoop-necked top, and beige kitten heels. Thick humidity had turned my blond hair limp, so I hid it under a pixie-style Dynel wig. I didn't look much like a hard-charging prosecutor, but I was neat and pulled together, ready for the most important job interview of my life.

My parents and brother, who'd flown in from Chicago the night before, were waiting downstairs in the living room with my husband, Ian Volner. We were headed to Colonial Williamsburg for a three-day holiday, but a call the previous day had added a stop on our way—at the Watergate special prosecutor's office.

We drove for ten minutes from our town house on 20th Street to a nondescript concrete-and-glass building at 1425 K Street NW. It sat on the edge of DC's red-light district, a tawdry grid of flophouses, neon-lit strip clubs, and dive bars, and a world away from the broad malls and stately, ornamented architecture of official Washington.

Ian parked the car, and I went inside. I took the elevator to the ninth floor and passed through security before being directed to a small office, where a dignified dark-haired man sat with the sleeves of his white shirt rolled up, studying documents at a wooden desk. He was James Vorenberg, a Harvard law professor; his friend and colleague Archibald Cox, the newly appointed Watergate special prosecutor, had brought him to Washington to help assemble a staff.

Vorenberg had asked to see me on the recommendation of Charles Ruff, my boss at the US Department of Justice, where I had been hired four and a half years earlier, straight out of Columbia Law School, becoming the first female attorney in the Organized Crime and Labor Racketeering Section. While still in my twenties, I traveled the nation arguing appeals, conducting grand jury investigations, and prosecuting and winning cases against some of the wiliest criminals in America. In every proceeding, I was the only woman lawyer up against seasoned male attorneys, who were bewildered by a "girl" in their ranks and had no clue how to treat me. I responded to their confusion and outright disdain by committing myself to tireless work, impeccable preparation, and steeliness during cross-examination. The long-term payoff was an excellent record, though my first two cases resulted in mistrials, starting in Alaska where I assisted Chuck Ruff in the prosecution of the powerful local teamster boss Jesse Carr, which ended when a juror's mother fell ill. In Boston I second-chaired the trial of the boxing promoter Sam Silverman for fixing fights and sparred—verbally—with the legendary Sugar Ray Robinson, a character witness for Sam. That trial concluded with a hung jury. From there, however, I went on to win a perjury conviction against two mob hit men in San Francisco and a spate of racketeering convictions against corrupt labor leaders in Detroit.

Archibald Cox had been appointed special prosecutor a week earlier by Attorney General Elliot Richardson, but he had started work only the day before my interview. He had decided to organize the office into a legal counsel's group and five task forces to investigate alleged misdeeds by the Nixon White House. One task force would look at illegal activity by the "plumbers" unit created by the White House to stop leaks, such as that of the Pentagon Papers. Another would explore the "dirty tricks" used to foil Nixon's rivals, including forging a letter under the name of Senator Edmund Muskie of Maine, a candidate for the 1972 Democratic presidential nomination, which defamed the state's French Canadians and hurt his candidacy. A third task force would prosecute illegal contributions to Nixon's presidential campaign, and a fourth would consider the president's interference in the antitrust prosecution of ITT Corporation. I was interviewing for the fifth and largest task force, the group that would investigate the Watergate cover-up and obstruction of justice.

I had heard that Cox was looking for smart, talented lawyers with good judgment, who were young and vigorous enough to endure crushingly long days and high-stakes pressure. And he needed them yesterday.

Like the rest of the nation, I'd been gripped by the Watergate scandal from the moment—less than a year earlier—when news broke of a group of men in business suits and surgical gloves, carrying fancy cameras and hundred-dollar bills, who were caught breaking into the Democratic Party's headquarters. I'd followed the stunning reporting on the case by Bob

Woodward and Carl Bernstein, of the *Washington Post*, with awe and a touch of wistfulness. My original ambition had been to be a journalist, and I still thought of news reporters as shining protectors of democracy. I'd been a news junkie for as long as I could remember. I majored in journalism at the University of Illinois at Urbana-Champaign, and as the chapter president of my sorority, Iota Alpha Pi, I started a rotation among the freshman pledges: every night at dinner one of them had to stand up and deliver a summary of the day's headlines.

The pioneering and glamorous TV journalist Nancy Dickerson was my idol. I met her when she spoke to the group of freshmen being honored for our achievement in campus activities. At the start of her career in the early 1950s, Dickerson had turned down a job as the women's editor of the *Washington Daily News* because, as she wrote in her memoir *Among Those Present*, she wanted to change the world and it was impossible to do that writing "shopping and food columns." She went on to cover Martin Luther King Jr.'s "I Have a Dream" speech and the assassination of President John F. Kennedy. I, too, wanted to avoid the so-called women's pages. Before meeting her, most of the working women I knew were teachers and social workers. Dickerson made me see other possibilities.

I got the idea that a law degree would be a stepping-stone to serious journalism from a book I read for a political science class, *Gideon's Trumpet* by Anthony Lewis of the *New York Times*. When I read on the back of the book—about a landmark case involving the rights of defendants to counsel—that Lewis had attended Harvard Law School I decided, not very logically, that law school would help me in journalism, too.

I hated my first year at Columbia Law and took a leave to

try working in journalism. To some extent, I was right about law school helping me achieve that goal: I was hired to write a political newsletter and help lobby the US Congress on behalf of the Assembly of Captive European Nations (ACEN), an anti-communist coalition representing nine nations that had come under Soviet domination after World War II. The work wasn't as stimulating as I'd hoped—though it may have made me an indirect hire of the CIA, as funding for the ACEN came from the Free Europe Committee, which was later revealed to be a CIA front organization. Also, I don't like leaving anything unfinished, so after a year I decided to go back to Columbia.

On my return, I warmed to the law, at least the advocacy part of it. Though I never excelled in academic legal studies, I won the national moot court competition for best brief and thrived in a course on trial practice, where I discovered I had a talent for thinking on my feet and for organizing and building the evidence that favored my client.

Winning cases in the real world thrilled me. I loved my job at the Department of Justice. Still, when James Vorenberg called, I was very interested. Overnight, I weighed the pros and cons. The Watergate break-in could be the start of a spectacular political crime reaching all the way to the president, or it could turn out to be nothing more than an odd burglary. But even if the investigation fizzled, my participation would likely amount to no more than a minor disruption in the flow of my career, and the timing was right for making a change. For aspiring trial lawyers like me, it was common to work at the Justice Department for five years to get great courtroom experience, and then to make the transition to private practice. After five years, the law of diminishing returns kicked in.

If you waited too long to join a firm, the partners would see you as overqualified to be an associate.

By morning, I'd decided. I wanted the job as an assistant Watergate special prosecutor.

◼

I had done no more than exchange a few pleasantries with Vorenberg when he looked intently at me and said, "When can you start?"

I was puzzled. "Don't you have any questions?" I asked. Didn't they need someone with years of experience? I'd done only appellate work during my first year as a Justice Department lawyer, so I had just three and a half years of grand jury and trial work.

"I've checked your background," Vorenberg said. "You have the winning record we want."

"It will take me a month to transition my cases at Justice."

Vorenberg's tone was adamant. "We need you today. If you're saying you need two weeks to be polite, don't worry, I can clear you to start right away."

Whatever qualms I had about being unprepared quickly dissipated. I'd been raised to think I could do whatever I set my mind to, and I'd learned to put aside my doubts and fears.

"I'm eager to start," I said, rising and shaking Vorenberg's hand.

◼

Outside, I made my way up the street to the white sedan parked at the curb. The scorching heat no longer seemed oppressive. Though my hair was soaked under my Dynel wig and my skirt was clinging to my legs, I had a sense of lightness, of a new adventure that would lift me high.

"I've got a new job!" I exclaimed, as I slipped into the passenger seat next to Ian.

My father beamed from the back seat. "That's great news!"

"Fabulous!" my mother chimed in, reaching forward to hug me.

Behind the wheel, Ian barely nodded. No kiss. No warm words of love and encouragement.

I'd grown used to my husband's indifference. He had never shown much interest in me romantically or in my work, and I'd been unhappy since the first night of our honeymoon, maybe even earlier. Still, I had no thought of leaving him. I'd been raised to believe that marriage was forever. In my mind, if something was wrong, it was *my* fault, and it was my responsibility to fix it.

Had James Vorenberg witnessed this scene, he might have had doubts about my judgment. And yet the qualities that kept me tied to Ian—a fierce sense of obligation, a willingness to ignore all roadblocks, and a refusal to give up— had also fueled my success at putting criminals away.

Two weeks later, at my farewell party at the Justice Department, my colleagues gave me a beautiful red-silk-and-gilt Chinese box. Inside were three brass balls and a note that read, "Because you have more than most men."

I never felt *ballsy*. I just worked hard and put up a brave, confident front.

2

ARCHIE AND THE GANG

The suite of rooms occupied by the Watergate cover-up task force on the ninth floor at 1425 K Street was as impenetrable as Fort Knox. Armed guards stood at the entrances, hidden ceiling cameras kept watch in the hallways, alarms monitored all the doors, and sensors detected the slightest movement. The drapes, made of specially designed metallic fiber to resist long-range snooping, were always drawn, though many of the offices, including mine, didn't have windows. It was easy to pass the entire day without seeing sun or sky.

To ease the boxed-in feeling, I tacked two posters to the walls by my desk: one featured a curtained window view of a bucolic landscape; the other showed a Peeping Tom with his nose pressed against the pane. The Peeping Tom poster was a gift from my trial partner, Richard Ben-Veniste.

Rick, as he was known, was thirty years old, just four months older than I. A native New Yorker, he'd grown up in a middle-class Jewish family like mine and had graduated from Columbia Law School a year before me. Before joining the trial team, he'd been an assistant US attorney in the Southern District of New York and chief of the special prosecutions section. He wore round wire-rimmed glasses under a mop of curly black hair and kept in shape by riding his ten-speed bike to work every day from his Georgetown apartment. He was brash, witty, cocky, and whip smart, and we became good friends. When I wore heels, Rick and I were also the same height—about five feet, seven inches. In fact, with a few tall exceptions (like Archibald Cox himself), the men on the special prosecutor's staff gave credence to the old Napoleonic cliché: their lack of height was matched by relentless drive and towering ambition.

Among the most driven was James Neal, the brilliant Tennessean and ex-Marine who headed our trial team. Jim had a strong, chiseled jaw and intense blue eyes, and he spoke in a rich drawl. He smoked cigars constantly, trailing ash in his wake and burning holes in his ties. He swaggered through the office, his barrel chest preceding him, in the manner of a man who knew he'd get what he wanted. His wife once joked that he strutted even while he sat. At forty-three, Jim had won several high-profile cases as a federal prosecutor, including a jury-tampering conviction against Jimmy Hoffa, the president of the Teamsters Union, in 1964. He was living temporarily in DC to get the obstruction task force up and running. He and Archie had agreed that afterward Jim would return to his hometown of Nashville and his brand-new law practice, leaving Rick and me to question all witnesses and get to the bottom of Watergate. If we could gather enough evidence for indictments against those responsible, Jim would be back for the trial.

From the start, Rick and I had a strong working relationship based on our commitment to the Watergate case and on our mutual affection and respect. Our temperaments complemented each other and helped us avoid conflicts that might have erupted over the divvying up and questioning of witnesses. I was patient and calm; Rick was bold and aggressive. He called me "Jilly Bean" and liked to tease me for what he considered my naïveté and ladylike primness.

As someone who struggled to overcome insecurity, I marveled at Rick's self-assurance. One day while walking down the hall together, we passed an office where Philip Heymann, a forty-year-old Harvard Law School professor whom Archibald Cox had brought in to help set up the office, was talking to a witness. Rick overheard Heymann mention "immunity," and a beat later he pulled the professor into the hall. "Don't ever talk to one of our witnesses again," Rick said in a sharp tone. "And don't ever mention immunity."

"Take it easy," Heymann said. He raised his hands palms outward and shook his head as he walked away.

I knew we wouldn't have to worry about Heymann interfering again.

■

The other members of the trial team were young men, most still in their twenties, who had been top students at top law schools. They had clerked for federal judges and Supreme Court justices and had worked as government attorneys and appellate lawyers. What they lacked in trial experience, they made up for in intelligence and commitment to hard work. Like soldiers in a foxhole, we trusted one another instantly. We were a band of brothers (and one sister) crammed into a tight warren of offices where we spent long hours bent over our desks. A sense of noble purpose charged our days. We knew we were part of history, which energized us but also led to some self-consciously grandiose moments. I recall one day when the usually down-to-earth George Frampton held up his briefcase, the same government-issued faux-leather case we all carried, and solemnly announced, "This will probably be in the Smithsonian one day."

George was twenty-nine, with thick brown hair, a medium build, and the kind of open face that signals mid-western friendliness. The son of a professor at the University of Illinois Law School, George had graduated from Yale University and Harvard Law School, where he'd been managing editor of the *Harvard Law Review*. After a stint as a volunteer lawyer in New York for the national anti-poverty program Volunteers in Service to America (VISTA), George had clerked for Supreme Court Justice Harry Blackmun during the arguments for the landmark case on abortion, *Roe v. Wade*.

One of our most important tasks in those early days was to establish the pattern of Nixon's meetings with his aides as the cover-up developed, and George spent hours poring over the president's phone logs and diaries. Gerald Goldman helped. Jerry had grown up in the Boston suburbs and had graduated from Harvard College and Harvard Law School, where he served on the *Harvard Law Review* and met his wife, Greer, one of the school's few female law students. At twenty-eight, Jerry was thin and dark-haired, with a bookish demeanor. After serving three years in the Coast Guard, he had clerked for Supreme Court Justice William J. Brennan and then worked in private practice in Washington before joining our team.

At twenty-seven, Lawrence Iason, the youngest member of our team, was just two years out of New York University Law School, where he'd been editor of the law review. Short, fair-haired, and bespectacled, Larry had been raised in

Hewlett, Long Island, and had graduated from Phillips Exeter Academy and Yale. Before arriving at K Street, he had clerked in Richmond, Virginia, for Judge Clement F. Haynsworth of the US Fourth Circuit Court of Appeals, an unsuccessful Nixon nominee for the Supreme Court. Larry spent his days going through transcripts of grand jury hearings and witness testimony and summarizing the material on index cards.

On our rare evenings off, we enjoyed meals at one another's houses and got to know one another's partners and significant others. But there was one member of the team who didn't participate. Peter Rient had grown up in Connecticut, the stepson of a US Court of Appeals judge for the Second Circuit. Dark-haired and bearded, Rient was thirty-five, the eldest member of our team after Jim Neal. We didn't know much about his personal life, except we suspected that he had a drinking problem. He'd graduated from Harvard College and Harvard Law School and had worked as an appellate lawyer in the US Attorney's office in New York.

Though not officially part of our trial team, two other lawyers in the office, Phil Lacovara, the counsel to the special prosecutor, and Carl Feldbaum, the assistant to deputy special prosecutor Henry Ruth, worked closely with us and played key roles in the work of the Watergate Task Force.

Stocky and round-faced, with a thatch of springy black hair and a large brush mustache, Phil Lacovara grew up in a devout Catholic home in suburban New York and graduated from Georgetown University and Columbia Law School, where he was at the top of his class, but turned down law review because of his family obligations. While an undergraduate, Phil had married his high school sweetheart, Madeline Papio, and at thirty was the father of seven children. He'd clerked for Judge Harold Leventhal of the US Court of

Appeals for the District of Columbia, worked as special assistant to Thurgood Marshall when the soon-to-be Supreme Court justice was US solicitor general, and, after a stint in a Wall Street law firm, became special counsel to the New York Police Department and then deputy solicitor general to Erwin Griswold.

It wasn't rare for laughter to ring out on the ninth floor, often caused by Rick's joking or one of Carl Feldbaum's pranks. At twenty-nine, Carl was slim, with a head of closely cropped light brown hair and the mischievous smile of someone who enjoyed practical jokes. He grew up in Philadelphia and had graduated from Princeton and the University of Pennsylvania School of Law. Before arriving at K Street, he had worked as an assistant attorney general in Philadelphia. A favorite prank of Carl's was to plant a water faucet tricked out to look like a microphone in a colleague's office and then watch the lawyer's momentary panic when he thought he'd been bugged.

◼

For the past year, there had been a steady drip of Watergate news, sparking a national craving for explanation of what was behind the odd crime. Although the White House had labeled the break-in a "third-rate burglary," I saw signs that it was a political crime. The first clue was that four of the five men arrested inside the Democratic National Committee offices were immediately identified as Cuban exiles who had worked as CIA operatives during the Bay of Pigs invasion of Cuba in 1961. Second, one of them had a notebook in which he'd written the name Howard Hunt next to a White House phone number. Then came the discovery that the fifth man arrested had used an alias, but was really James W. McCord, Jr., an ex-CIA operative and electronics expert with a contract to provide security for the Committee to Reelect the President, aptly known as CREEP.

The incident on June 17, 1972, had actually been the second break-in at the Democratic National Committee headquarters. The burglars had first struck in May, intending to tap the phone of the Democratic Party chairman, Lawrence O'Brien, and that of R. Spencer Oliver, the executive director of the Association of State Democratic Chairmen. As part of their dirty tricks campaign, they hoped to collect information embarrassing to the Democrats that the Republicans could use to their advantage in the 1972 presidential campaign. They succeeded in gathering material from Oliver's phone, but they failed to pick up any of O'Brien's conversations. They concluded the tap on his phone wasn't working and went back to replace that bug.

The *Washington Post*'s reporting of these facts, combined with the subsequent arrest of G. Gordon Liddy, the mastermind behind the Watergate break-in, and E. Howard Hunt, the scheme's coordinator and personnel recruiter, suggested the involvement of the White House and CREEP. At the time of the break-in, Hunt worked for the White House, and Liddy worked for CREEP. But there was no other evidence to link the president or his campaign to the crime, and Nixon won re-election in November 1972 in a landslide, carrying forty-nine states and an overwhelming popular-vote margin.

In January 1973, just after the break-in trial started, the four Cuban Americans and Hunt pleaded guilty. As the trial continued against Liddy and McCord, the mounting evidence called into question the White House's repeated denials of involvement in the burglary.

On January 30, 1973, ten days after Nixon's second inauguration, McCord and Liddy were convicted of conspiracy and wiretapping charges; the jury deliberated for only ninety minutes. Several days later, Judge Sirica told reporters he hoped Congress would investigate, as there was more to Watergate than had come out at the trial.

"More" didn't begin to describe it.

Hoping for leniency on the eve of his sentencing, James McCord sent a letter to Judge Sirica on March 19, which the judge read in open court. McCord made clear that the trial had been a sham and that key witnesses had perjured themselves in exchange for promises of clemency and financial support for their families should they go to prison. "There are further considerations which are not to be lightly taken," McCord wrote. "Several members of my family have expressed fear for my life if I disclose knowledge of the facts in this matter, either publicly or to any government representative. Whereas I do not share their concerns to the same degree, nevertheless, I do believe that retaliatory measures will be taken against me, my family, and my friends should I disclose such facts." Still, he had decided to come forward, he wrote, "in the interests of justice . . . and restoring faith in the criminal justice system."

McCord's letter put the lie to White House denials of involvement and unveiled a colossal effort to obstruct justice, a contemptible abuse of power by the very government officials charged with safeguarding our democracy and legal system. McCord said that "political pressure" had been "applied to the defendants to plead guilty and remain silent," that "perjury occurred during the trial," and, most tantalizingly, that "others involved in the Watergate operation were not identified during the trial, when they could have been by those testifying."

Our investigation eventually proved all that and more. Immediately after the arrests, the president and his top aides had tried to use the CIA and FBI to prevent investigators from tracking the currency found on the burglars to a cashed campaign donation check that had been deposited to the bank account of one of the Cubans. Cash from campaign contributions was later used to pay for the burglars' silence. We would also prove that witnesses from the White House and CREEP had perjured themselves by giving false statements to the FBI, to the Senate, and to us, and had coached other witnesses to commit perjury.

Another clue to the political nature of the Watergate break-in came on December 8, 1972, a month before the burglars' trial, when $10,000 in cash was found in the purse of Dorothy Hunt, the wife of Howard Hunt, after she was killed in a plane crash in Chicago. Talk abounded that Dorothy was on her way to deliver hush money to the burglars' families. No one could explain where the money had come from. A flurry of stories appeared in the press implicating the president's closest aides and advisors in a vast cover-up to suppress the truth.

With the evidence of wrongdoing mounting, in February 1973 the US Senate created the Select Committee on Presidential Campaign Activities, which quickly became known as the Senate Watergate Committee. In May, the Senate refused to confirm Nixon's nominee for attorney general, Elliot Richardson, until he agreed to name an independent special prosecutor to handle the Watergate investigation and promised not to fire him except for cause. After Richardson's first two choices turned him down, Archibald Cox, a sixty-one-year-old Harvard Law School professor and former solicitor general of the United States, accepted the position on May 18.

I understood the overwhelming public desire for an

independent prosecutor. Americans didn't trust presidents to investigate themselves, and ever since the Reconstruction Era following the Civil War, special prosecutors have been appointed to ferret out high-level corruption, the Teapot Dome scandal under President Warren G. Harding in the 1920s being a prime example.

On May 17, the day before Cox was appointed and a week before I was hired, the Senate Watergate hearings began under the chairmanship of Senator Sam Ervin, a portly, white-haired Democrat from North Carolina who'd been born in the nineteenth century and never quite made it into the twentieth. A committed segregationist, Ervin had opposed civil rights legislation, and just a few months before the Watergate break-in, he had voted against the Equal Rights Amendment. Though he'd graduated from Harvard Law School and had a razor-sharp mind, Ervin talked in a folksy manner and described himself as "just a country lawyer." He peppered his questions with Bible quotations and sometimes pulled a copy of the Constitution from a pocket in his jacket to wave dramatically at Nixon's men as they testified before his committee. Thousands of Americans joined the Sam Ervin Fan Club, which sold mugs, T-shirts, and calendars emblazoned with the senator's smiling face. He also produced a spoken-word album, *Senator Sam at Home*, in which he told anecdotes and drawled song lyrics, including those of Simon & Garfunkel's "Bridge Over Troubled Water."

Archibald Cox's office was at the far end of the ninth floor from mine, but I often saw him as he strode down the hallway in his three-piece suit, starched shirt, and bow tie. He was gray-haired, slender, and six feet but he looked even taller. He had a fifties-style crew cut, ramrod posture, and a gaze that bore into students, lawyers, and judges who didn't have their facts straight. Passing him in the hallway, I was drawn back to my days as a middling law student and often felt too intimidated to start a conversation with him.

Among Harvard law students, Archie had a reputation for being boring and stiff, but when he talked about the law with us he was engaging and expansive. All of us experienced what Carl Feldbaum called Archie's Abe Lincoln moments. These were times when the special prosecutor would give a stirring reflection on the meaning of the US Constitution and the importance of honoring its fundamental principles. I recall once when the subject of presidential power came up during a staff meeting, Archie leaned back in his chair with his interlaced hands cradling his head and gave us an eloquent disquisition on *Marbury v. Madison*, the case that established the US Supreme Court as the final arbiter and interpreter of the Constitution. As we listened, our jaws went slack and our eyes moistened and we forgot the work waiting on our desks, which seemed at that moment far less important to our lives that what Archie had to say about the law and American history.

Archie wasn't someone you chatted up. Carl Feldbaum, whose office was close to Archie's, had more of an opportunity than most of us to talk to him privately, and sometimes the special prosecutor was astonishingly candid. Once when they discussed the Supreme Court, Archie told Carl that he'd probably argued before the high tribunal a hundred times. "I'd always done meticulous work and was fully prepared," Archie said. "But every time I had to go to the Supreme Court I'd wake up in the morning, go to the bathroom, and throw up."

Not even Carl would dare make a Nixon joke in front of Archie. At a dinner with our press officer, James Doyle, one evening, Archie's wife, Phyllis Cox, made a disparaging

remark about Nixon, and Archie frowned at her as if he'd bit-
ten into a sour lemon.

I never went to Archie's office to ask him a question
unless I thought he was the only person who could answer it.
But when I did seek him out, he always made me feel that he
was glad to help, that I was an important member of the trial
team. It didn't matter to Archie that I was a woman or that
my undergraduate degree came from a state school. He cared
only that my ideas were sound, based on rigorous thought
and study.

Since our work started almost simultaneously with that
of the Ervin Committee and our investigations overlapped, we
kept a black-and-white TV in a back room of our office tuned
to the Senate hearings, which were broadcast live that spring
and summer. We needed to know what each witness was saying under oath to the committee to be sure it was consistent
with what they or other witnesses had told us. We also had
to make sure that the committee wasn't granting immunity
from prosecution to any individuals who we thought should
be indicted. The junior staff took turns monitoring the hearings, taking notes and alerting us if anything important happened. The goal of Ervin's committee was very different from
ours. The senators were investigating whether new laws were
needed to prevent future Watergates. Our goal was to determine whether existing laws had been broken, and, if so, to
prosecute those responsible.

3

THE WATERGATE BOY

For our trial team, the first task was to master the mountain of documents that had landed at our door. We started by reading records of the burglary investigation and the transcripts of the burglary trial. We kept up with the ongoing press reports, checked out rumors, and, most important, reviewed documents and interviewed witnesses. White House and CREEP officials, eager to avoid indictment as the evidence against the administration mounted, started clamoring to talk to us in the hope of receiving more lenient treatment. One of these men was Jeb Stuart Magruder.

I met Magruder on my first day on the job, when his lawyer brought him to our office to discuss a plea deal. Magruder, a young member of Nixon's inner circle, had worked as a White House communications aide before becoming deputy campaign chairman for Nixon's reelection. He was tall, athletic, and good-looking, with abundant dark brown hair and droopy, long-lashed blue eyes. He looked much younger than his thirty-eight years.

We settled into chairs in Jim Neal's office, and Jim asked

whether anyone wanted coffee. Magruder and his lawyer turned to me, the only woman in the room, and simultaneously said, "I'll take mine black." Jim fixed his gaze on Magruder. While George Frampton—the junior lawyer in the room—ran to fetch coffee, Jim drawled, talking around his cigar, "Not very smart insulting a major player in deciding the terms of your plea agreement."

I was used to sexist assumptions. What I wasn't used to was Magruder's utter amorality. He had lied and lied and lied. To the FBI, to Justice Department investigators, to a federal grand jury, to Judge Sirica. His name had first come up during the burglars' trial in January, when he testified under oath that he knew nothing about the outrageous plan cooked up by G. Gordon Liddy to sabotage the Democrats, which would culminate in the DNC break-in.

Magruder also said on the witness stand that he'd instructed all of CREEP's employees "not to do anything embarrassing or illegal that could make the president's reelection difficult." Magruder said this with a straight face, while maintaining eye contact with the prosecutor questioning him, and with his voice firm. Lying was as natural to him as breathing.

As part of his offer of information preliminary to a plea deal, Magruder now told us that he had known about the break-in and cover-up from the start and that it was part of Liddy's grand spy scheme. He'd been present on January 27, 1972, nearly five months before the break-in, when Liddy presented his bizarre intelligence plan at a meeting in the opulent Justice Department office of the US attorney general, John N. Mitchell. Mitchell had run Nixon's 1968 campaign and would soon step down from his cabinet post to head CREEP full-time. Also attending this meeting was John W. Dean, the White House counsel.

Liddy was at the time a lawyer for CREEP's finance committee, having previously been a member of the White House "plumbers" unit. Now, under the carved cathedral ceilings and surrounded by historic murals and mosaic floors, Liddy illustrated his scheme with a complicated chart set up on an easel. He called the plan Gemstone, with each element named for a different jewel. One involved drugging and kidnapping anti–Vietnam War protesters, such as Abbie Hoffman, and holding them hostage in Mexico until after the election. Another proposed luring delegates at the 1972 Democratic National Convention in Miami onto a yacht moored in front of the Fontainebleau Hotel. On the yacht would be plenty of call girls and, of course, hidden cameras ready to record embarrassing behavior.

The Gemstone plan would cost $1 million, and Mitchell vetoed it, not because it was illegal and ludicrous, but because it was too expensive. After several tries, Liddy came up with a cost-efficient scheme that could be pulled off for just $250,000, an amount acceptable to Mitchell. The revised plan involved photos and phones, not hostages and hookers, and it led directly to the Watergate break-in.

Magruder had had the five-inch-thick Gemstone file, filled with materials related to the scheme, in his office for several months, until Mitchell asked him to destroy it after the Watergate burglars were caught. He was well familiar with its contents. But it took weeks of painstaking questioning before he would tell us about any of the plotting. Even then, he resisted telling us everything he knew, though he would have to give us more details and more corroboration of his story if he ever hoped to get a plea agreement.

You might think lying was part of Magruder's DNA. He came from a long line of criminals, stretching back to his ancestor Alexander Magruder, who arrived in America from Scotland in 1651 as an exiled prisoner. During the Civil War, Magruder's great-grandfather, a Washington, DC, shoe store owner, was jailed for running a boot-smuggling operation for the Confederacy. In 1921, Magruder's grandfather went to prison for embezzling from the shipyard corporation he headed.

Magruder grew up in the New York City borough of Staten Island, where his father owned a print shop and never had trouble with the law. He graduated from Williams College in 1958, after serving a stint in the Army; then he moved to the Midwest, where he became involved in Republican politics. In Chicago in 1962 he worked for the successful campaign of Donald Rumsfeld for Congress and went on to work for Barry Goldwater's 1964 presidential campaign. He joined Richard Nixon's campaign in 1967, and two years later he landed a job in the White House as a special assistant under H. R. "Bob" Haldeman, Nixon's chief of staff. Magruder quickly became one of the president's closest advisors, and, in 1971, a top executive at CREEP.

Jeb Magruder's life fell apart on May 18, 1973, when James McCord testified before the Ervin Committee. The convicted Watergate burglar said he had decided to tell the truth to Judge Sirica when he opened a newspaper and saw a photograph of a smiling Magruder at the very time he, McCord, faced years in prison. He told the committee that Magruder and Mitchell, with the help of John Dean, had planned and approved the Watergate break-in and then invented a cover-up story in an elaborate conspiracy to obstruct justice.

No witness in my experience had affected me the way Magruder did. I was stunned by the ease with which he dissembled, even as he tried to clear himself. He was a slippery confabulator, and I came to the conclusion, based on our many hours of conversation, that he had no moral center. He didn't understand that what he had done was wrong, not even when he finally admitted to having burned the Gemstone file in his fireplace at home in the middle of a scorching Washington summer not long after the burglars were arrested. Magruder didn't think there was anything odd about this or that he had anything to apologize for. It was normal for him to do the expedient thing, to get rid of the file, never mind that his wife and children were asleep upstairs.

"Jeb, did you even stop to open the damper? You could have burned the house down. Didn't that occur to you?" I asked him one afternoon.

"It wasn't the smartest thing I ever did," he said.

I detected a slight smirk on his face and felt he was just telling me what he thought I wanted to hear.

Magruder wasn't telling us the *whole* truth. Still, we needed him badly. He was the only key figure in the planning of the break-in and the early development of the cover-up whom we were likely to secure as a witness, and he was the bedrock of any case against his former boss, John Mitchell.

◼

On June 14, a couple of weeks after he talked to us, Magruder testified before the Ervin Committee, where he told a similar albeit embellished story. In another instance of deflecting blame for his actions, he said that his judgment had been corrupted by the political left. At Williams College in the 1950s, he had admired William Sloane Coffin, Jr., a clergyman and peace activist from whom he took a course on ethics. Years later, he saw Coffin urging young men to break the law by burning their draft cards to protest the Vietnam War. He reasoned that the Nixon men were justified in also breaking the law for *their* cause.

Sitting at the witness table, Magruder was the very picture of boyish contrition. The senators felt sorry for this attractive young man, his brilliant career now in tatters, and they pitied his pretty wife, Gail, who sat loyally nearby, looking heartbroken. "I believe you have comported yourself in an admirable fashion before this committee," Senator Joseph Montoya, a Democrat from New Mexico, told Magruder. "I want to say to you that the tragedy of Watergate is that it has affected many fine young men who dedicated themselves to a President. . . . I want to wish you well in your future endeavors."

Senator Ervin himself congratulated Magruder on his courage in coming forward to atone for his sins. "In spite of your very unfortunate state at present," said Ervin, trying to be kind, but not making much sense, "you have got about the greatest asset any man can have. You have a wife who stands behind you in the shadows where the sun shines."

All that was missing was a choir singing "Hallelujah."

Millions of Americans watched these tributes on TV and read the encomiums for Magruder that poured in from the press. I wasn't buying any of it. I had spent enough time interviewing the man to know better. He offered no verbal apologies and he showed none of the typical signs of guilt and remorse, no stricken looks or slumped posture, no clenched hands or trembling voice. He looked composed, even smug, with the corners of his mouth turned up and his eyes sparking with satisfaction.

A few days after his Senate testimony, Magruder came back to K Street without his lawyer, and I questioned him closely. "Okay, Jeb. Help me to rely on you," I said.

Prosecutors should be unemotional in questioning witnesses. Carefully worded, neutral questions keep the temperature cool and are most effective in probing for the truth. Where were you sitting? Who was in the room with you? What time was it?

I had started out with the assumption that Magruder would eventually be truthful and that I would learn valuable things if I asked the right questions. But after talking to him at length, I began to doubt that was correct. Still, Magruder insisted, "I've told you everything."

It's a good thing my office didn't have a window, because there were times I would have flung him through it. He was a major part of the scaffolding of our case, but I couldn't hang much brick on the rickety structure he'd given me. I needed a steadier foundation. He'd told us that Mitchell had approved the break-in, but we couldn't go to court with just Magruder's words. After weeks of questioning, Magruder finally implicated others in the cover-up, including Nixon's campaign finance chairman, Maurice Stans, a former secretary of commerce who had raised $62 million for the president's reelection. Magruder also said that Gordon Strachan, an assistant to Bob Haldeman, knew about Liddy's plan. And, most important, Magruder told us that John Mitchell had approved the Watergate bugging scheme at a meeting in Key Biscayne, Florida, in late March 1972. But Magruder stopped short of implicating the president himself.

I couldn't shake the feeling that he was withholding information. Often, when I questioned Magruder, I could feel my chest tightening and my voice turning harsh and scolding. I'd take a deep breath and speak to him gently. I sensed that he was a witness who needed coddling, who needed to be told, "Jeb, you're doing a great job." No one else in the office would have had the patience for this approach. Certainly, Rick's aggressive style never would have worked with Magruder.

I asked Magruder for diaries, calendars, and memos that would confirm his story. And I interviewed a parade of witnesses who might corroborate his version of events.

Most of them came voluntarily to my office. I talked to secretaries who might have heard something or who could explain visitor lists and phone logs. I also interviewed four aides who worked with Magruder on Nixon's reelection campaign and who he claimed had been at the Key Biscayne meeting, where the plans for the Watergate bugging had been discussed.

But these witnesses gave conflicting accounts. Magruder's story wasn't checking out, and I didn't feel comfortable offering him a plea deal. I pressed on, interviewing more witnesses, reviewing more documents, calling Magruder back again and again to go over his testimony.

I worked late into the night, as did the rest of our team. Typically, when I walked to my car, the neighborhood prostitutes were on the street. They would stare at me with puzzled expressions, wondering why a blonde in a miniskirt and heels was carrying a briefcase. One night, another young woman who worked in the special prosecutor's office, a lovely redhead, stood in the doorway waiting for her husband to pick her up. A car passed by once, then twice. The third time the car rolled by, the driver yelled out his window, "Honey, if you're working tonight, you better get out here, closer to the road."

The prostitutes were gone when I returned in the mornings at eight. Upstairs in the Bat Cave, as we started calling our office, we were as isolated as Batman in his subterranean command center and just as protected from outside snooping—or so we thought. One hot morning that summer, while sitting at my kitchen counter reading the *Washington Post* before heading to the office, I saw a front-page story that froze me with shock. From above the fold, the headline screamed, "Approval of Bugging Unresolved," over a story that read:

> Special prosecutor Archibald Cox and his staff have been unable thus far to obtain testimony corroborating Jeb Stuart Magruder's allegation that John N. Mitchell approved the Watergate bugging plan at a meeting in late March, 1972.
>
> According to documents received by The Washington Post, the special prosecutor's office is still grappling with sharp conflicts in the testimony of four witnesses as to meeting dates, the number of persons who attended the crucial meeting and whether or not a decision to go ahead with the bugging was actually made at this meeting.
>
> The issue is significant because it holds the key to one of the major, unanswered questions of the Watergate investigation to date. Is Mitchell guilty of approving the bugging as Magruder claims, or is he innocent because he specifically rejected the bugging proposal as he contends?

The article went on to describe two confidential memos about Magruder that a colleague had written and addressed to me. The memos contained an analysis of evidence that I'd requested. Now the *Post* was blasting their contents across the front page for the world to see. There was a serious security breach in our office. How had the newspaper gotten that copy? Had other documents leaked? Had I done something careless? As usual, I blamed myself.

I dressed quickly and drove downtown. Everyone in the office had seen the story and was just as upset as I was. But while we analyzed all the possibilities and speculated about the source, Archie Cox took matters into his own hands. He called the *Post*'s executive editor, Ben Bradlee, an acquaintance through their mutual friendship with President John F. Kennedy, to demand an answer. Bradlee was cagey, but wanted to help. "If you ever tell anyone I told you this, I'll deny it, but Archie, you've got a trash problem," he said.

It turned out that a member of the cleaning crew at our building had walked into the *Post* newsroom and, without revealing his name, handed a few of our memos to the political reporter John Hanrahan. "If you want more," the man said, "just come tonight to the loading dock behind the special prosecutor's office."

We'd been dumping our trash in clear plastic bags every night, and apparently an eagle-eyed worker had spotted the special prosecutor's letterhead amid the foam coffee cups, Coke cans, and cigar butts. After Archie's call with Bradlee, we bought a shredder, and there were no more leaks.

▣

I finally managed to find enough witnesses to corroborate Magruder's story, and on August 16 I met the former White House aide and his lawyer at court, so Magruder could enter his plea.

The US District Court was housed in an immense, unfriendly building on the northeast corner of Constitution Avenue and Third Street NW. A six-story limestone block built in 1950, it seemed designed to be as intimidating as possible: cold marble floors; tall slab walls; windowless courtrooms that sealed off the participants in legal cases from all life outside.

As we rode the elevator to the second floor, I studied Magruder. He looked tan and fit from playing tennis in Blue Ridge Summit, a bucolic area of Pennsylvania where he and his family were spending the summer in a rented house. Magruder had been forced to quit his job as director of policy planning at the Commerce Department—a post-election reward—when he began talking to us, but he still worked. He had started a one-man consulting firm he called Metropolitan Research Service, intending to use it as a springboard to an eventual management job in a major corporation. It amazed me that anyone would hire Magruder for advice on how to run their business, but he had no trouble lining up a few lucrative accounts, including the Sea Pines Company, a resort in Hilton Head, South Carolina. He also engaged a speaking agent who had arranged a tour of college campuses in the fall for which Magruder would be paid $1,500 per lecture to talk about the moral lessons of Watergate. His pose as the poster boy of humble contrition had paid off most handsomely in a $100,000 book deal from the publisher Atheneum to write his memoirs.

■

The elevator doors slid open, and we made our way through the crowded hall to the courtroom. We took our seats at the prosecution table and waited for Judge Sirica: Maximum John, as he was known for his sentencing record. Magruder knew what he was up against.

A onetime amateur boxer, the son of an immigrant barber from Naples, Sirica had been appointed to the US District Court by President Eisenhower in 1957 and had become chief judge in 1971. He had gone to Georgetown Law School straight from high school, which was possible in DC in the 1920s. His lack of a college education showed in his less than refined courtroom manner. Short-tempered and outspoken, he often ignored normal courtroom procedures. He questioned witnesses himself and badgered lawyers. He'd been criticized in the press for turning the Watergate burglars' trial into an inquisition, but his toughness had also helped move the case forward. To Sirica, the bending of courtroom rules was a small price to pay. "I have no intention of sitting on the bench like a nincompoop and watching the parade go by," he said.

We were the first case on the docket, and promptly at nine a.m. Sirica entered the courtroom. At sixty-nine, he was short and stocky, with deep folds in his olive skin, salt-and-pepper hair, and bushy eyebrows like caterpillars. He frowned at Magruder. "You understand you are facing a jail sentence of five years and a $10,000 fine for your role in the Watergate scandal," Sirica said.

Magruder bent his lanky frame to reach the microphone and lowered his eyes. His long lashes brushed his cheeks as he spoke in a soft voice. "Yes, your honor."

Sirica leaned forward on his elbows. "No one has coerced you into giving testimony," the judge continued.

"No, your honor."

My heart was thumping. In my office, Magruder had agreed to plead guilty to one count of conspiracy to obstruct justice, in exchange for cooperating with us fully. But I worried that when the time came, he wouldn't actually say, "Guilty." In his heart, he still thought he hadn't done anything wrong. It would be just like him to slip out of our grasp. I saw our case against Mitchell and the rest of Nixon's men crumbling, along with my future. I saw the press blaming me—a woman!—for not being tough enough to bring Magruder to heel.

Judge Sirica read the conspiracy charge against Magruder; it included a long list of crimes, from plotting the break-in and lying to the FBI to encouraging others to lie and secretly raising hush money to buy the silence of the Watergate burglars.

"How do you plead?" Sirica asked, his expression impassive.

"Guilty, your honor," said Magruder, his voice barely above a whisper.

A current of relief coursed through me.

Sirica postponed sentencing until the end of our investigation so he could evaluate how cooperative Magruder had been with us.

Flashbulbs popped, and microphones were shoved toward us as I hurried Magruder out of the courthouse.

"Mr. Magruder, have you thought about what it's going to be like in prison?" a reporter shouted.

Magruder stopped on the sidewalk to answer. "I will accept the sentence whatever it is," he said. "But in the meantime I would like to give some lectures to tell people that these types of things have no place in American politics."

I fought the urge to roll my eyes.

Magruder didn't tell reporters that he'd signed a major book deal. He would be the first disgraced Nixon man to write a book about his role in Watergate. He would have to write it fast, before his sentencing, and it would have to be approved by me. I would read the manuscript before it went to press to ensure that Magruder hadn't written anything that could jeopardize our case. He had to tell the truth, to me and to his readers, or he'd be going to prison for a very long time.

4

NINE CONVERSATIONS

"There are tapes! Nixon recorded everything!" George Frampton shouted from the hall.

I leaped from my desk. A small crowd had gathered around George to hear his report of what just happened on Capitol Hill. That morning it was George who was listening to the Ervin hearings on our black-and-white TV, and he'd just heard a witness drop a bombshell that would change the course of the Watergate investigation.

Alexander Butterfield, a former Nixon aide and Air Force colonel, testified that the president had planted listening devices in the White House. Butterfield himself had supervised the Secret Service technicians who installed the voice-activated bugs in 1971 at Nixon's request. Six tiny microphones were embedded in the president's desk. Microphones were also stashed in Nixon's personal telephones in the Oval Office, in his hideaway at the Executive Office Building, in the Lincoln Sitting Room of the residence, and at the presidential retreat at Camp David. Butterfield said that Nixon intended the tapes as a record for posterity.

In the president's inner circle, only Butterfield, who'd been in charge of Nixon's daily schedule, and Bob Haldeman, the president's former chief of staff, knew about the devices. The Secret Service had installed them at night and on the weekends when the staff was gone. It also fell to the Secret Service to change the tapes when they ran out and to lock them away in a vault at the Executive Office Building.

"We've got Nixon now!" George yelled.

Our team moved from the hall to Jim Neal's office, our eyes wide with excitement. I felt my face tingle with the anticipation of what this could mean, but I was not as confident as George. The tapes could just as easily ruin us as make our case. It all depended on how closely they corroborated the testimony of our chief witness, the former White House counsel, John Wesley Dean III. At thirty-four, Dean was the youngest of Nixon's top aides and the first to have acknowledged the immorality and illegality of Watergate and come clean about the cover-up. He'd been fired at the end of April, at the same time Haldeman and Ehrlichman were forced to resign; Nixon had not let him take any files.

Dean had been talking to us for several weeks, and he had just completed a weeklong stint testifying before the Ervin Committee, all without knowing that during his time at the White House he had been taped. In his five days as a witness, Dean went much further than Jeb Magruder had, implicating a dozen or so of Nixon's men and the president himself in the cover-up. Dean had testified that Nixon knew about the cover-up and participated in it, spelling out the president's instructions to pay hush money and offer clemency to the Watergate burglars. Dean spoke calmly, in an almost robotic monotone, and he displayed an astonishing memory for the smallest details.

Soon afterward, Haldeman made his own appearance before the Ervin Committee, in which he asserted that the conversations Dean described hadn't taken place. The public believed Haldeman over Dean. According to a Gallup poll, half of the Americans who watched Dean's testimony on TV thought he was lying, a judgment reinforced in the press by conservative journalists who viciously attacked him.

A whiff of opportunism had swirled around Dean since the start of his career, and questions arose about his motives. Was he just trying to save his own skin, or did he sincerely want to do the right thing? As he spoke from the witness table in the Senate chamber, peering out from behind his round tortoiseshell glasses, Dean looked the very model of preppy rectitude, fair-haired, fit, and handsomely dressed in an expensive suit. His stunning twenty-seven-year-old wife, Maureen, known as Mo, sat behind him in designer clothes, her platinum hair pulled into a severe chignon and her icy runway-model air hiding her emotions.

The Deans were the Ken and Barbie of Watergate, beautiful and perfectly groomed, but also cool and remote. The public, treated every day throughout Dean's testimony to images of them on TV and in the newspapers, didn't quite trust their polished veneer. As the case unfolded, and I got to know Dean, I saw beyond the slick surface to the tormented young man underneath. He'd ridden to the top of Washington life only to end up publicly disgraced, facing a prison term and financial ruin.

Just five years older than me, John Dean had grown up, as I had, in the buttoned-down Eisenhower fifties. He was a fellow Midwesterner (in his case, from Ohio and Illinois) who had gone to law school and married young. His first wife, Karla Hennings, was the daughter of a US senator, but they divorced in 1970, after just eight years of marriage and one son. By this time, Dean had joined Nixon's inner circle. After writing volunteer position papers for Nixon's 1968 presidential campaign, he was rewarded with the post of deputy to Attorney General John Mitchell, and he became Nixon's White House counsel when John Ehrlichman, who'd held the job since Nixon's election, moved up to become the president's chief domestic advisor.

Around the time of his divorce, Dean met Maureen Kane in Los Angeles, where she'd been raised, and they were married in October 1972. Reporters digging into her past discovered that she'd been wed twice before and had worked as a stewardess, a model, and an insurance agent. Dean admitted to the Ervin Committee that he had taken $4,850 of $15,200 in leftover campaign money entrusted to him and stashed it in his office safe for their Florida honeymoon. He later replaced the money with a personal check, he testified, "and I've got the stub to prove it."

At the White House, Dean's job included writing legal briefs to support the administration's positions on such issues as executive privilege. He also worked on more personal tasks: plans for the Nixon library in Yorba Linda, California; financing for the president's property in nearby San Clemente; and the Rose Garden wedding of Nixon's daughter Tricia to Edward Cox in June 1971. After Watergate broke, however, Dean's most important job became coordinating the cover-up.

In July 1973, Dean was still negotiating with us over his plea deal and he was at K Street nearly every day. Though he was Jim Neal's and Rick's witness, he frequently came to my office to chat and we found it easy to talk to each other. Dean saw my frustration in getting enough corroboration to make

Magruder a credible witness, and he sympathized, noting Magruder's callowness and bad judgment. "Looking back, it's impossible to believe that Jeb even got hired at the White House," Dean said.

Of course, some people said the exact same thing about Dean.

Jim was in charge of questioning Dean and thrashing out arrangements with his lawyer. Rick participated in this process, as he would take over management of Dean when Jim returned to Nashville. But Jim, Rick, and Dean had reached a standoff. The Senate had given Dean what's known as use immunity, which meant we could try him only on criminal acts we hadn't learned of from his testimony at the Ervin hearings. Dean refused to tell us anything without *total* immunity, which our office declined to grant him. We knew Dean wouldn't be an effective witness at trial if he got away with no punishment for his role in the Watergate cover-up. No one was more adamant than Archie that Dean needed to plead to something. But Dean's attorney was equally adamant that Dean would prevail and should not plead. The negotiations proved tense, as Jim and Rick were determined to find a way to satisfy Archie without losing Dean.

◼

As usual, Dean was in our office on the day of Butterfield's testimony when we learned of the tapes. "Now you'll see I was telling the truth," he said.

Despite my concern about what the tapes would hold, I believed Dean. The fact that he didn't know Nixon was taping him enhanced his credibility, in my view. Unlike Magruder, Dean seemed to understand that what he had done was wrong. Although my view was not universal, I thought his remorse was sincere, and he was convincingly candid about the corruption he'd seen and participated in. He said he'd urged Nixon to end the cover-up. When the president didn't heed his warning—but after the release of James McCord's letter to Sirica implicating Nixon's aides—Dean offered himself to federal prosecutors, first at the US Attorney's office and then at ours.

In Jim Neal's office, we planned what steps to take. Jim astounded me by announcing that he thought Butterfield's testimony was a setup. He suspected that Butterfield had been directed by Nixon to divulge the taping system as part of a shrewd strategy to discredit Dean and our entire investigation. "It's bound to be a ruse," Jim warned. "If the tapes don't show a damn thing, we'll all be out of a job."

I didn't accept Jim's theory for a minute. Not that I didn't think the president capable of planning such a trap—he wasn't called "Tricky Dick" for nothing. But Nixon wasn't acting like a man with the upper hand or a plausible strategy. We'd heard talk that he'd been drinking heavily. He hadn't given a press conference in four months, and he was spending more and more time away from Washington, at Camp David and at his waterfront retreat in Key Biscayne.

There was also evidence that the president was breaking down physically. On the Thursday before Butterfield testified, Nixon was hospitalized at Bethesda Naval Hospital with viral pneumonia and a fever of 102 degrees. Anyone can fall ill, but it was hard not to conclude that Nixon's compromised physical strength reflected his anguish over Watergate. We knew, though, that as long as the president was breathing, he would never let up in his fight against us. We were locked in a battle to the death.

One thing was certain—we had to get hold of the tapes

as soon as possible. Even if Jim was right, we had to know the truth. Working around the clock, we analyzed which tapes to subpoena, drawing on information provided by Dean, White House meeting logs, and the desk diaries of Haldeman and Ehrlichman, which they had turned over to us. The logs and diaries would prove critical to our success. By showing exactly when Nixon had met with his chief aides, they enabled us to identify specific conversations that would corroborate Dean's testimony about the involvement of Nixon and his men in the cover-up. We would have to show beyond a reasonable doubt that the requested conversations involving the president were part of a criminal conspiracy, not a discussion of politics or policy. If we couldn't, then the president could successfully invoke executive privilege and prevent the tapes from ever being heard.

We quickly narrowed the list to conversations that we were most confident centered on Watergate. The first one occurred on June 20, 1972, three days after the break-in, when Nixon met in his hideaway office in the Executive Office Building with Ehrlichman and Haldeman, his German shepherds, as the press dubbed them. The meeting began with just the president and Ehrlichman. After Haldeman arrived, the three men conversed together for a brief period. Then Ehrlichman left, and Haldeman and Nixon spoke alone, with the secret tape system churning and Haldeman taking notes on a yellow legal pad.

Also on the list was a conversation on March 21, 1973, that we believed was key to Nixon's knowledge of the cover-up. We knew from Dean's Senate testimony and his conversations with us that on that day he told Nixon there was "a cancer on the presidency," which had to be removed lest it destroy him. Dean also laid out details about the ongoing obstruction, including the need to keep the burglars quiet. He testified that the president had responded by asking how much it would cost. Dean told him $1 million paid out over two years. Nixon assured him, Dean testified, that it would be no problem getting the money in cash.

The fight over the tapes aggravated something that had been bothering me all along. It distressed me to think that the president might have participated in illegal activity, let alone that we were now close to proving it. I was raised to respect the office of the president, even if I didn't agree with his politics. It was sickening to consider that Nixon had actually engaged in the kinds of sleazy activities familiar to me from my years prosecuting mobsters: intimidating witnesses, paying bribes, lying to law enforcement officials.

Archie Cox thought we were getting ahead of ourselves, and that we should ask politely for the tapes before slapping the president with a subpoena. We knew Nixon wouldn't voluntarily produce the tapes, but Archie wanted to try. He called us into his office to explain his decision. "We're facing a situation unprecedented in constitutional history, and we should proceed carefully and thoughtfully," he said. It was another Abe Lincoln moment, when Archie pointed out that respecting the Constitution and the humanity of a witness (even a criminal president) took precedence over the expediency of our investigation. On July 18, Archie sent a letter to Nixon's lawyer Fred Buzhardt requesting eight tapes. At the same time, Sam Ervin also demanded four tapes for his Senate probe, all of them conversations between the president and Dean. Nixon refused both requests on the grounds of executive privilege. "Executive poppycock!" thundered Ervin when reporters asked him about it.

We had no choice now but to subpoena the president to

turn over the tapes, though how to do it posed a dilemma. "We can't just walk into the White House, knock on the Oval Office door, and hand the document to Nixon," I said when the trial team met in Jim Neal's office to ponder our next step.

We wasted no time. Phil Lacovara, the head of Archie's legal research team, arranged a meeting with Buzhardt. On July 23, just one week after we learned of the tapes, Lacovara delivered our carefully crafted subpoena, this time demanding nine conversations, to Nixon's lawyer, who accepted it and signed his name with the notation "on behalf of the President." We had acted fast, but the president's response was even faster. It took him just two days to inform Judge Sirica that he would not comply. Two more days passed, and we were back in court.

■

By midday on July 27, the mercury had risen to 92 degrees. The heat hadn't seeped through the granite walls of the federal courthouse, though, and the windowless grand jury room had the metallic chill of the typical over-air-conditioned government office.

When Archie entered with me and several members of the trial team, our grand jury was seated in wooden chairs with tablet arms, like those used by schoolchildren. Most of the twenty-three jurors were middle-aged, and they had to dodge in and out of jobs and family obligations to serve. Seventeen of them were black, and thirteen were women. Their foreman, Vladimir Pregelj, a forty-six-year-old refugee from Yugoslavia, worked as an archivist at the Library of Congress. He was dressed in a pair of mod patterned slacks and sported a gray Vandyke beard.

By now, this grand jury had served for more than a year,

and the jurors understood their role perfectly. We selected documents for their consideration, interrogated witnesses in their presence, and recommended actions for them to take, such as issuing subpoenas and indictments. They took notes in spiral notebooks that were locked in a courthouse safe at the end of each day and returned to them when they next took up their duties. The jurors were, in theory, a check on the special prosecutor since the ultimate decision about whether to subpoena a witness or indict a defendant rested with them. If they believed we had enough evidence to justify our request for the tapes, they would grant us the right to them. If not, that would be the end of it.

The jurors sat rapt as Archie read them Nixon's letter, which argued that it was "wholly inadmissible" for the courts to compel a president to *any* action. Then Archie explained why that was not legally or constitutionally correct and why the tapes were crucial to our investigation. When he was done, the grand jury voted unanimously to petition Judge Sirica for an order demanding that Nixon "show cause why there should not be full and prompt compliance" with our subpoena.

We marched the twenty jurors (three were absent that day) to Judge Sirica's courtroom, where they took seats in the front benches, standing as the clerk read their names in a formal poll of their votes. Reporters and spectators got their first look at them, and the next day the jurors' names were printed in the *New York Times*. It moved me deeply to see the courage of these ordinary Americans. They knew what was right, and they were unafraid to challenge the president of the United States, the most powerful man in the world.

Archie handed Sirica the proposed order, and the judge signed it at the bench. The burden now was on Nixon to show why he should be exempt from the rule of law.

Outside, pedestrians who recognized Archie stopped to stare. Photographers and newsmen surrounded him, clogging the sidewalk and impeding our progress to the street. "What do you think of the president's refusal to honor the subpoena?" a reporter demanded.

"I think it's quite wrong," Archie answered in a clipped, professorial tone, as his eyes searched the curb for our car. The black Rambler was nowhere in sight. "Where's the damn car?" Archie muttered. He clutched his briefcase with one hand, while he waved furiously to hail a taxi. It was a familiar scene that summer. Archie might succeed in forcing Nixon to turn over the tapes, but he had trouble getting the office interns to pick him up on time.

5

SATURDAY NIGHT FEVER

With or without the tapes, we vowed to find the truth about the Watergate cover-up. While we waited to see what Nixon's next move would be, we continued interviewing witnesses and seeking more evidence to support our case. Our twelve-hour days stretched to sixteen hours and spilled into the weekend. Takeout containers and foam coffee cups overflowed the trash cans. Dinner dates were broken; calls from family and friends went unreturned.

Nixon's stubborn fight to deny us the tapes was costing him support even with his political base. He tried to explain his position in a televised speech to the nation on August 15, arguing that he was withholding the tapes for the good of the presidency. "If I were to make public these tapes, containing as they do blunt and candid remarks on many subjects that have nothing to do with Watergate, the confidentiality of the office of the President would always be suspect," he said.

The public was unconvinced. The latest Gallup survey showed that Nixon's approval rating had sunk to a record low of 31 percent, lower even than President Lyndon Johnson's ratings during the most heated days of the Vietnam protests.

Two weeks later Judge Sirica heard arguments on our motion requiring the president to show cause why he should not turn over the tapes. He then ordered Nixon to turn them over—but not to us: to himself. The judge also ruled that the Ervin Committee did not have a right to the tapes, since the Senate was conducting a legislative oversight hearing, not pursuing a criminal or judicial investigation.

Until now, Sirica's willingness to favor the pursuit of evidence over traditional legal standards had worked in our favor. We were wary of his ways, however, so we were careful not to request anything that he might approve on gut instinct only to have a higher court reverse his ruling, with the result of tainting the rest of the case we had built. In this case, we also had to be careful about objecting to Sirica's decision to give himself the tapes. We didn't want to anger him by challenging this ruling. But we had no choice: we needed to hear those tapes ourselves. We couldn't do our jobs if we were relying on a secondhand account—that would be hearsay and inadmissible. And so we petitioned the US Court of Appeals for the District of Columbia Circuit. Archie argued our appeal in September, and on October 12 the court ruled that we, not the judge, had the right to the tapes and ordered Nixon to turn them over to us. Once again, the president refused.

Our struggle for the tapes unfolded against a world wracked by escalating turmoil. On October 6, Yom Kippur, the holiest day in the Jewish calendar, Egyptian and Syrian forces launched a surprise attack on Israel, raising the risk of a confrontation between the Soviet Union and the United States. The situation nearly exploded when each superpower tried to send equipment and supplies to its respective allies in the conflict.

Four days later, as we waited for the tapes, and the fighting in the Middle East continued, Vice President Spiro Agnew suddenly and unexpectedly resigned. Agnew had been under investigation by the Justice Department for crimes unrelated to Watergate. Going back to the 1960s and his days as Baltimore County executive and, later, governor of Maryland, Agnew had demanded kickbacks in exchange for local architectural and engineering contracts. Even as vice president, he took money from Maryland businessmen whose contracts were up for renewal, meeting them in the White House basement, where they handed him envelopes of cash. At the same time, Agnew was also trying to influence the awarding of some federal contracts. To avoid jail and additional charges of criminality, he pleaded no contest to one count of tax evasion and left office in disgrace.

Invoking for the very first time the Twenty-fifth Amendment—enacted in the wake of President Kennedy's assassination to allow for the smooth transition of power—Nixon nominated a new vice president. His choice was House Minority Leader Gerald Ford, a country-club Republican congressman from Michigan. Washington insiders speculated that Nixon had chosen Ford because he was likable enough to be easily confirmed by Congress and lightweight enough that the Senate would never vote for Nixon's impeachment should it come to that, lest Ford become president.

With war raging in the Middle East, the nation facing a constitutional crisis over the tapes, and Nixon's presidency on life support, many of us in the special prosecutor's office worried that the White House would try to shut down our investigation. Without telling Archie, Rick and I and others in the office started making copies of documents, including memos and transcripts of interviews with witnesses that provided clear evidence of White House wrongdoing. Every night for several days, we carried out the copies in our briefcases. I stashed my trove of documents in a large cardboard box in the attic of my 20th Street town house.

◼

Friday, October 19, was the height of fall color in Washington. In my neighborhood, the propeller-shaped leaves on the ginkgo trees had turned gloriously gold. Downtown, the parkways were ribbons of yellow chrysanthemums, and the White House lawns shimmered like green silk. I felt a hint of hope in the air with the soft, cool autumn.

After a six-month struggle, John Dean had ended his fight for total immunity, and Archie and I were on our way to court, where Nixon's former White House counsel would plead guilty. I was sitting next to Archie in the back seat of the Rambler as he reflected on the situation Dean faced. "Think how differently things would have turned out it if Dean had taken another path," Archie said in a thoughtful and sympathetic tone. This led him to reflect on a friend of his, a judge, whom he greatly admired for the man's honesty and integrity. "He could have made a lot of money in private practice," Archie said, "but he displayed his character by choosing to serve the public good. If only Dean had followed that path of selflessness."

George Frampton had collected all the evidence we had against Dean, and we analyzed how to prove that at least some of it preceded Dean's testimony at the Ervin hearings so we wouldn't violate the use immunity granted him by the Senate. We joked about sending a couple of prosecutors to an Alaskan village where there was no TV signal, to quarantine our evidence before Dean testified. In the end, after a great deal of research and analysis, we came up with a way around the use immunity by identifying one minor segment of the cover-up that we knew about independent of Dean's Senate appearance: Dean's offer of clemency to the Watergate burglar James McCord in early 1973, in exchange for McCord's guilty plea at the original Watergate trial.

We told Dean that we would try him on that charge if he refused to plead guilty to one felony count of obstruction of justice. Though he'd have to spend some time in prison, we assured him it would be nowhere near the maximum penalty of five years.

In court, Sirica read the charges against Dean; then the clerk took over. "How do you plead?" he asked.

"I plead guilty," Dean replied in a firm voice. He had disregarded the advice of his attorney, who argued that we could not overcome the use immunity he had been granted and urged Dean not to accept the plea.

As in the case of Jeb Magruder, Sirica deferred sentencing until Dean had completed his cooperation with us. How valuable Dean would be depended on the tapes we were still awaiting. If the tapes didn't corroborate his testimony, Dean's credibility as a witness would be destroyed. It would be Dean's word against Nixon's, and there was no telling how a jury would react.

◼

That same day, the White House offered a compromise on the tapes so ludicrous it seemed like a joke. Nixon suggested that we let Senator John Stennis, a Democrat from Mississippi, listen to the tapes and compare his report to a transcript prepared by the White House. Stennis was elderly, nearly deaf, and weak from a gunshot wound suffered during a recent mugging at his Capitol Hill town house. *Time* magazine caught the absurdity of the proposal in a photograph of Stennis with his hand cupped around his ear. The caption read "Technical Assistance Needed."

Even apart from Stennis's physical difficulties, any White House transcript authenticated by him would be hearsay and therefore inadmissible as evidence in court. Nixon's proposal was not only ridiculous, it was in direct violation of the Court of Appeals ruling. James Doyle, our smart, tough press officer, argued that if the public understood what was at stake, we'd have their support. A dark-haired, Boston-bred Irish American, Doyle understood the power of the press because he had been a reporter himself. He had come to K Street from the *Washington Star*, where he had served as national correspondent. Earlier, as the Washington bureau chief of the *Boston Globe*, he had won a Pulitzer Prize for breaking a story about an unqualified nominee for federal district judge, which led to the withdrawal of the judge's nomination.

Doyle's office fielded an average of five hundred press calls a day. Pink message slips blanketed the staff's desks. Jim knew the quickest way to turn reporters against you was to ignore them. He and his staff tried to honor as many requests for comment and interviews as they could, and now Jim urged Archie to explain to the press his position on the tape transcripts.

Archie agreed, so Doyle scheduled a press conference for the next day, October 20, a Saturday.

At one o'clock, Archie walked to the front of a large room at the National Press Club with his wife, Phyllis, who had driven in from the couple's temporary home in McLean, Virginia. Blinking into the photographers' flashbulbs, he squeezed Phyllis's hand and whispered something to her.

He then took a seat at a cloth-covered table in front of a blue backdrop and an unfurled American flag. He wore a gray tweed suit, a blue button-down shirt, and a regular-length maroon-and-white-striped tie. Perhaps he thought his usual bow tie too jaunty for this solemn occasion.

"I read in one of the newspapers this morning the head-line, 'Cox Defiant.' I don't feel defiant," Archie said. "I hate a fight. But some things I feel deeply about, and I hope I can defend them steadfastly. I'm not looking for a confrontation. I'm not out to get the president. I'm concerned that I don't appear to be getting too big for my britches. But in the end, I thought I had to stick with what I thought was right."

Archie spoke for thirty minutes. He was eloquent, moving, and humble in explaining why we needed the tapes, why we had a right to them, and why the "Stennis compromise" was unacceptable. At the end, he patiently answered reporters' questions. As I listened to Archie from my seat in the second row, I considered a personal dilemma. I had a ticket for a flight to New York that afternoon with Ian for a family wedding, and a rare day off. I had discussed this trip with the trial team before the press conference and they all urged me to go. They reasoned that nothing major happened in Washington on the weekend, and besides, what could the president possibly do in retaliation? It was unlikely I'd miss anything. Still, I hesitated; but in the end, I left for the airport straight from the press conference and caught the shuttle to New York. In Manhattan, we went to the St. Moritz Hotel on Central Park South, dressed, and left for the wedding.

The bride was my husband's cousin. I can't recall any details about the ceremony or the reception, only the vision it brought of my own wedding on August 21, 1965, at the Covenant Club, a Jewish club on Dearborn Street in downtown

Chicago, whose huge, opulent ballroom glowed with crystal chandeliers and gilt-topped columns draped in dark green velvet swags. My parents had been married here during World War II, at a time when Jews were barred from most private clubs in the city. We weren't members, but relatives who belonged arranged for us to use it. I liked the idea of exchanging vows with Ian in the same place where my parents had been wed.

Ian Volner and I had met at Columbia Law School in 1964, when I was a first-year student and Ian was in his final year. He was tall, fair-haired, and handsome and far more sophisticated than I. He'd grown up in New York, in Croton-on-Hudson. His father was a real estate developer, his mother had worked at IBM and was studying for a master's degree at Columbia University. I liked Ian's family but was not close to them except for his aunt Ruth, his father's sister. She was a part-time actress who lived alone in Greenwich Village, was welcoming to me, and, among other acting gigs, appeared in a horror film called *Violent Midnight*; a film with Gina Lollobrigida, *Fast and Sexy*; and, during our marriage, *Annie Hall*, in which she played Woody Allen's aunt.

Ian's brilliance dazzled me. He was an editor at the *Columbia Law Review*, an honor limited to the top students in each class, and when we started dating he already had a job offer from the prestigious New York law firm Paul, Weiss, Rifkind, Wharton and Garrison. He didn't care that I hailed from the Midwest. Some of my classmates who'd grown up in the East and graduated from Ivy League schools made me feel like a naive hick. A cloud crossed their faces when I told them I'd earned my undergraduate degree from a Big Ten school. Their eyebrows rose at my Chicago accent and my Midwestern ways, such as calling soft drinks "pop" instead of "soda." One classmate I tried to befriend stopped speaking to me after I asked her where her alma mater, Mount Holyoke, was located.

Most important to me, Ian shared my exuberance for life. He smiled when I squealed with excitement at seeing the Statue of Liberty and the Empire State Building for the first time or stared in awe at the Gothic reliquaries at the Cloisters in Upper Manhattan. He delighted at my eagerness for new adventures. Once he took me skiing at Van Cortlandt Park in the Bronx. We rented poles, leather boots, and tall wooden skis and spent the afternoon sliding (or for me, mostly falling) down a modest hill sprayed with artificial snow.

It didn't seem to matter to Ian that I was an indifferent student of the law. I'd been at the top of my class at the University of Illinois, but I was mediocre at Columbia. I found it hard to apply myself to subjects in which I had no interest, and I almost flunked the final exam in Development of Legal Institutions. I hadn't read the materials and I sometimes skipped class, a first for me.

I wasn't exactly a role model for women in the law, a shockingly small group. I was one of only fifteen women in my class of three hundred; nationwide, women made up just 4 percent of the legal profession.

It was hard to put much effort into studying torts and contracts, because I still hoped to become a journalist. I was encouraged in this by a new wave of feminism I could feel around me, energized by—among other things—Betty Friedan's bestseller *The Feminine Mystique*. Published in 1963, the year before I graduated from college, it described the suffocating lives of suburban housewives and their widespread malaise, "the problem that has no name."

I yearned to work and be part of the world. But I also longed for intimacy with a man I loved. A few months after Ian and I started dating, when we were getting serious, I returned early from winter break to spend time alone with him while my roommate was gone. I was eager to sleep with him, but Ian astonished me by saying he respected me too much and wanted to wait until after we were married.

That should have been a warning, though at the time "nice girls" were supposed to be virgins. When one of my college sorority sisters got pregnant, she left school in disgrace. Sex was still a taboo subject. I didn't ask my friends whether they slept with their boyfriends or whether my chaste relationship with Ian was normal. I wondered whether there was something wrong with *me* for having such desires, but I ignored my sense that all was not well. I was living my life by the "beyond a reasonable doubt" standard I had just learned in my criminal law class, and since I didn't have that level of proof that Ian was wrong for me, I said yes when he proposed in the spring. We went to New York City's Diamond District on 47th Street to shop for a ring. A diamond was beyond Ian's budget, but other stones were also sold there; we found an opal ring for $35. I loved the ring and wore it proudly. Still, my sense of unease continued throughout our engagement.

After Ian's graduation, he remained in New York to study for the bar exam, and I headed home to Chicago to plan our wedding and work for the summer. Before leaving, I'd applied for and been granted a year's leave of absence. Now I'd have time to evaluate whether law school was right for me and to earn money for tuition if I decided to return. Ian and I agreed that once we were married, my father should no longer pay for my schooling.

That summer I worked as a social worker for the Department of Public Aid at Cook County Hospital. My job involved questioning women on welfare who were about to give birth. While they screamed in pain in the dirty, crowded hallway, I asked them the names of their babies' fathers and whether these absent men would be contributing to the infants' care. I didn't know whether I'd become a mother myself. I had no strong desire for children, and Ian and I had not discussed the issue, just as we'd avoided the subject of our nonexistent sex life.

As the day of our wedding approached, my doubts intensified.

Two nights before the wedding, I drove to O'Hare Airport to pick up Ian, his parents, his sister, and his aunt Ruth in my father's white Buick convertible. I hadn't seen Ian in nearly three months, and I hardly remembered him. We barely embraced. I felt nothing. It disturbed me that I wasn't joyous and excited, as I thought a bride should be. My unease continued through the rehearsal dinner the following evening.

The next day, driving to the Covenant Club with my younger sister Robin, my maid of honor, from our home in Skokie, I felt nauseous. We were late, so Robin sped up, her eyes darting around as she looked for a drugstore. Then a police car pulled us over. I explained the urgent situation to the officer, and he peered inside the car, where my gown lay on the back seat like a white silk, pearl-beaded shroud. Instead of giving us a ticket, he escorted us to the drugstore. "Good luck!" he said before driving away.

The wedding was perfect; my first night with Ian less so. We stayed at a hotel overlooking Lake Michigan. Beyond the windows, the lake stretched to the horizon, calm and blue. Sailboats bobbed on the surface, as a party of gulls flew above.

I changed in the bathroom into a fluttering white peignoir and slipped under the sheets next to Ian. What followed was awkward, quick, and not at all satisfying.

◼

Despite my efforts, our sex life never improved, which left me feeling unloved and undesirable. Now, eight years later, as I sat with Ian at his cousin's wedding, watching the tipsy revelers and the beautiful bride, so happy and hopeful as she glided across the parquet in a froth of satin and tulle, my heart felt as heavy as stone. Since joining the special prosecutor's office in May, I hadn't had a moment to reflect on the disaster of my own marriage. I took a sip of champagne and pushed away these painful thoughts, only to have them replaced by worry over Watergate. I was relieved when the reception ended around midnight, and we returned to the St. Moritz.

As soon as I stepped into the hotel lobby, I knew something terrible had happened. The night clerk darted from around the front desk with a frantic look on his face and thrust a slip of paper at me, a message from George Frampton in Washington. "Cox fired," the clerk had written in an urgent hand. "Office seized by the FBI. Call immediately."

6

THE MORNING AFTER

I called Rick from my hotel room. "It's unbelievable," he said in an angry tone. In the background I heard my team members talking, sounding agitated; a loud voice I didn't recognize was barking orders.

"Who is screaming at George?" I asked.

"FBI agents," Rick replied.

I dropped onto the bed and listened with a sinking feeling as Rick recounted the night's shocking events—a cascade of firings that would soon be known as the Saturday Night Massacre. Nixon was not moved by Archie's eloquence and logic, and a few hours after the special prosecutor's press conference, the president ordered Attorney General Elliot Richardson to fire him for daring to insist on getting the tapes. Richardson refused to carry out this order; he resigned instead. That made William Ruckelshaus, Richardson's deputy, the acting attorney general. Ruckelshaus also refused to fire Archie, and followed Richardson out the door. Now the third-ranking official at the Department of Justice, Solicitor General Robert Bork, became the acting attorney general. Bork had no problem executing Nixon's order, and he fired Archie. Soon after, at nine p.m., on a directive from the president himself, the FBI swooped in to occupy our office. They were still there keeping an eye on things as I talked to Rick.

"Were we fired, too?" I asked.

Rick, in a rare moment of not being sure of everything, sighed deeply. "I don't know," he said.

After a sleepless night, I caught the first shuttle to Washington on Sunday morning and went straight to the office. Cars and television trucks clogged K Street. I stepped over snakes of black cables as I pushed my way through the network news crews who were blocking the entrance to the building. Upstairs, the friendly guards who'd been with us since the start of our work were joined by a lineup of menacing FBI agents. I showed my green ID to one of them, and he allowed me into our suite of offices. I felt a lot older than when the ID photo of me with the pixie hairstyle had been taken, just months earlier.

The ninth floor looked like a crime scene. The desks and phones had been taped up, the file cabinets padlocked. Though earlier we'd taken home copies of key files as a precaution against just this sort of event, the office still held material that had yet to be presented to the grand jury, and I worried that we wouldn't have access to it. In my office, I threw my trench coat on my chair and started to peel the tape from a desk drawer where I kept my notes, when an FBI agent stopped me. "I wouldn't do that, Miss," he said in a threatening tone.

The sound of ringing phones mixed with the clickety-clack of the telex machine as it spewed messages of support from across the nation. Peering into Archie's now empty office, I saw secretaries sorting telexes and telegrams by state into cardboard boxes they'd arranged on the special prosecutor's conference table.

I joined the rest of the staff from the five task forces and supporting teams—lawyers, secretaries, paralegals, assistants—who'd gathered in a large anteroom, balancing files and notebooks on their laps.

"Welcome home," said Rick, his voice edged with cynicism, as I settled next to him on the floor.

"This is a coup, like in a banana republic. Nothing like it has ever happened in America," one of the lawyers said.

The newspapers were filled with stories that our office had been abolished, but Jim Doyle, our press officer, didn't think so. "We've been folded into the Justice Department, like you fold eggs into a cake. But we've gotten nothing on paper," he said in a comment he later repeated to reporters.

"Does this mean we'll be moving to Justice headquarters?" I asked.

Doyle shrugged. "Nothing's certain."

That afternoon, Rick, Carl, and I, along with several others, gathered at the Georgetown house where our colleague Chuck Breyer was housesitting. We talked about—and firmly rejected—the idea of quitting in protest of Archie's firing. We weren't going to make it easier for Nixon to kill the investigation of his wrongdoing. Rick had shared a compelling story from his childhood when, after being bullied, his mother told him "to kick 'em in the shins and always fight back." We would stay and do our jobs.

◼

Two days later, on Tuesday, October 23, our status was still uncertain. Outside, the weather was mild and clear. The sun glittered over the city's marble monuments like crystal, and a fresh breeze stirred the air. In the office, the anger of the previous days had settled into disbelief. Around noon, Archie came in to say goodbye, and we gathered in the anteroom outside his office as he spoke. "I have been spending some time thinking over something to say and never got beyond that point," he began. "Perhaps we've been saying all the things that needed to be said during the past few months. Perhaps, as in most important things, there is nothing to say. I think we tried to conduct this investigation by working with integrity, impartiality, fairness, and care. I do think it important that the work go on being done. I cling to the faith that its merit will appear to the American people and those who make decisions for them. And that you will be able to continue to do what you came here to do."

He told us he'd never come in contact with a group with more professional skill and dedication. "I hope that for all of you, as it certainly was for me, that this was a place . . ." He paused. "I'm not sure that 'fun' is the right word, but a place where there were real satisfactions, where we had a sense of coherence, of everybody helping everybody else. And that was enormously important to me. Just as your friendship and support was over the last week. I don't know quite how to thank you all for that."

When he finished, the room erupted in applause. "We should quit in protest!" someone shouted.

Archie shook his head. "You shouldn't do that," he said. "You should stay unless and until you're fired."

A few people cried softly, and a couple of women rushed forward to kiss Archie on the cheek. Archie himself looked as if he might cry. He hurried out, not lingering to share the cupcakes and punch that one of the secretaries had brought for the occasion.

The American public overwhelmingly opposed Archie's firing. Editorials denounced Nixon's action as the behavior of a dictator "who considers himself sole judge of the law and who uses the power of his office to purge independence from the executive branch and to supersede the mandate of the courts by arbitrary exercise of his will," as the *New York Times* put it.

The president's approval rating sank to a record low of 24 percent.

Archie's dismissal also revived campus activism, which had seemed all but dead after the withdrawal of the last American troops from Vietnam earlier that year. Student protests against Nixon's firing of the special prosecutor were not as zealous as the response had been to the escalation of conflict in Southeast Asia, or to the 1970 shooting of four students at Kent State University by the Ohio National Guard. Nevertheless, the protests were strong and consistent, taking the form of widely circulated petitions, rallies, and plans to form a delegation to lobby Congress for the appointment of a new special prosecutor.

I felt a deep kinship with these students. I wasn't much older than they were, and I shared their idealism. Like the campus protesters, I was appalled by Nixon and his generation of power-mad politicians who'd allowed a series of disasters to befall the nation and the world, from the McCarthyite witch hunt of the 1950s and the Bay of Pigs invasion in 1961, to the Vietnam War and Watergate.

I wasn't that far from my own activist days. As a freshman at the University of Illinois I was a member of the Young Democrats who had brought John Kennedy to campus during the 1960 presidential campaign. During my junior year in 1963, the year Martin Luther King Jr. gave his "I Have a

Dream" speech at the Lincoln Memorial in Washington, I organized a student symposium on civil rights and civil liberties. I took a course in constitutional law to help me make better arguments at the symposium. I also joined Students for a Democratic Society, or SDS, which organized a lot of protests at colleges across the country.

Years later, I was in my last semester at Columbia Law School during the April 1968 campus revolt organized by Mark Rudd, the fiery head of Columbia's SDS chapter. For a week, students occupied five university buildings, including the administration offices and the library, until the police evicted them in a predawn raid that resulted in seven hundred arrests. Campus demonstrations and picket lines outside academic buildings continued through the spring. Undergraduate classes were suspended for a while, though our law school courses carried on. We didn't want to cross the picket lines, but the New York State Bar Examiner said we would not be allowed to take the bar exam if we missed too many hours of class. I don't recall where all our classes were held, though I have a distinct memory of taking my final trial practice exam in the basement recreation room of an off-campus apartment building, where we sat in tiny chairs at little tables meant for small children.

Later, while working at the Justice Department in Washington, I marched in several candlelit parades in front of the White House to protest the Vietnam War. If one of the FBI agents or undercover cops in the crowd had recognized me and reported me, I could have lost my job.

Given my history of active protest, it might have been easy to label me as "out to get" Nixon, but that would be inaccurate. My colleagues and I were just doing our job of uncovering the truth and seeking justice, as I had done in prosecuting mobsters and labor racketeers. Win or lose, the goal was to nail down the facts, whatever they proved. Win or lose, a fair outcome was what mattered. Political affiliation was irrelevant.

For me and many other Americans, the linkage between the White House and Nixon's reelection committee, on the one hand, and the Watergate break-in, on the other, was undisputed. James McCord's letter to Judge Sirica implicating the president's men in the break-in and subsequent cover-up, and John Dean's testimony at the Ervin hearings describing the obstruction of justice in granular detail, had put the lie to Nixon's denials.

To ensure that the public didn't think Rick and I and our colleagues were just wild, liberal kids intent on bulldozing the presidency, Jim Doyle set up interviews for us with the media. Doyle thought that if the public got to know us, they would trust us. I went along with the interviews, though the end results often stung. Whereas reporters noted Rick's admirable "aggressiveness" in fighting for justice, his repu-tation as a "tough prosecutor," and his passion for ending government corruption, most journalists writing about me focused on my appearance. One story described my makeup, down to my pink eyeshadow. Other articles referred to me as "the miniskirted lawyer." The headline over a profile of me in the *Cincinnati Enquirer* blazed "The Leggiest Watergate Lawyer." Plus, the press usually portrayed Rick as the head of the trial team. True, he was technically the leader now that Jim Neal had returned to Nashville, but Rick always treated me as an equal partner and I never regarded him as my boss.

I had more to worry about than the annoying stories. I didn't know if I even had a job. But since no one had told us we were fired, we continued our work. On Tuesday afternoon, after Archie's farewell, we were back in court. Judge Sirica had called a hearing so that Nixon's lawyers could formally respond to the Court of Appeals decision ordering the president to give us the tapes. The paneled courtroom overflowed with spectators—court buffs, Justice Department officials, a group of Navy officers, and packs of reporters from around the country. Earlier, before the massive doors were unlocked, Sirica's clerk had sneaked in eight law students from his alma mater, Catholic University. When a young woman from the Howard University School of Law complained, the clerk let in her group too.

Two of Nixon's lawyers, Leonard Garment and Charles Alan Wright, sat at one counsel table. Garment's curious gaze traveled over the crowd, as Wright nervously downed glasses of water. At the opposite counsel table—a sturdy wood rectangle meant to seat six—Rick and I squeezed in with nine other lawyers from the special prosecutor's office, bumping our knees and elbows like kids playing musical chairs. Our leaders, Archie Cox and Jim Neal, were gone. It was now a children's crusade.

Time dragged as we waited for Judge Sirica. We tried to keep our faces neutral and ignore the chattering from the spectators behind us. I distracted myself by studying Nixon's lawyers. As the evidence against the president mounted, he'd grown his legal team, bringing in Wright, an expert on court procedure from Texas, and Garment, a respected Wall Street litigator who'd once been Nixon's law partner. Wright struck me as arrogant and distant, but I liked Garment. He always said hello and treated Rick and me as fellow professionals, not the evildoers or witch hunters the other White House lawyers made us out to be.

Judge Sirica entered late, at 2:05 p.m. He looked even sterner than usual; his brows were knitted together, and the folds in his skin seemed to have deepened.

"All rise," intoned the bailiff.

Sirica took his seat and put on his reading glasses. For the next ten minutes, he droned into a microphone the mandate of the United States Court of Appeals for the District of Columbia Circuit. Almost two months had passed since the judge issued the original order for Nixon to turn over the tapes. The president had not let up his fight to hold on to them, culminating in the firing of Archibald Cox.

Removing his glasses, Sirica asked Wright to stand. The room was so quiet I could hear the reporters' pens scratching. Wright looked pale; tension charged the air. Speaking softly, Wright told Sirica that Nixon would comply with the order to turn over the nine taped conversations. "This president does not defy the law," Wright responded.

Before I could fully absorb his words, the reporters dashed toward the exit. Sirica banged his gavel, ordering them back to their seats.

"Mr. Wright," said the judge, "the court is very happy the president has reached this decision." Sirica paused, smiling at the lawyer, then continued, "Anything further?"

"No, your honor," said Wright.

The judge banged his gavel. "Court is adjourned."

I was pleased, but, ever the pragmatist, I knew it was way too soon to celebrate. We didn't have the tapes yet.

◼

After Rick and I and the rest of the lawyers from our office returned to K Street, we gathered around a conference table in one of the ninth-floor offices to await a visit from the man who'd fired Archie Cox—Acting Attorney General Robert Bork.

When Bork arrived, he was accompanied by Henry Petersen, head of the Justice Department's Criminal Division, whom Bork had designated to oversee our office. Bork had a beefy build and frizzy carrot-colored hair, with a matching scraggly beard. "I want you to continue your work," he said. He stood close to the door, as if positioning himself to flee as soon as possible.

"Why did you fire Archibald Cox?" demanded Carl Feldbaum.

Sweat beaded Bork's forehead above his black-rimmed glasses. "I had ten minutes to make up my mind, and if I didn't do it, somebody else would have. So here I am," he said.

But I wondered if that was true. After Bork, there was no clear line of succession at the Department of Justice. If Bork, like Richardson and Ruckelshaus, had refused to fire Cox, it's likely that Nixon would have been thwarted, at least temporarily, in his zeal to get rid of the special prosecutor. Eventually, yes, he'd have hired another attorney general and gotten his way. But now Bork would go down in history as a toady who had done a corrupt president's bidding instead of what was right for the nation.

I was surprised and disappointed to see Henry Petersen, my former organized-crime section chief, standing next to the bearish Bork. Henry had become head of the entire Criminal Division and, we were told, was now our designated leader. He was a square-jawed ex-Marine with ramrod posture, wearing a dark suit. The yellow nautical knots patterned on Petersen's ship-themed blue tie struck me as a fitting symbol for the tangled mess we were in.

I had a history with Petersen that now came flashing

back. While working for him, I noticed that the men who had started after me were trying cases while I was kept arguing appeals despite my being hired as a trial attorney, which was my passion. I wasn't sure how to get a trial, but decided that confronting Petersen was my only way forward. "Henry, you hired me as a trial attorney. What's going on?" I demanded.

Petersen sputtered his answer. "But . . . we try cases against the Mafia. You'd be in the courtroom with made mobsters, and, well, you're a girl. You'd be more vulnerable."

"Didn't you notice I was a woman when you hired me as a trial attorney?" I fumed in response.

I shouldn't have been surprised, though. Earlier, at my first meeting of all the section attorneys, Petersen paused before playing one of the first legal wiretaps ever recorded, looked up and said, "Jill, we'd all understand if you want to leave the room. There's some very harsh language on this."

I said I had heard worse in my sorority house and stayed put.

Despite my clashes with Petersen over his sexist attitudes toward women lawyers, I'd never had a reason to distrust his judgment on the law. Now, as he stood next to Bork, I had to wonder.

Petersen cleared his throat. "If you want to lose your jobs, you are going to have to quit. You won't be fired," he told us. "For you to quit would be a moral and professional disservice to yourselves and the country. This case cannot sustain another change in personnel."

It was as if he had heard the beginning, but not the end, of our discussion on Sunday. We had already rejected the idea of quitting.

Though Petersen was saying all the right things, I felt uncomfortable. I couldn't shake the feeling that he was on

Nixon's side, not ours. No sooner had Bork and Petersen left, when Rick broke the sour mood. "Nixon's Bork is worse than his bite," he said, making me laugh.

■

A feeling of exhausted relief carried me through the following days. I would never forgive Robert Bork for firing Archie, but our mission was still on track. We'd dodged a legal confrontation with Nixon that no one wanted and that should never have happened, and after all the legal wrangling and public uproar, we were at last awaiting the tapes.

A week later, on the Monday two days before Halloween, I arrived at work to find a small pumpkin on my desk. Inserted in the top was a telex message—one of hundreds that had clattered out of our Western Union machine. I don't recall exactly what it said, except that it was a bolstering sentiment from a supporter. That morning everyone in the office was greeted with a similar message-in-a-pumpkin on their desk, courtesy of Carl Feldbaum, who had gone with his wife, Laura, to a Safeway the night before and bought up the store's entire supply of pumpkins—enough to fill two grocery carts. Carl had slipped into the building in the middle of the night to deliver the pumpkins and distribute the messages, which he retrieved from the boxes in Archie's now empty office.

That Halloween, though, the treats did not protect us from Nixon's tricks. The day after we got our pumpkins, Rick went to court with Hank Ruth and Phil Lacovara to meet with Judge Sirica and Nixon's lawyer about the procedure for transferring the tapes from the White House vaults to the court. Nothing important was expected, just technical details, so I didn't go with them. Instead I stayed at the office, preparing to interview still more witnesses.

Two hours passed, and I looked up to see Rick standing in my doorway, his face white with fury. "Two of the damn tapes are missing!" he said in an anguished tone.

"What?" I was sure I hadn't heard him correctly.

"Nixon claims they don't exist."

In the middle of explaining to Sirica how the tapes would be turned over, Nixon's lawyer Fred Buzhardt blurted out that two of the conversations we wanted had never been recorded at all. One call, Buzhardt claimed, had been made on a phone in the residential section of the White House that wasn't included in the recording system. During the other conversation, in the Executive Office Building, Buzhardt said the tape system had malfunctioned.

"It's unbelievable," I said. The bad news had raised my voice an octave higher. This was astounding.

All the conversations were crucial to our investigation, as we believed they held evidence of Nixon's involvement in the cover-up. We had only asked for nine, so the removal of two was a significant loss. The first missing tape was of a telephone call between the president and John Mitchell, the man we believed had approved the Watergate break-in, three days after it happened. The second recorded Nixon's face-to-face meeting with John Dean in the Executive Office Building. Dean had told us that during that conversation he admitted to Nixon he was talking to federal prosecutors.

The next morning, the White House sent a taping system expert to our office to explain how the equipment had broken down. To our surprise, the technician denied there was any malfunction, as Buzhardt had claimed. Without sharing that information with Buzhardt, we got him to agree to a hearing that very afternoon to put what we labeled "helpful facts" on the record. But at the hearing we were surprised yet again:

the technician now said that there was indeed a malfunction. On cross-examination by Rick, however, he admitted that he had changed his testimony because, before he came to court, Buzhardt had told him there was a malfunction. That revelation, which strongly suggested witness tampering, was the first of many disasters for the White House lawyers. Normal procedure would have been for us to continue questioning witnesses in secret before the grand jury, but Sirica said he wanted "the facts and circumstances" of the missing tapes to "be made a matter of public record." So he ordered that the day's public hearing continue.

For the next week, Rick and I cross-examined a parade of Secret Service technicians and White House aides who had knowledge of the president's taping system. This was the public's first opportunity to see us in action as prosecutors. Our painstaking questioning revealed a shocking carelessness in the handling of the tapes before and after the system's disclosure at the Ervin hearings that showed the White House's significant vulnerability. The Secret Service was responsible for removing the fully recorded tapes from the machines—which were stashed in a cabinet in their basement locker room below the Oval Office—replacing them with new tapes, and labeling the completed tapes before putting them away in a secure storage area at the Executive Office Building. The Secret Service also was charged with keeping track of the tapes, but their record keeping was haphazard and extremely sloppy. Part of the log of who had borrowed the tapes had been scratched in pencil on a torn piece of brown grocery bag. We also learned that the return of more than thirty tapes removed from storage had never been logged.

Under our questioning, the president's men insisted that

the crucial April 15 conversation between Nixon and John Dean hadn't been recorded because the tape had run out. They explained that there were backup machines, which were supposed to pick up when a tape ended, but the switchover had failed in this instance. They also stuck to their story that the conversation between Nixon and Mitchell three days after the break-in hadn't been recorded.

From Sirica's scowl, I could tell he was as skeptical as we were.

◼

Toward the end of the week, things got more interesting when two White House aides testified that the person who knew most about the tapes was Nixon's longtime secretary, Rose Mary Woods.

John C. Bennett, a retired general who was the deputy to General Alexander Haig, Bob Haldeman's replacement as White House chief of staff, told Judge Sirica that fourteen tapes of presidential conversations had been in Rose's office for several months while she worked on transcribing them. Some of the tapes had since been returned to storage in the Executive Office Building, though eight tapes were still in her office.

Another White House aide, Stephen B. Bull, testified that some of the tapes had left the White House entirely on two occasions. Bull said he took a dozen tapes to Camp David on the weekend of September 29 and 30 for Rose to review. Bull said that Nixon and Rose listened to a tape in Rose's cabin while Bull, working in an adjacent room, listened to another tape, trying to find the exact location of the subpoenaed conversations. Rose later accompanied the president to Florida, taking some of the tapes with her so she could continue work on transcriptions at Nixon's home in Key Biscayne.

At that point, Judge Sirica interrupted Bull's testimony to issue an order that Rose Mary Woods be summoned as a witness.

Rick had cross-examined Bull and also taken the next witness, Alfred Wong, an expert on the taping system from the Secret Service Technical Division. I felt that Rick was taking a disproportionate share of witnesses, and though he had a year's more trial experience than I, I saw no reason for this. During my time at the Justice Department, I had learned that I needed to stand up for myself. After Petersen refused to give me a trial because I was a "girl" and would be more "vulnerable" to mobsters in the courtroom, I raised the issue with Charles Ruff, my supervisor and mentor. Ruff took action, and that was how I got my first trial. He asked to have me as his second chair in the labor racketeering case against Jesse Carr, the powerful head of the Teamsters in Alaska. It turned out I *was* more vulnerable than the men—to the weather. Federal court rules prohibited women attorneys from wearing pants, even in Anchorage where the temperature was typically 30 below. Like Ginger Rogers, who had to do everything Fred Astaire did, only backward and in high heels, I had to be as good as the male lawyers while freezing to death in a skirt and hose.

I didn't hesitate to act on that lesson now. During a courtroom break, I took Rick aside in the hallway. "I'm taking the next witness, and from now on, we'll share equally," I said.

Rick shrugged. "Fine," he said.

I don't think he had intentionally shut me out. He just didn't stop long enough to realize he was stepping on my toes.

7

SECRETARY OF MORALE

The next morning, November 8, 1973, I sat with Rick in Judge Sirica's brightly lit courtroom as we awaited the day's first witness. Because the burden of proof was on the White House to convince Sirica that there was no deliberate wrongdoing in the missing tapes, Nixon's lawyers controlled the flow of witnesses. We had no idea who would appear until a little after ten, when the bailiff called Rose Mary Woods. A few moments later, the president's secretary pushed through the swinging gate at the bar and took her seat in the witness box. She wore a wool dress, pearls, and heavy powder that didn't hide the flush of indignation spreading from her neck to her temples.

Rose was a "chain of custody" witness, called by the White House to shed light on her handling of the two missing tapes. Her aggrieved manner, though, suggested she considered the entire proceeding an outrage.

Under questioning by Samuel J. Powers, a Florida lawyer newly hired by the White House to bolster its beleaguered legal team, Rose described her struggles in transcribing the tapes. The quality was so poor, she said, that it was difficult to hear conversations over ambient noises that registered loudly. Dishes clattered. Band music from a ceremony on the South Lawn wafted in. When the president put his feet up on his desk, it sounded like a bomb exploding.

Rose told of driving to Camp David on the morning of Saturday, September 29, with Steve Bull, the aide who managed the president's calendar and was assigned to cue up the tapes to where the subpoenaed conversations began. She said she worked nonstop on transcribing the tape that contained a ninety-minute conversation from June 20, 1972, involving Nixon, Haldeman, and Ehrlichman. Bull gave her a machine with this tape already in it, and she worked in her cottage until three a.m. on Sunday, sleeping only three hours, and working again from six a.m. until "the Nixons were kind enough" to ask her to dinner in the first family's lodge. "It is one of the very few [Sundays] in my life I did not attend mass because I was trying to finish this job," she said. Nevertheless, after twenty-nine hours of work, she was unable to complete the transcription. Rose seemed intent on casting doubt on the usefulness of the tapes, as if to diminish the importance of the fact that two were missing.

Then it was my turn to cross-examine her. I started slowly, with basic questions. How had she learned about the taping system? The same way the rest of the world had, she said, through Alexander Butterfield's testimony at the Ervin hearings. How did she get the assignment to transcribe the tapes? The president had asked her "to be available for a special task," and "of course, I would always do it for him," she added. Rose looked hard at me, her green eyes defiant. It was an expression I'd often seen from hostile witnesses, and the message was clear: *I'm not giving you a damn thing.*

Despite her hostility, she spoke softly, muffling her words. Judge Sirica had to ask her numerous times to "speak a little louder."

I pressed on, asking her to describe the procedures she followed in handling the tapes and making transcripts. Cross-examination is a craft, like cooking or writing or playing the flute. Good trial lawyers operate on instinct, bolstered by training and preparation. During my first trial, as the second chair in the racketeering case against Jesse Carr, I had prepared the entire case and read every bit of documentation and analysis we had—and even so, I was staggered by my boss Chuck Ruff's withering cross of the Teamsters boss.

"How did you know what to ask him?" I whispered when Chuck had finished and was sitting next to me at the prosecution table.

"Easy," he said. "When you start the cross, the words just come out of your mouth. You know what to ask."

It helps to be well prepared and have a gift for thinking on your feet. Becoming expert at cross-examination, however, requires something that applies to any skill—practice. By the time I encountered Rose Mary Woods in the witness box, I had only a bit more than three years of trial experience—but that was enough to give me a solid grounding in technique. I proceeded without hesitation.

As my cross of Rose progressed, she grew increasingly agitated. "I told you, I don't remember," she snapped, after I repeated a question she had avoided answering. When I asked her whether Steve Bull had given her any instructions on how to operate the recording machine, her anger flared. "It says on and off, forward and backward, and I did catch on to that very fast," she said, her voice edged with sarcasm.

"Were there any precautions taken to assure you would not accidentally hit the erase button?" I asked.

Rose glared at me. "Everybody said be terribly careful. I don't believe I am so stupid that they had to go over it and over it. I was told if you push that button it will erase, and I think I used every possible precaution to not do that."

"What precautions specifically did you take to avoid recording over it, thereby getting rid of what was already there?" This turned out to be a prescient question.

"What precautions?" Rose snapped. "I used my head. It is the only one I had to use."

Her answer would come back to haunt her.

◨

Of all the women in Nixon's life, Rose spent the most time with him, more even than his wife. She had been with him through twenty-two roller-coaster years, boosting his ego, advising him, nurturing his ambitions, and protecting him from troublesome people and distractions. There was much to draw them together: a fierce work ethic, an obsession with privacy, a remarkable rise from humble beginnings, and an early bout with tragedy. Nixon had grown up in Whittier, California, the son of a devout Quaker mother and a father who ran a small grocery store and gas station. His two younger brothers had died of tuberculosis as children, and when a spot was found on Nixon's lung, his parents feared that he, too, would succumb to the disease. They forbade him to play sports, though the spot turned out to be a pneumonia scar.

Rose was born four years after Nixon, in 1917, the middle child of five in a strict Catholic home in Sebring, Ohio, that sat across the street from the church where her parents had married. As a teenager, she suffered a mysterious illness that caused her to drop out of school briefly. Soon after graduating from high school, her fiancé, who had been the school's basketball star, died of spinal meningitis. Rose never got over the loss and never married. For several years she worked as a secretary for the Royal China Company, a pottery-making enterprise that employed her father as foreman and, later, as personnel director. During World War II, to escape memories of her fiancé, she moved to Washington, where she got a job in the Office of Censorship and became known for her astonishingly fast typing and shorthand skills. In 1947, she landed a position on the House Select Committee on Foreign Aid, which studied the needs of war-ravaged European countries to allocate funds under the Marshall Plan. One of the committee members was Richard Nixon, a newly elected Republican congressman from California. As a secretary to the committee, Rose handled Nixon's expense reports, which she admired for their neatness and accuracy. He in turn admired Rose's efficiency. When Nixon won a Senate seat in 1950, he asked Rose to become his secretary. Nixon hired her despite her warning, "I'm a Democrat and a Catholic."

Rose's loyalty was unfailing and absolute throughout the most important moments of Nixon's career. She was with him during the "Checkers Speech" on September 23, 1952, when Nixon's candidacy as Dwight Eisenhower's vice presidential running mate was threatened after the *New York Post* accused him of abusing a political expense fund by accepting gifts from wealthy donors. Nixon told sixty million Americans watching on TV and listening on radio that "regardless of what they say about it," the family intended to keep one gift—a black-and-white cocker spaniel that his six-year-old daughter, Tricia, had named Checkers. When Nixon heard that Eisenhower, unsatisfied by the speech, demanded a deeper explanation, he dictated a telegram of resignation to Rose. As she left the room, Nixon's campaign manager ran after her, grabbed the telegram from her hands, and ripped it up. "You didn't need to do that. I wasn't going to send it anyway," Rose said.

Rose stood by Nixon throughout his vice presidency in the Eisenhower years and his time in the political wilderness after he lost the presidency to John Kennedy in 1960 and then the governorship of California to Pat Brown in 1962. She served as Nixon's secretary in his private law practice, moving with him to Los Angeles in 1961 (where she drove a turquoise convertible), then to New York in 1963. When Nixon became president, in 1969, his first staff appointment in the White House was to hire Rose as his personal secretary. He assigned her a small office very near the Oval Office. Almost immediately, she clashed with Bob Haldeman, the president's chief of staff, who tried to usurp her power as gatekeeper and cut off her access to Nixon by moving her to the Executive Office Building, which is separated by a wide driveway from the West Wing. Rose fought back, securing a larger, more elegant space in the West Wing. Though not attached to Nixon's office, it was just steps away, through a private corridor. After Haldeman was forced to resign in the wake of disclosures of his role in the Watergate cover-up at the end of April 1973, Nixon elevated Rose's title from "personal secretary" to "executive assistant."

Over the years, as Rose typed Nixon's speeches and guarded access to him, she became his confidante and advisor. When he was vice president, the *New York Times* called her "Nixon's Real Enforcer" and his "de facto Chief of Staff." She was a "super secretary" who had several secretaries of her own. Rose helped Nixon prepare and edit many of his most important speeches, including the speech on November 3, 1969, in which, instead of announcing the end of the Vietnam War (as he'd promised on the campaign trail), he called on "the great silent majority of Americans" to support him in a gradual troop reduction as the fighting continued. She accompanied Nixon on his historic trip to China in 1972, and regularly traveled with him and his family to their homes in Key Biscayne and San Clemente; on Air Force One, she strapped her typewriter to a table spread over her lap so she could work without interruption through takeoffs and landings and unexpected turbulence.

Without a husband or children of her own, Rose turned to the Nixons as her surrogate family. She was close to Pat, with whom she sometimes shared clothes, and to Tricia and Julie, who called her Aunt Rose. The family feeling extended to Rose's brother Joe Woods, a former FBI agent who became the sheriff of Cook County, Illinois, and to whom Nixon gave his discarded suits.

Rose shared Nixon's hatred of the news media. She once poured a drink on the head of a reporter who'd written unkindly about "the boss." Before Watergate, though, her own press had been favorable. In 1962 the *Los Angeles Times* named her "Woman of the Year"; she was the first secretary to ever receive the honor. In 1971 *Ladies' Home Journal* tapped her as one of the "75 most important women in America," a group that included Joan Baez, Margaret Mead, Coretta Scott King, Katharine Graham, and Joyce Carol Oates.

Her lifestyle was more like a cabinet member's than a secretary's: long, stressful hours at work cushioned by a posh apartment and a glittering social life. She earned more than many White House aides, including Alexander Butterfield, Nixon's deputy chief of staff. Her $36,000 annual salary allowed her to live in a two-bedroom condominium at the elegant Watergate, as did John Mitchell. Rose was a frequent guest at Washington parties. She loved to dance, her chief stress reliever. Dressed in elegant, floor-length gowns, she twirled away at embassy balls and state dinners with her frequent companion, the gay lobbyist and public relations executive Robert Gray.

Observers of Nixon and Rose, wrote Madeleine Edmondson and Alden Duer Cohen in their book *The Women of Watergate*, "marveled at the 'instant communication' they achieved while working at top speed, their almost telepathic relationship. Often Rose knew what Nixon had in mind before his sentence was half formed. . . . She was almost an extension of Nixon's will."

Perhaps her most important role was Secretary of Morale. Rose was attuned to every nuance of Nixon's emotions and moods. "You keep telling me I say everything is great, but the speech was absolutely beautiful," Rose told the president after a televised speech about the Vietnam War on April 7, 1971, in a telephone conversation caught on Nixon's secret taping system.

"It was pretty good, actually," Nixon responded, as if to convince himself. Protests against his policies in Southeast Asia had been raging across the nation, and his voice was tinged with anxiety. In the speech, Nixon had assured the nation that the end of America's involvement in Vietnam was near; in fact, it wouldn't come for almost another two years.

Rose told the president of the many calls she had received praising the speech. She reported that Admiral Thomas Moorer, the chairman of the Joint Chiefs of Staff, "thought it was so great, that you struck just the right note and that all the military people would appreciate it."

Rose said that she had also gotten a call from Paul Keyes, a writer for the hit TV show *Laugh-in*, where Nixon had made an awkward appearance in 1968 in a bid to appeal to younger voters. "Paul thought it was marvelous, one of the best speeches you ever made," she gushed.

"You didn't hear from any cabinet officers?" Nixon asked.

Rose wasn't going to lie to the president, but neither was she going to let the conversation end on a negative note. "A lot of them probably don't want to talk to *me*," she said.

Nixon seemed satisfied with her answer, signing off, "OK, hon, bye."

In another era, Rose might have been chief of staff herself, in which case the cabinet members would have eagerly spoken to her. But in her time ambitious women had limited options beyond traditionally female jobs as nurses, teachers, and secretaries. There were a few women like me—pioneers in fields reserved for men—but most of us were a generation younger than Rose.

◼

When her testimony in Judge Sirica's courtroom concluded, Rose hurried outside into the cold afternoon, pushing through the crowd of journalists and photographers. "Miss Woods, do you still think President Nixon is an honest man?" a reporter asked, shoving a microphone in her face.

"That is a rude, impertinent question," she shot back, adding emphatically, "The answer is yes."

8

THE LADY LAWYER

As public outrage over the Saturday Night Massacre continued into November, President Nixon finally approved the appointment of a new Watergate special prosecutor, Leon Jaworski. At sixty-eight, Jaworski was a conservative Democrat from Texas who had voted for Nixon and headed one of the nation's largest law firms, the Houston-based Fulbright & Jaworski.

From the start, I was suspicious of Leon. Unlike Archie, who had been selected by the attorney general, Leon was selected by the president and his new chief of staff, Alexander Haig. If Nixon really wanted to undo the damage he'd caused by firing Archie Cox, why didn't he just bring back our revered leader? Archie was still in Washington, and he had recently testified before the Senate Judiciary Committee, which was investigating his dismissal. Archie told the senators of our frustration in getting the White House to release the tapes and other documents, and he talked candidly and clearly about the important investigative work that remained. The Watergate case, he said, was "nowhere near done."

My wariness of the new special prosecutor only increased

when Leon came to K Street the first time to talk to the staff. In Texas, he was known as "Colonel," the Army rank he'd held during World War II, but he didn't look the part. Stocky and white-haired, he had a fleshy, broad-nosed face and shrewd brown eyes. He was dressed in an elegant dark suit, with a green silk handkerchief folded in his breast pocket, and a spotless white shirt.

A group of about eighty people crammed into the file room to hear Leon's opening remarks, which didn't alter my feelings about him. He started off by saying that he had met with Haig, but had avoided an appearance of impropriety by refusing to meet with the president, and proudly announced, "I believe I can get the job done because I have greater independence than Archie Cox had."

How arrogant, I thought. I took his slight of Archie personally.

"You're not implying that Archie didn't think we were independent?" said Hank Ruth, who had been Archie's deputy and was now Leon's. He clearly shared my feeling.

Earlier in the week, the *New York Times* reported that Leon had actually turned down the job before Archie took it. "I didn't think at the time the independence was there as it is now," Leon told the paper. Leon now explained to us that Robert Bork had written a new provision into the Justice Department's regulations requiring the approval of both Republican and Democratic congressional leaders before the special prosecutor could be dismissed. That was all to the good, but it seemed impossible that we would ever have the warm, trusting relationship with Leon that we had had with Archie.

We were young, liberal, and Ivy-educated, and we felt a natural affinity with Archie's Eastern academic sensibility. I thought Leon's *otherness* as a Texan wheeler-dealer in big oil and fast money would prevent us from getting too close to him or trusting him completely. Still, there was no denying that Leon's skill as a trial attorney could be helpful if we ever got to that point.

A champion debater in high school, Leon entered Baylor University at fifteen and the next year was admitted to the university's law school. He got his professional start in Waco, Texas, at the height of Prohibition, defending bootleggers and moonshiners, winning cases before bone-dry juries and judges. In 1929 he lost a notorious case defending a black tenant farmer accused of murdering a white couple, but his expert handling of witnesses in that case got him noticed by the legal big shots in Houston. Before he turned thirty, he had made partner at one of the city's most prestigious firms, Fulbright, Crooker, Freeman and Bates.

Leon's confidence and courtroom flair worked magic with juries. Once in a capital case, he hid a knife in his pocket. During his closing argument, he produced it and tried to hand it to a juror. "If you are going to send this man to the electric chair, then you might as well walk over there and do the deed yourself," he said, as the juror recoiled from the shiny blade. Leon had made his point, and the jury voted to reduce the convicted man's sentence to life.

As the chief prosecutor for the Army's War Crimes Trials Section in 1945, Leon convinced a jury to convict several citizens of Russelsheim, Germany, who had stoned to death six American prisoners of war. He also prepared a series of cases that resulted in the hanging of Nazi guards at Dachau. Based on his Army work, Leon was asked to join the prosecution at Nuremberg, which he declined, on the grounds that the legal procedures were too confused, particularly the general Nuremberg charge. As he told *Esquire*, "I couldn't understand why they had to charge Germany with waging an aggressive war. They didn't need that. They had the clearest of cases in crimes against humanity. Calling a war of aggression a war crime—I knew *that* was sure to come back and haunt us some day."

After the war, Leon returned to Houston, where he became active in politics. He managed the litigation that allowed Lyndon B. Johnson to run simultaneously for the Senate and the vice presidency in 1960. He also became friendly with Governor John Connally and later served on the legal staff of the Warren Commission, which investigated the assassination of John F. Kennedy. As president, Johnson asked Leon to be his attorney general, but Leon turned him down. "It just *bothers* me if I can't be in a position to pursue my own independent judgment," Leon told *Esquire*. "You know you're not your own master if you serve in a cabinet."

By the time he arrived in our offices, Leon was the rich and powerful head of an immense national law firm, the patriarch of a family of three children and many grandchildren, and the owner of a three-hundred-acre ranch in the hill country outside Austin where he raised his beloved prize quarter horses. In the year before becoming the Watergate special prosecutor, he had served as president of the American Bar Association. At the time, the journal *Juris Doctor* wrote of Leon that "there appears to be no fierce sense of moral outrage at social justice gnawing at his gut." Yet, as the *New York Times* commented, "none who know him doubt that his reverence for the law is profound."

He deserved more respect than we gave him.

◼

During his first meeting with us, Leon's tone was that of an elder scolding unruly children. He'd heard that we'd been discussing the Watergate case with outsiders and told us that this practice had to stop. "What you learn in these offices must be held in sacred confidence. It is not a fit subject for repetition outside these walls," he said. "What I mean is that it is not a fit subject of idle gossip at a cocktail party."

I never discussed Watergate with outsiders, and I didn't think my colleagues did either. Yet for the first time—other than the incident the previous summer of the *Washington Post* getting hold of our trash—there were suspicions of leaks from our office. To this day, I have no idea where the leaks might have come from. During the first week of his tenure, Leon threatened to have the staff sign affidavits swearing they had not leaked information to reporters and would not do so in the future. It was a hollow threat meant to scare us. He never followed up on it, but it showed his distrust of us and added to our wariness of him.

In addition, Leon told us that we were over-aggressive in the grand jury and that some of us should be fired. Rick was sure that Leon was looking straight at him when he uttered those words, and he was sure that Haig had criticized him to Leon during their meeting.

"We are just doing our jobs and doing it right," Rick retorted. "We're not rude and we're not pulling any punches."

We were all relieved when Leon added that he had decided not to fire anyone.

Even if it was true that Haig had spoken ill of Rick to Leon, there was another reason for their strained relationship. Rick's brash, cocky style clashed with Leon's Southern courtliness. Actually, Leon was just as cocky as Rick, but the older man's high confidence was hidden under a veneer of good-ol'-boy charm. His arrogance was less well disguised, at least in my view. I thought Leon egotistical for having declined a role in the Nuremberg prosecutions, for having refused President Johnson's offer to become attorney general, and for having turned down the first offer he had received to be special prosecutor and then boasting about securing from Bork more independence than Archie had. As I got to know Leon better, my view softened.

In contrast to his feelings about Rick, Leon liked me and enjoyed showing me off as a kind of surrogate daughter. He took me out to lunch with his friends, and he brought me to the Washington office of Fulbright, Crooker, Freeman, Bates and Jaworski to meet his partners. He always introduced me as "the lady lawyer." I wasn't overly sensitive to language, and I usually let sexist comments slide by without comment. But being called a "lady lawyer" aggravated me. It implied that a woman practicing law was different from a male lawyer, and somehow less.

Once, as we left a gathering with some of Leon's acquaintances, I said gently, "It wasn't really necessary to introduce me as a lady lawyer."

Leon looked surprised. "But you're so special. I'm proud of you and want everyone to know it," he said.

"Leon, they *saw* me," I protested. "If you just introduce me as a lawyer, they'll know."

Still, he continued to introduce me as the lady lawyer no matter how often I asked him not to. I knew he meant no disrespect of my abilities. In fact, he had so much confidence in my skills that he wanted to push Rick out and have me take over the trial team by myself in Jim Neal's absence. Or perhaps he thought—incorrectly—that he could control me more easily than he could Rick.

The incident that prompted Leon's plan to oust Rick started on Wednesday, November 21, the day before Thanksgiving. Two of Nixon's lawyers, Fred Buzhardt and Leonard Garment, showed up at K Street, the first time they'd been to our offices, and in a private conversation with Leon, revealed a startling new development. In addition to the two missing tapes among the nine we'd subpoenaed, the lawyers said they'd recently discovered a problem with a third tape.

An eighteen-and-a-half-minute section of the crucial conversation between Nixon and Haldeman on June 20, 1972, had been wiped out. Where there had once been talk, there was now only a steady hum. The lawyers blamed the gap on Rose Mary Woods. "I see no way this could have been done accidentally," Buzhardt told Leon. He and Garment had questioned her, he went on, "and she has no defense."

In telling us about the gap before its existence was revealed in court, the lawyers hoped to minimize its value as bombshell news while also giving us the appearance that they had nothing to hide.

Immediately, Leon called Judge Sirica, and a few hours later the three lawyers, with Rick, Hank Ruth, and me in tow, gathered in the judge's second-floor courtroom at the federal courthouse. As Sirica glowered, Buzhardt explained the problem with the third tape. The judge ordered that the seven tapes, including the one with the gap, be turned over to him no later than Monday morning. He also ordered another hearing to investigate.

As usual, a pack of reporters waited outside the courthouse. We had been warned many times not to speak to the press, but when a reporter shouted a question about what possible violations of law could result from this new information about the tapes, Rick nevertheless responded.

"There is potentiality of obstruction of justice or contempt of court and I want a hearing into the matter by the court."

It infuriated Leon that Rick had defied the order not to talk to reporters. Soon afterward, he called me into his office to say he wanted me to take over the task force myself. "I don't trust Rick. I trust you," he said.

I wouldn't hear of it. "We're working well," I said. "You should leave things alone."

"I'll think about it," said Leon.

That was the end of it. He never brought it up again.

By now, Rick and I were a celebrated team, anointed by the press as wunderkinds, the nation's best hope to bring down the corrupt president. Photographers loved snapping us as we walked to and from court, carrying identical faux-leather government-issue briefcases and sometimes wearing similar tan trench coats. The contrast of Rick's black curls with my blond locks and peachy complexion made for striking pictures that seemed to echo our courtroom styles: Rick was hot and combative, I was cool and steady. Out of court, we worked well together, too. Both of us were determined to explore every lead, interview every witness, and analyze every angle in our quest for the truth. It was an immense, exhausting job that tested the limits of our strength and endurance.

In my private life, though, I was hardly a star. My marriage to Ian continued to be miserable. Ian had not been supportive of me and my work going back to our first years together and my time at the Justice Department. One example occurred when I was arguing in the Second Circuit Court of Appeals in New York to uphold the conviction of several gangsters who had stolen a shipment of Whirlpool appliances. The three-judge panel was led by Chief Judge Henry Friendly, a revered legal mind who was frequently discussed as a potential Supreme Court nominee, though this never came to pass. Before I even had a chance to say "May it please the Court," Judge Friendly berated me and announced he wouldn't consider the evidence in my appendix because I had presented it in the standard format used by the Department of Justice instead of in the style of the Southern District. Not being able to argue using the facts in the appendix was a serious loss, but I controlled my distress and proceeded calmly and successfully, eventually winning the case. Once I exited the courtroom, though, I felt my anger exploding and my eyes welling up. I made it to the adjacent lawyers' cloakroom, but I was unable to find a ladies' room for privacy—the nearest one was on a different floor—and my tears erupted in front of the lawyers gathered nearby. I found a pay phone in the hall and, still weepy, called Ian at his office for comfort.

He yelled at me for crying in public.

I couldn't understand his reaction. I hadn't cried or yelled obscenities in the courtroom. I had acted professionally until I was outside the court. And so it fell to my law school classmate Rena Gordon, who had come to court to hear my argument, to console me.

Given his own success as a lawyer, it was unlikely that Ian was jealous of my career. If he resented my working because he really wanted a traditional wife who would stay home and raise children, he never said so. In any case, I did fulfill many functions of a traditional wife: decorating our Washington town house, grocery shopping, and cooking. I didn't have time for laundry or cleaning, or any interest in them, so I had help for those tasks. As for raising children, I didn't have a desire to become a mother, and having a child with Ian was never a possibility, since our marriage was so dysfunctional.

We rarely made love. I bought sexy lingerie in an attempt

to attract him. When that failed, I urged him to consult a therapist with me. Then I pretended I wasn't interested in physical intimacy either, hoping it would relieve the tension in case Ian felt pressured. Nothing helped. Finally, I started going to bed after Ian was already asleep to avoid feeling rejected night after night. But our problems weren't just sexual. I let Ian control me and be psychologically abusive. I turned over my paychecks to him, giving him sole power over our finances. Most of the time I used work as an excuse not to think about my unhappiness. One day, though, while I was still at the Justice Department, after parking my car illegally on the edge of the National Mall—the city tickets were cheaper than any nearby garage—I set out across the vast lawn toward my office, when I was overcome with hopelessness and sorrow and began to cry. I walked around the Mall and couldn't see any solution to my misery. I didn't want to live alone, and I didn't want to live with a roommate. My parents and the couples I knew growing up were not openly affectionate, and I didn't have a romantic view of marriage. I didn't think a different husband would be an improvement.

Divorce seemed unthinkable. Though it was becoming more common in the 1970s, in my mind divorce still meant failure. Every fiber in my being strove to avoid it. I spent a good part of my life feeling daunted, but I always forged ahead in spite of my fears and lack of confidence. This attitude had gotten me through my school years and my career so far. Somehow, I hoped, it would get me through life with Ian.

To find the love and support I craved, I would have to go outside my marriage.

9

KURT

Gold light seeped through the curtains of my bedroom window, grazing the long, well-built form of the black-haired man lying next to me in bed. Flinging the covers aside, I rose, donned a robe, and padded downstairs to the kitchen. I made a pot of coffee and sat at the Formica counter, looking through the *Washington Post.* As the caffeine coursed through me, I heard a stirring upstairs, then the tread of bare feet on the floorboards—my lover, Kurt Muellenberg, heading to the shower.

Kurt and I had taken advantage of Ian's being out of town to spend a rare night together, choosing to sleep at my 20th Street house instead of Kurt's Georgetown home because I needed to be available if my office—or my husband—called.

A divorced father of three sons, Kurt was tall and handsome, with thick, wavy hair, an endearing gap in his front teeth, and startlingly blue eyes. He had been born in what was now East Germany, and as a young man he had fled to the West after the Communist takeover following World War II. Kurt and I met at the Department of Justice, when he was an organized crime prosecutor before becoming the section chief. We had been secret lovers for two years.

The night before, we'd both worked late and arrived at my house tired from the long day. If I had thought about it, I would have recognized the enormous risks of spending the night with Kurt at my house. Nixon's men could have had the place under surveillance. Telephoto lenses could have peered through my windows. But I didn't think about it. My affair with Kurt existed in a realm outside Watergate, a romantic world of love and safety I relied on for strength.

An element of our relationship that hung in the air that night was the misery of my home life. Kurt had ended his own unhappy marriage years before, and it baffled him that I stayed with Ian.

"Why don't you leave him?" he asked me now in his thick German accent.

It was a question he often asked, and I had no answer.

"I don't know," I said. Why I stayed through the first years of my marriage was a mystery to me, and by the time of Watergate I was too busy to think hard about it or make any big changes in my life. Work gave me a perfect excuse to do nothing. Moreover, I was good at compartmentalizing and suppressing my unhappiness and fears.

I had never imagined that I would be an adulteress. Looking back, I see that I was attracted to Kurt from the moment we met as colleagues in 1969, but the affair didn't begin until more than two years later, in November 1971, when we found ourselves in Detroit together. I was in town for a grand jury hearing investigating a construction union accused of demanding kickbacks. Kurt was prosecuting a notorious mob swindler on perjury charges. The mobster was represented by the celebrity attorney F. Lee Bailey.

At the end of the day we ran into each other in the hall of the federal courthouse, and Kurt invited me to dinner while his jury was deliberating. We went to the Anchor Bar, an infamous mob hangout that had recently been raided by police seeking to break up a gambling ring. I had never been there and never would have gone there on my own, but it was close to the courthouse and Kurt enjoyed the bar's colorful outlaw ambience. Toward the end of our meal, he got a call that the jury in his case had reached a decision, and I returned with him to the courthouse. The jury brought in a guilty verdict: Kurt had won his case. He was in a buoyant mood as we said goodnight in the lobby of the government-rate Sheraton Cadillac Hotel, where we were both staying. No sooner had I reached my room than the phone rang. It was Kurt, asking if he could come up to talk to me. He said he wanted my advice about one of his cases.

A few moments later, there was a knock on the door. As soon as I opened it, I knew advice wasn't what Kurt wanted. He stepped into the room, pushed the door shut behind him and, putting his arms around me, he drew me close.

◼

From that night on, we met regularly, at lunch and on the weekends, either at my house when I knew Ian wouldn't be home, or at Kurt's place. Sometimes we took walks together at Hains Point Park in Southwest Washington or Glens Falls Park in Maryland. We went to out-of-the-way restaurants like the Old Angler's Inn in Maryland where we could talk and be together far from prying eyes. I always felt happy and relaxed with Kurt.

I told no one about the relationship except one of my girlfriends, a young lawyer named Maggie Fraser who worked at what was then the US Department of Health, Education and Welfare. Maggie and her friends, who soon became my friends, sometimes dined out with Ian and me, so she saw and heard how my husband belittled me—calling me "fat peach," and cutting me off when I was talking. Though she was impressed by Ian's intelligence, Maggie thought him arrogant and condescending and more interested in playing the big shot than in getting to know my friends. He always picked up the check—as a partner in a prestigious law firm, he had more money than any of us, who were all government lawyers—which led Maggie to call him "Mr. Aloha."

I don't recall if Maggie told me directly how she felt about Ian, but I must have sensed it, and that gave me courage to confide in her about Kurt. Years later, I found out how dismayed my friends and family were about my marriage. Ian's mistreatment of me was obvious to most people close to me, but no one said anything for fear of offending me—and I blocked seeing the reality.

On paper, Ian was an ideal marriage partner, a brilliant, sophisticated man who shared my religious and cultural heritage. Yet it was Kurt, the foreigner from a disgraced nation, in whom I found solace and support.

Kurt was horrified by the Nazis and felt extreme guilt about the Holocaust. He strove to put the war behind him. If I'd known his background before I'd come to know him, however, it might have given me pause. Kurt's father had been killed fighting for the Nazis, and Kurt himself had been conscripted into the Hitler Youth as a child. He once was forced with his unit to watch a public hanging of Jews who had escaped from Buchenwald, the concentration camp near his city of Jena. He recalled seeing Jews dragged from their homes never to be seen again, and he'd had firsthand experience of Kristallnacht, the night of November 9, 1938, when the Nazis torched synagogues and Jewish homes, schools, and businesses across Germany. The apartment building where his family lived, next to his father's butcher shop, had once been a synagogue. That night it was bombarded with bottles by an angry mob because of a Star of David that was still embedded in the brickwork of an outside wall.

Kurt was just thirteen when the war ended. The Soviets who soon occupied Jena were as brutal as the Nazis, and at seventeen, leaving his family behind, he escaped to the West.

For my part, I didn't think of Kurt as German. He had struggled and suffered to get to America and become a citizen, and he was kind, humorous, and generous. He made me feel interesting and desired.

◼

My parents would have been shocked that I was cheating on Ian. Thinking about this saddened me and added to my guilt, so I suppressed it. As the beloved eldest child in a close-knit Jewish family, I had never disappointed my parents or given them any reason to doubt my character.

Growing up, my entire world existed mostly within a few blocks of Buena Park, a warm, friendly neighborhood on Chicago's north lakefront. My father, Bert Wine, was an accountant; my mother, Sylvia, a stay-at-home mom. We lived in a small apartment on Gordon Terrace, where my parents slept on a pullout couch in the living room while my younger sister, Robin, and I shared the one bedroom. My brother, Stevie, arrived when I was eleven, and we moved to a three-bedroom apartment on Clarendon Avenue a block away. For most of the rest of his life, my maternal grandfather, Max Simon—who before retiring owned an old-school tavern in the Chicago Loop with brass spittoons and a polished wood bar—lived with us. My mother's two sisters lived on the same block, and her brothers lived nearby. My siblings and I walked to and from Graeme Stewart Elementary School, named after a turn-of-the-twentieth-century philanthropist, and came home for lunch every day.

As young children, my friends and I liked to run around on a grassy median strip near the lakefront that we reached by crossing busy Marine Drive. Our parents worried about our safety, so my father organized and raised the money to build a playground on Gordon Terrace, where the traffic was slow and scant. Daddy delighted in arranging surprises for us. One Halloween he hired an actor to dress like the Lone Ranger and ride onto the playground on his horse, Silver. I was dressed like a Spanish señorita that year, and I remember my thrill when the masked hero, who I was sure was the *real* Lone Ranger, hoisted me onto Silver and led me around the playground's baseball field.

My family went to synagogue on the high holidays, held Seders to celebrate Passover, and had a big party with our relatives on Hanukkah, but otherwise we were not observant. Before my grandfather Max gave up his house on South Spaulding Avenue, we gathered there every Sunday with my mother's siblings, their spouses, and my ten cousins. When my grandfather moved in with us, the weekly tradition continued at our home. My parents taught me to honor our Jewish heritage, but they also wanted me to know people outside our community, and one summer they sent me to a racially integrated YWCA sleepaway camp, where I canoed, played games, and made lanyards with girls of all colors and religions.

This was the mid-1950s, the calm before the social storms

of the 1960s. I knew that just a decade earlier millions of Jews had been murdered in the Holocaust, but my parents never spoke about how it had affected our family. Itzak Wein, one of my father's cousins from a branch of his family that had remained in Europe, lost his parents and siblings, all gassed at the Belzec concentration camp in Poland. The American Wines sponsored Itzak's emigration to the United States, and I saw him at family gatherings in Chicago. He was an uneducated, broken man who had managed to escape the Nazis by joining first the Polish army, then the Soviet army, from which he'd fled. Whenever we children asked what had happened to him or why he had black numbers tattooed on his arm, the adults hushed us. "He doesn't want to talk about it, and you don't want to know these things," they'd say.

At the time, there was a cultural reticence about unpleasant truths, a need to cling to a vision of prosperity and happiness. For women, the 1950s were also years of little opportunity and social constraint. It was the Golden Age of the Housewife, when most married middle-class white women didn't work outside the home. My mother didn't even have a bank account of her own and relied on my father to give her money for groceries and other necessities. She seemed content, though, with her role. I never heard her express regret at her situation or a desire that I follow a different, more independent path. In fact, I don't remember ever having a conversation with my mother about life or dating. It was understood that I would go to college and marry someday, but beyond that we didn't discuss my future. That said, I did have a few models for nontraditional career women. My mother's youngest sister, Ethyle, had had a job as the Chicago director of B'nai B'rith, the global Jewish community services organization, until she married. I remember going to the airport to see Aunt Ethyle off on business trips. The idea of a job that would take you to far-off places seemed impossibly glamorous to me.

I loved school, and was an excellent student. Even as a child, I was an avid reader. I devoured Booth Tarkington's *Seventeen*, and the Cherry Ames and Nancy Drew mystery books with their girl detective heroines who led exciting lives packed with action and adventure. I had an inchoate sense that I would also do something interesting with my life, but I had no idea what that would be.

Early on, I learned not to let my fears and doubts interfere with my goals, and to show confidence in myself even if I didn't feel it. In seventh grade, I'd been nominated for class president. We voted by putting our heads down on our desks and raising our hands for the candidate of our choice. When the teacher saw me vote for another student, she halted the balloting and called me out of the room. "If you don't have the confidence to vote for yourself, you shouldn't run," she said.

It wasn't lack of confidence. I'd been raised to believe that it was unladylike and improper to be too brazen, and I thought that included voting for myself. But my teacher showed me a different perspective, and I changed my vote. Whether or not that decided the election, I won. To this day, though, I still consider what is ladylike before acting, even if I end up ignoring it.

For years I studied ballet with Edna McRae, a nationally known teacher who trained many professional dancers. Several times a week, I took the bus downtown to the historic Fine Arts Building, which had been home to artists' lofts and musicians' studios since the Jazz Age. After my classes, I returned home by bus, sitting in the last row where I did my homework while eating a dinner cooked and packed by my mother. McRae strove for perfection, rapping our legs and arms with a rod to prod us into higher extensions and wider turnouts as a pianist played waltzes on a baby grand in the corner. I progressed enough in my ballet studies to dance *en pointe*. I also took piano lessons to complement my ballet, but I never had much talent in either, and when I became interested in boys, I dropped the lessons.

At the end of the summer of 1956 my parents, brother, and sister moved to a house in Skokie, twelve miles northwest of Chicago. Having skipped half a grade, I wouldn't graduate from Graeme Stewart until February 1957, so I stayed behind in Buena Park, moving in with my unmarried Aunt Mildred, a social worker, who lived next door to us on Clarendon Avenue. After graduating, I joined my family and entered Niles Township High School.

The suburbs did not have graduations in February, so my midyear start put me in classes with students who had flunked, a serious constraint on forming friends in a new school where I knew no one. Still, I dove into activities, joining the Scribbler's Club and the Science Club, and moving on in the next years to working on the yearbook and becoming president of the Teachers of Tomorrow Club (despite having no plans to teach).

Though I never lacked for dates, I wasn't part of the in crowd, the top clique of uber-cool fashionistas, athletes, and hipsters that ruled teenage social life. I was also unhappy with my looks because of my nose, the bumpy Simon proboscis I'd inherited from my mother's side of the family. Among middle-class Jewish girls in the 1950s, nose jobs were almost a rite of passage, like getting a driver's license or your first pair of high heels. Many of us had bought into the myth that beauty meant a small, upturned nose, and I had no trouble

convincing my parents to pay for the surgery. When my soph-
omore year in high school started, I looked like a new person.

My grades, activities, and beautiful new nose, however,
didn't protect me from disappointment freshman year at
the University of Illinois, when I failed to be accepted by the
sorority of my choice. I joined Iota Alpha Pi instead, which, as
it turned out, should have been my first pick: it was perfect for
me. My sorority sisters were smart, interesting young women
who are still treasured friends.

During my senior year I became engaged to a charm-
ing Canadian student who had arrived at the University of
Illinois from Australia, where his father worked for International Harvester. I'd met him my junior year at a fraternity
party. After our engagement, he transferred to Roosevelt
University in Chicago for reasons he kept vague. Then, a few
months before I was to graduate, I came upon a letter in the
glove compartment of his Volkswagen Beetle, revealing the
truth—he had flunked out. I was distressed that he hadn't
been straight with me, and I broke our engagement. With
no wedding or job in my immediate future, I applied to law
school, and there, of course, I met Ian. Unfortunately, our
relationship, too, would be marred by lies—some of them my
own.

◾

After dressing and eating breakfast, Kurt and I sneaked out
of the house, hoping not to be seen by my neighbors. Taking
separate cars, we drove off to work. It would be another long
day for me, as I moved closer to facing off in court with Rose
Mary Woods over the biggest mystery of Watergate so far.

10

THE DAYS OF WINE AND ROSE

The revelation of an eighteen-and-a-half-minute gap in the tape from June 20, 1972, gripped the nation when the story broke the day before Thanksgiving, and for weeks afterward the papers were filled with news about this latest bombshell in the Watergate scandal. The obliterated conversation between Nixon and Haldeman had come to symbolize all that was corrupt about the Nixon White House. Though the president had insisted in a speech earlier in the month that "I'm not a crook," it seemed probable that he or someone close to him had tampered with the tape. His lawyers were quick to divert attention from the president by pointing a finger at his secretary, and on Monday morning, November 26, a crowd swarmed the federal court to hear Rose Mary Woods answer for it. By the time I arrived at eight, the line stretched from the entrance, down the steps to Third Street, and along Constitution Avenue toward the Capitol. Sleeping bags, backpacks, and empty takeout containers littered the sidewalk.

Promptly at nine, US marshals opened the towering carved-wood doors to the sixth-floor ceremonial courtroom, and the public flooded in. Every seat immediately filled. Since there was no jury for today's hearing, the marshals allowed reporters to sit in the jury box. I spotted a few famous faces—Dan Rather, the aggressive CBS News White House correspondent, and his counterparts at the other networks, Sam Donaldson from ABC and Tom Brokaw from NBC. Also present were two up-and-coming female reporters who would soon make their mark on television news—Lesley Stahl and Connie Chung. The once-aspiring journalist in me thrilled to see them.

As I organized papers at the prosecution table, I felt a tap on my shoulder. Turning, I found myself face-to-face with Anthony Lewis, the brilliant *New York Times* columnist. Lewis was in his midforties and slender, with a hairline that receded from the tops of his ears. He told me he'd read an interview I'd given recently in which I had said that his book *Gideon's Trumpet* had inspired me to go to law school.

"I'm glad you liked my book," Lewis said. "I just wanted to say hello."

"Oh, hello," I stammered, redness spreading over my face. Couldn't I think of anything interesting to say? I was very familiar with Lewis's work. Why was I so tongue-tied?

Lewis gave me a gentle smile. "Good luck today."

I nodded, growing flustered with the thought that I might not get the right words out for the rest of the morning despite my thorough preparation. During the long Thanksgiving weekend, I'd read and reread the transcripts of Rose's November 8 testimony. I memorized every detail so I could spot inconsistencies with whatever she might say today, and identified points to use in questioning her about her handling of the June 20 tape. Her previous statements took on a different meaning and importance now that she was accused of tampering with crucial evidence. I also had carefully reviewed Bob Haldeman's notes of the June 20 meeting, two stapled, handwritten pages torn from a yellow legal pad; Rose's typed transcript; and the president's daily diary, which catalogued his every move, visitor, and phone call.

We knew Rose had used two different machines—a Sony and the more up-to-date Uher 5000—to transcribe the tape that had eighteen and a half blank minutes. Since the gap could have been created on either machine, I asked the White House to produce both. The Sony and the Uher, marked with manila evidence tags, now sat on the prosecution table, two squat, silent suspects.

The White House had also turned over—finally!—the seven existing tapes of the nine we'd requested, and they were in Judge Sirica's chambers, locked in a safe provided by the National Security Agency. An NSA guard kept vigil around the clock outside the judge's door. We still hadn't heard them and didn't even have copies of them in our possession.

The subpoenaed conversations represented just a fraction of what Nixon had actually taped. Before dismantling the system after Butterfield's testimony in July, the president had recorded thousands of hours of activity in the Oval Office and in the other bugged areas of the White House and Camp David. Not all the recorded sounds, however, were speech. The taping was activated by sounds of any kind—one reel contained nothing but hours and hours of a ticking clock.

Turning back to my notes, I heard the rustle of spectators behind me but ignored their chatter. Out of the corner of my eye I saw a lone empty seat in the front row—the one I'd reserved for Ian. His failure to appear didn't surprise me. My husband never missed an opportunity to belittle me. Today's hearing might be the best show in town for most

Washingtonians, but to Ian it was just another way to slight me and let me know my work didn't matter. I'd long ago learned to suppress the hurt his rejection caused me. Often, I didn't even notice his demeaning treatment. I only wished Kurt could have been there in Ian's place. But, of course, there was no possibility of saving a seat for my lover.

Just then the bailiff's voice rang out, snapping me back to the proceedings. "All rise! This court is in session, the Honorable Judge John Sirica presiding."

The door from the judge's robing room opened; Sirica settled himself behind his tall bench and nodded to the crowd to sit. When the clerk called Rose Mary Woods, a buzz rippled through the courtroom, quickly quieted by a stern glance from Sirica. Nixon's secretary walked down the aisle toward the witness box, wearing a wool dress, a brightly colored patterned scarf, and black pumps. She moved more hesitantly and looked paler and more fragile than in her previous court appearance, and I couldn't help feeling sorry for her.

She also was no longer accompanied by White House lawyers. Late on Thanksgiving afternoon, Alexander Haig had called Rose at home to tell her that the White House legal team would no longer represent her. Despite her nearly quarter century of unfailing devotion to Nixon, it looked as if the president was forsaking her. She immediately phoned Charles S. Rhyne, a prominent Washington trial attorney and former president of the American Bar Association who was a close friend and law school classmate of Nixon's, and they had met over the holiday weekend. At sixty-one, Rhyne was tall, slim, and bespectacled, with a ski-jump nose that resembled Nixon's and wavy gray hair. Rose's choice no doubt pleased Nixon, who surely counted on Rhyne to prevent her from saying anything in court to hurt him. Just to make sure, four members of the president's legal team were on hand, squeezed shoulder-to-shoulder around the defense table to keep their eyes on the proceedings.

At the prosecution table, I too was surrounded by colleagues, including Rick, George Frampton, Jerry Goldman, and Leon. A few days earlier, Leon had used his appearance before the Senate Judiciary Committee—testifying on the question of whether future special prosecutors should be appointed by the courts or by the president—to praise our team. He told the senators that "excellent ground work was laid" in our early efforts with Archie Cox. We were "professional," "objective," and "dedicated," he said, contradicting widespread rumors in the press that he thought us spoiled kids out to get the president. Still, we didn't completely trust Leon, and his presence added to my jagged nerves. I felt the weight of an immense and somber responsibility—getting to the truth about the eighteen-and-a-half-minute gap. Also, I felt the added pressure to perform well as the only woman on the team.

The stakes were high for me, but they were higher still for Rose. She was the only suspect in this criminal investigation. We were gathering evidence to determine whether she had obstructed justice by deliberately destroying evidence or whether she had committed perjury by lying about it during her November 8 testimony. Both obstruction of justice and perjury were federal crimes punishable by stiff jail terms, as several figures in the Watergate scandal, including Jeb Magruder and John Dean, had already discovered.

I stood, smoothed my skirt and cleared my throat, then gave Rose her *Miranda* warning. "Miss Woods, I would like to advise you of your constitutional rights," I said, the first time I'd spoken those words to a witness. "You have a right not to answer questions, which may tend to incriminate you. Anything you do say in response to any question may be used in a court of law as evidence against you. Do you understand that?"

"Yes, ma'am," she answered in a soft voice.

I could have mumbled the words, and Rose would have understood. Thanks largely to police shows on television, the *Miranda* warning is so thoroughly embedded in our culture that most Americans know they are not under any compulsion to talk to law officers or prosecutors. From the tight set of Rose's jaw and the contempt flashing in her green eyes, I knew she would not be giving up anything voluntarily. Whatever I would learn from Rose today I would have to pull out of her.

I was about to violate the first rule a prosecutor learns: Never ask a witness a question unless you already know the answer. A surprise response can ruin your theory of the case. At this point, though, I had no theory. Nor did I have any idea what Rose would say. All I had were questions: Did she erase any part of the June 20 tape? If so, how exactly did she do it, when did it happen, and was it done by accident or deliberately? My job was to get Rose to narrate the sequence of events in her own words, to establish whether her story made sense or whether it conflicted with her prior testimony or any known facts.

The tape with the suspicious gap was a recording of a two-hour-and-twenty-five-minute conversation involving Nixon, John Ehrlichman, and Bob Haldeman in the Executive Office Building, the first time the president had spoken to either of his top two aides since the Watergate break-in. The conversation started at 10:25 a.m., with Ehrlichman and Nixon discussing matters unrelated to Watergate. At 11:20

Haldeman joined them, and the three men discussed a possible political trip to the West, including South Dakota, where Pat Nixon's parents had been married. Nixon mentioned that his in-laws had later moved to Ely, Nevada, where Pat was born. At 11:25 Ehrlichman left, and Nixon was alone with Haldeman. At that exact point, the recorded conversation abruptly ended. For the next eighteen and a half minutes, there was just a low, steady hum.

But Haldeman's notes, which were in front of me marked as Exhibit 61, revealed that the subject discussed immediately after Ely was Watergate. "Your honor," I said, turning to Judge Sirica, "the portion of the tape obliterated is the portion related to Watergate. Nothing prior to the Watergate discussion or subsequently was erased from that tape."

A hubbub rose from the crowd.

Leonard Garment, from Nixon's legal team, jumped to his feet. "I object strenuously to Mrs. Volner's characterization," he said.

"Haldeman's notes," Sirica huffed, "speak for themselves."

I read the notes out loud, and as I did, the court stenographer typed Haldeman's words. Later, they would be transcribed into the official record. The notes reflected sketchy, abbreviated thoughts, but to anyone familiar with Watergate, as the news-devouring spectators jammed into the courtroom were, they broadcast cover-up:

Be sure EOB office is thoroughly checked re bugs at all times. What is our counterattack? PR offensive to top this. Hit the opposition with their activities. Point out libertarians have created Public callousness. Do they justify this less than stealing Pentagon Papers, Anderson file, etc.? We should be on the attack for diversion.

Nixon and Haldeman were indeed plotting a PR offensive. Why, they asked, was the break-in at the Democratic National Committee any worse than the theft, by the activist Daniel Ellsberg, of the Pentagon Papers, which detailed the history of American involvement in Vietnam? Or worse than the leak, by the journalist Jack Anderson, of a memo by an ITT executive who had given a sizable donation to Nixon's presidential campaign in hopes of derailing an antitrust prosecution?

When I returned to questioning Rose, she insisted that she had never heard any of this on the tape. I guided her now through the events she claimed led to the gap, a convoluted and unbelievable story that from time to time had the spectators whispering and shaking their heads.

The tape at the center of this drama contained six hours of conversation in the Executive Office Building, but Rose was told to work only on the subpoenaed segment. Stephen Bull, who had taken over responsibility for the tapes from Alexander Butterfield, had placed strips of white paper at the start and end of the section Rose was to transcribe. It had taken Bull hours to locate the relevant point on the tape for Rose, and because the recording was of poor quality it took her hours more to transcribe just one paragraph. To catch every word accurately, she said, she had to constantly back up and replay the tape, pressing buttons on the Sony machine each time. She also had to deal with a headset that was too big for her. After twenty-nine hours of work at Camp David over the weekend of September 29–30, she had transcribed less than one hour of conversation. When she helicoptered back to DC on that Sunday night, she hadn't reached the section where Haldeman joined the conversation.

Continuing her testimony, Rose said that she resumed

work on the tape in her White House office on Monday morning, October 1. Soon after, her complaints about the equipment resulted in the Secret Service buying her a new machine with a foot pedal and a smaller headset—the Uher 5000.

Around one p.m., she was listening through the new headphones and typing on her IBM Selectric when the phone rang at the opposite end of her desk. Before answering the phone, she said, she hit a button on the Uher and removed her headphones. She added that she also must have kept her foot on the pedal as she talked.

Who, I asked, had called? Clenching her teeth and becoming defensive, Rose said she couldn't remember. After all, she asserted, her voice rising, she handled not only fifty phone calls a day on a nine-button phone but also a mountain of mail, some of it demanding the president's immediate attention. Notwithstanding her crowded day, it seemed to me a feeble excuse. How could she forget who had interrupted the nation's most crucial typing job?

Rose had three secretaries to help her, but her chief assistant, Marjorie Acker, was out recovering from a serious operation. Moreover, she was exhausted from her marathon typing session over the weekend. It was perfectly logical, she argued, given the constant interruptions and her fatigue, that when the phone rang and she answered it, she might have accidentally hit the Record button, while pressing the foot pedal.

As soon as she hung up the phone, Rose saw that the Record button was depressed, and she panicked. She immediately rewound the tape to where she'd been transcribing. When she listened, she heard a steady hum right after "Ely," the last word she remembered hearing before the interruption. She couldn't say how long the hum lasted because, she insisted, she had listened to it for just a short time. *If I were the president's secretary, I'd want to know exactly how big my mistake was,* I thought.

The only way Rose could explain the sound, she said in a plaintive tone, was that "through some error on my part, some way in turning around to reach one of my phones, which buzzes and buzzes and buzzes, I pushed the Record button down. Now, whether I held my foot on the pedal or whether [it] stuck down I couldn't tell you. I thought [the phone call] was something like four and a half minutes, and I so told the president as soon as I could go in to see him."

I asked her the significance of keeping her foot on the pedal after pressing Record. She responded that this combination was the only way to erase conversation on the Uher; there was no Erase button.

Rose said she was frantic when she heard the buzz. She stared at the knob on her desk that lit up red when the president had someone with him. As soon as the knob flashed off, she dashed into the hall that separated her office from Nixon's and entered his inner sanctum.

"What did you tell the president you had done?" I asked.

"That I'd made a mistake."

"What was your mistake, Miss Woods?"

"Having the Record button down."

"What would the effect be of having it down?"

"There would be no effect, if I also didn't have my foot on the pedal."

"You then realized immediately you might have erased part of the tape?"

"I realized there was a gap in the tape."

It turned out to be eighteen and a half minutes long, but Rose was sure the Record button was pressed only during her phone call, which she said was four or five minutes at the most.

The five Watergate burglars who broke into the Democratic National Committee's headquarters on June 17, 1972. From left to right, James McCord, Virgilio Gonzalez, Frank Sturgis, Eugenio Martinez, and Bernard Barker. Caught in the act, McCord used an alias when he was arrested to conceal the connection between the burglars and the Committee to Re-elect the President (CREEP), where he was the security chief.

A courtroom artist's rendering of me questioning Jeb Stuart Magruder, a top executive at CREEP and a former White House aide. Magruder was one of the first Nixon administration officials to reach a plea agreement with the Watergate special prosecutor's office.

Former White House counsel John W. Dean with his wife, Maureen, around the time of his testimony before the Senate Watergate Committee. Dean's remarkable recall of White House meetings helped me and my colleagues piece together the different elements of the Watergate cover-up.

My yearbook photo (notice the pin) from Niles Township High School, outside Chicago. As a student at the University of Illinois, I had the idea that a law degree would be a stepping-stone to a career as a serious journalist.

On August 21, 1965, I married Ian Volner at the Covenant Club in Chicago. Ian and I met during my first year at Columbia Law School. It was not long into our marriage that difficulties emerged.

[AP Images / Jim Palmer]

James Neal was in charge of the trial team investigating the Watergate cover-up. Jim got the task force up and running before returning to his law practice in Nashville, promising to come back for the trial but leaving our group of young lawyers to question witnesses and gather evidence for possible indictments.

[AP Images]

Watergate special prosecutor Archibald Cox, seen here with me on our way to a court hearing, was a hero to all the young lawyers who served under him.

[AP Images / Charles Tasnadi]

Richard Ben-Veniste (at right, with dark hair and glasses) was my trial partner. Our different temperaments—I was patient and calm; Rick was bold and aggressive—complemented each other and helped us avoid conflicts that might have erupted over the divvying up and questioning of witnesses.

I met Kurt Muellenberg (center) while we were both working as Justice Department lawyers, and our friendship soon turned into much more. Here we are in the post-Watergate years at a reception with Secretary of the Army Clifford Alexander.

Another day in court, this time with Rick, special prosecutor Leon Jaworski (who replaced Archie Cox after the Saturday Night Massacre), and Carl Feldbaum.

Judge John Sirica of the federal district court in Washington oversaw the Watergate grand jury. He was at the center of all the crucial legal battles, and his steady hand made it possible for justice to be done.

"The Rose Mary stretch." Rose Mary Woods, President Nixon's secretary, sought to demonstrate how she may have accidentally erased eighteen and a half minutes of an Oval Office conversation by reaching for the phone in her office. No one was convinced.

Photos like this one, taken after I oversaw Rose Mary Woods's demonstration in her White House office, often accompanied newspaper stories and headlines identifying me as "the miniskirted lawyer." No one ever commented on what my male colleagues were wearing.

CBS News correspondent Dan Rather and I sold kisses in a booth at the "Counter-Gridiron" carnival, which was held to protest the exclusion of women from the prestigious Gridiron Club.

After the Supreme Court ruled that President Nixon had to release the Oval Office tapes to the special prosecutor's office, Rick and I arrived at federal court in Washington to pick them up.

In the summer of 1974, Marvel Comics featured two guest characters in *The Incredible Hulk*: the crusading young lawyers June Volper and Ben Vincent, who battled an invasion of humanlike monsters at the White House.

Richard Nixon resigned the presidency on August 9, 1974, making one final "double-V" gesture before boarding the presidential helicopter for the last time.

In the fall of 1974, several top former Nixon administration officials faced justice. Pictured here before Judge Sirica are John Ehrlichman, H. R. Haldeman, Gordon Strachan, Kenneth Parkinson, Charles Colson, John Mitchell, and Robert Mardian. Colson pleaded guilty and Strachan was granted a separate trial, but the other five were tried together, with our team prosecuting the case. All but Parkinson were found guilty.

During the administration of President Jimmy Carter, I served as general counsel of the US Army, the first woman to hold the position. I was often the only woman in the room, as this meeting photo shows.

As Army general counsel, I got to ride in a spy plane with ejector seats, and I even did a couple of practice parachute jumps—though off a training platform, not out of a plane.

As my marriage to Ian broke up, I reconnected with my high school boyfriend, Michael Banks, who still lived in Chicago. On January 12, 1980, Michael and I were married in our new home in Evanston.

Years after the Saturday Night Massacre, several members of our task force reunited in Washington for dinner. From left to right are Larry Iason, Jerry Goldman, Rick, me, Jim Neal, Susan Kaslow, Peter Rient, and George Frampton, with Carl Feldbaum, who had been the assistant to deputy special prosecutor Hank Ruth, at the far right.

"And you might have caused [it]?" I asked about the gap.

"I might have," said Rose, her tone turning heated, "but I wasn't sure then, and I'm not sure now."

I felt a jolt of surprise. A tingling sensation spread from my chest, down my arms and legs. Had she really said "I'm not sure" about erasing the tape? The White House lawyers said they could find no innocent explanation for the missing minutes, and that only Rose could explain them. Had the lawyers been careless in preparing her or in listening to her explanation? The president was her life. The press often referred to Rose as his "office wife." But apparently she wasn't going to be his scapegoat and take responsibility for causing the entire gap. A rush of admiration for her burst of independent spirit spiked inside me, but I kept my face a neutral mask, as I'd been trained to do.

"What did the president say to you when you told him of the missing section of the tape?" I asked.

"He said not to worry about it, that is not one of the subpoenaed tapes. It is too bad, but don't worry about it."

I was stunned. The Haldeman segment was clearly included in the subpoenaed June 20 tape. The idea that it wasn't was absurd, and the idea that this was the president's response was equally unbelievable.

Rose had previously testified that Al Haig had called her at Camp David just as she was setting up to transcribe this tape. I had her notes of that call in my hand, and I read them aloud to the court: "Cox was a little confused in his request re the meeting on June 20. It says Ehrlichman-Haldeman meeting—what he wants is the segment on June 20 from 10:25 to 11:20 with Ehrlichman alone."

This message raised a jumble of possibilities. Did the president and Haig know about the gap before they gave the tape to Rose to transcribe? Had they concocted the story about the subpoena to keep Rose from discovering the hum? If Rose believed that the Haldeman conversation wasn't part of the subpoena, why was she so upset when she discovered she'd "mistakenly" erased it? Why did she feel compelled to immediately rush into the Oval Office to tell the president about it?

Our subpoena requested "all tapes and other electronic and/or mechanical recordings . . . relating to a [m]eeting of June 20, 1972, in the President's Executive Office Building ('EOB') . . . involving Richard Nixon, John Ehrlichman, and H. R. Haldeman from 10:30 a.m. to noon (time approximate)."

That language seemed clear. Any possible confusion was eliminated three weeks later, when we got access to the White House logs that detailed the timing of all meetings with the president. Based on this information, Archibald Cox sent a memo in August to Judge Sirica spelling out even more precisely what we wanted on the June 20 tape. Archie's memo said the meeting under subpoena included "when Ehrlichman and then Haldeman went in to see the President." Archie also specified that "the time of the meeting was from 10:20 a.m. to approximately 12:45 p.m."

That memo was delivered to the White House more than a month before Haig told Rose to disregard the Haldeman segment. There was no way that Nixon and Haig did not understand what we wanted. Samuel Powers, the Florida trial attorney who had joined Nixon's legal team that month, later testified under oath that when he looked at the subpoena, he knew without a doubt that the Haldeman-Nixon conversation was covered.

Questions about the scope of the subpoena aside, we had other important issues to probe: Had Rose or someone else erased the tape? How? And was the erasure accidental? I was convinced that someone, acting alone or with another person, had deliberately erased the tape, obliterating eighteen and a half minutes of Nixon's first known discussion of Watergate with one of his top aides. During the Camp David weekend, Nixon had visited Rose's cabin to check on her progress as she transcribed the June 20 tape. While there—so she had testified on November 8—he spent a few minutes listening to the tape and moving "the buttons back and forth" on the recorder. This raised the possibility that the president, who was clumsy and notoriously inept at mechanical tasks, had erased the tape himself. Had she meant to come so close to incriminating Nixon?

Whether he or Rose, or the two of them together, had erased the tape, or someone else entirely had done so, I was certain that Rose had lied on the witness stand on November 8, more than a month after she'd discovered the gap and told Nixon about it.

I asked the court reporter to read Rose's response from that earlier hearing in answer to my question about the precautions she used to avoid accidental erasures. Even as the court reporter read the words in a professional monotone, Rose's hostility burst out. "I used my head. It was the only one I had to use."

The crowd murmured disapproval, and Judge Sirica's eyes widened in disbelief. It shocked him that Nixon's secretary could be as coldly duplicitous as the president's high-level men. "Didn't you think it important on November 8 to tell everything you knew had happened?" Sirica asked Rose.

She gazed at him with an imploring expression. "I would say, your honor, that I would today, but I didn't then. . . . It was my first time in a courtroom. I was petrified," she said in a quiet, ladylike voice.

She hadn't sounded petrified at all on November 8. She'd sounded arrogant and defiant.

When I asked her now whether she reported to any of Nixon's lawyers "the fact you erased a part of the tape," her anger flared again. "You call it an erasure, I call it a gap. I never did hear any word on that tape."

Her lawyer leaped to his feet. "The witness testified she does not know if she erased anything. She doesn't know if there was anything there to erase," Rhyne said.

The fencing match over terminology would continue throughout Rose's testimony, as Rhyne objected every time I used the word "erasure."

At the end of the day, Rose had very cleverly deflected suspicion from anyone else, while admitting very little. She remained unyielding and unapologetic in her conviction that withholding information about the missing minutes was perfectly legitimate. Perhaps she would accept responsibility for four to five minutes of the gap, but no more.

To believe that Rose had accidentally caused even a minimal erasure on the June 20 tape, you had to believe that she made two simultaneous mistakes: as she reached to answer the phone, she would have had to keep her foot on the pedal of the Uher machine after pushing the Record button down. I tried to visualize her doing both but thought it very improbable, the more so because she said she had her left foot on the pedal, which further constrained her reach as she tried to grasp the ringing phone with her left arm. The next day I would ask Rose to demonstrate her "accident"—first in court and then in her White House office. The result forever put the lie to her outrageous story.

11

TWO LADIES ARGUING

It was the kind of powerfully dramatic moment that is commonplace in TV trials, but almost never happens in real courtrooms. On the stand, under my guidance, Rose Mary Woods demonstrated how she might have accidentally erased part of a subpoenaed Watergate tape by pushing the Record button on her Uher machine while pressing the floor pedal with her left foot and reaching to answer her ringing phone. But even with her equipment within easy range inside the witness box, she couldn't do what she described. She barely lifted her hand to point to the headphones on the ledge next to the Uher, and her foot came off the pedal. The tape stopped cold, and her lie was apparent to everyone in the courtroom. The reenactment in her White House office later that afternoon, as she stretched the length of her executive-size desk to reach her phone, proved even more damning to her claim that the erasure was inadvertent. Most Americans who saw pictures of the "Rose Mary Stretch" completely rejected her story.

In the coming weeks, the photographs taken at the White House showing the president's secretary in a series of wild contortions sparked ridicule throughout the nation. "Doing the Twist While Erasing the Tape," clucked a tagline in *Newsweek*, which put Rose and the now famous picture on the cover with the headline "Rose Mary's Boo Boo." A cartoon by Herblock in the *Washington Post* showed Rose collapsed on a stretcher, her limbs twisted like tangled spaghetti, as two medics carried her into a hospital emergency room.

Secretaries across America wrote me letters pointing out that there was no way the tape could have been erased in the manner Rose described. "I know! I've been transcribing tapes and working with a Uher 5000 machine forever," read a typical letter.

Newsweek quoted Rose's lawyer, Charles Rhyne, complaining to friends that the president and his men had thrown her "to the wolves." One day in court, I heard Rhyne swear under his breath at Buzhardt and Garment, murmuring, "Those bastards," as they strode through the swinging gate at the bar. Rhyne clearly thought the president's lawyers had exploited Rose's loyalty to Nixon to make her take the blame for the gap, and he refused to sit with them, placing himself at a separate table. Nixon was wrong if he had thought Rhyne would protect him above his client.

The day after the photographs were taken in Rose's office, I was back in court with her once again on the witness stand. When she first appeared in Judge Sirica's court on November 8, Rose had held her chin up haughtily and glared at me with hard, cold eyes. Now her shoulders slumped and her gaze darted around anxiously. She knew she might face criminal charges. To judge by the scowl on Sirica's face, he looked ready to turn Rose over to the grand jury now and be done with her. Let the good women and men of the Watergate panel, twenty-three ordinary citizens, decide her fate.

And that was before I had finished questioning her.

When I held up one of the photographs of Rose's "stretch," she lashed out, accusing me of posing her in a deliberately awkward way to make her look ridiculous.

"Miss Woods," I replied, hearing my voice rise in outrage and disbelief, though I strove to remain calm. "I didn't ask you to pose for any photographs, and I would like to correct your statement."

"I'm sorry, I can't agree with you," Rose snapped.

Before I could respond, Judge Sirica interrupted. "All right. We have enough problems without two ladies getting into an argument," he scolded.

The courtroom erupted in laughter. The blood drained from my face and I froze at the podium. It wasn't the first or last time Sirica's reflexive sexism interfered with my questioning of a witness. I was used to this kind of thing, and not only from the Watergate judge. In my early days as a prosecutor, male opponents sometimes tried to use my gender and youth to undermine my credibility and the jury's trust. They would refer to me as "the young lady" instead of "my esteemed colleague" as they addressed the male lawyers. Or I'd hand them a piece of evidence and, sniffing the air next to me, they'd say, "What a lovely perfume," just loud enough for the jury to hear. Even worse, one judge in an organized-crime case in California was so flummoxed by having a female lawyer in the courtroom that he refused even to acknowledge me as a woman. He referred to me as a "gentleman" and addressed me as "*Mr.* Volner."

One person who wasn't laughing was Angelo "Angie" Lano, the black-haired, dark-eyed FBI agent for our office.

Earlier that morning I had noticed Angie sitting in the spectator seats, and during the break that followed the laughter,
he asked to see me in private. From his furrowed brow, I knew
he had bad news for me. We met in the anteroom outside
Sirica's chambers.

"The engineering expert just came from your house,"
said Angie in his distinctive Maryland accent. That morning,
while I'd been cross-examining Rose, the expert had taken
apart and examined my telephones and concluded that they
likely had been bugged. The night before, after the police officer responding to the burglary told me there was resistance
on my phone line, I called Angie. I feared that the burglary
was a cover for placing or removing phone taps, a theory now
confirmed by crossed wires inside the phones and scratches
on the screws, all discovered by the expert.

"Just like the Watergate break-in," I said.

"Exactly," said Angie, shaking his head.

"Was it the plumbers?" I asked.

"I don't know," said Angie. "But it's a good bet."

The fact that the Watergate burglars were behind bars
didn't mean the White House had disbanded its covert operation to stop leaks and spy on its enemies.

Despite my fear that personal conversations might have
been overheard, I took a deep breath, blocked thoughts of it,
and went back to court. I concluded my questioning of Rose,
and Sirica dismissed her as a witness.

At the next break, a group of reporters rushed up to com-
miserate with me about Sirica's sexist comment. I'd almost
forgotten about it in my distress over Angie's news. I appreci-
ated the reporters' sympathy, and I answered their questions
politely. But in the coming days, their stories put a crazily
false spin on my courtroom confrontation with Rose, por-

traying it as a catfight engineered by Rick, who was cast in the role of my Svengali. Unaware of the fact that Rose was my witness not because of any action by Rick but because I had stood up for myself, and ignoring the fact that Rick and I were partners who were exactly the same age, a reporter from the *Philadelphia Inquirer* called me Rick's "female protege" and wrote that "the verbal hair pulling contest" between me and Rose was the result of Rick pitting "female against female" for the sake of courtroom drama. I felt a stab of pain at this misrepresentation.

Sirica's interference in my skirmish with Rose had one positive effect. After a detailed account of it appeared in the press the next day, three hundred students from Columbia Law School, my alma mater, signed a letter of protest to Judge Sirica complaining about his sexist treatment of me. It was the only time I ever got support of this type.

When Sirica read the letter, he called me to his chambers and apologized. He intended no disrespect of me, he said. He just didn't like high tension in his courtroom.

My cross-examination of Rose raised my profile in a way that also drew attention to Ian as "Mr. Jill," as one writer put it—a label that, needless to say, enraged him *and* me. He agreed to talk to a *New York Times* journalist who was writing a profile of me, but the resulting story overflowed with his not-so-subtle putdowns. Under the insulting headline "A Lawyer in Miniskirts," the *Times* quoted Ian describing me as "a fairly vain woman" and "a quietly competent" person with "a reasonably stable personality . . . once she belted me with a hairbrush when I told her that a procedure she was pursuing I considered fascistic."

The story ended with a completely untrue anecdote that came not from Ian but from one of my "admirers." The day before Thanksgiving, according to this unnamed source, my office had been frantically trying to reach me, but "the calls were unsuccessful," because I "was in a department store buying clothes." Actually, I was in my office working.

I began to understand why Nixon hated the press.

The day after the burglary at my house, I had gotten a call from Connie Chung of CBS News. She wanted to send a television crew to my house to film how the burglars had broken in. "Absolutely not!" I told her.

But Chung persisted. I couldn't make her understand why I didn't want to broadcast to the world how to break into my home, which was empty all day while I was in court and my husband was at work. She gave up only when Leon called a high-level CBS executive and got him to drop Chung's story.

■

The tapes hearing continued, with Rick questioning several of the president's men. As Sirica looked on, I detected a glimmer of fatherly pride in the judge's eyes. The way Rick moved in the courtroom reminded him, he once told Rick, of Tony Canzoneri, an Italian boxer who was a champion in three weight divisions. This was a high compliment. He also thought Ben-Veniste was an Italian name, and we reasoned that it couldn't hurt to have Sirica regard Rick as his *paisan*.

Though Rick's style was very different from my own, our courtroom manners complemented each other. He respected my quiet persistence, just as I admired his brashness and wit. Rick's skills were on full display in his cross-examination of Fred Buzhardt, the head of the president's Watergate defense team. Under questioning by Rick, Buzhardt admitted that he and several of the president's lawyers had entered Rose's office on the evening of November 14, after she'd left for the day, and had performed tests of their own on the June 20 tape. That meant they had withheld their knowledge of the gap from the court and from us for at least a week. In court, Rick's body language was as assertive as his interrogation of witnesses. After asking a question of Buzhardt, he turned away from the lawyer and, looking out at the spectators, paced in front of Sirica's bench. The effect, as our astute press officer Jim Doyle observed, was to convey to Buzhardt "that the questions were more important than the answers, that after each answer there would be another question, like a mortar shell landing in the witness box."

Buzhardt sat hunched in his chair, as if cowering from Rick's verbal assault, as he described how he and a group of Nixon's lawyers used Rose's Uher machine to play the tape several times. At least once, he said, they did this while Rose's typewriter and Tensor desk lamp were switched on. They noticed that the missing section of the tape contained two distinct sounds—the first, a rather loud hum, dropped noticeably in volume after about five minutes. At this point, Buzhardt lowered his voice to a near whisper, as if he were trying to become invisible. Judge Sirica asked him to speak up, and Buzhardt said that the "buzz" during the first few minutes of the gap was caused by electrical interference from Rose's typewriter and lamp as she was erasing the tape, though he offered no explanation for why the humming noise changed. He said he still believed that Rose had deliberately erased the entire tape, emphasizing, however, that this was only his "belief" and "not a real certainty."

Rather than leading us closer to a solution to the mystery, Buzhardt's testimony added to our confusion. Was that his goal? Speculation ran wild about who had caused the gap, the most bizarre being the "devil theory" put forth by Alexander Haig, Nixon's chief of staff, when he testified.

Under questioning by Rick, Haig said that he had concluded that Rose had, indeed, erased the first four minutes or so of the tape. As for the remaining fourteen and a half minutes, Haig said that for a while he suspected that "perhaps some sinister force had come in . . . and taken care of the rest of the information on the tape." (I wondered if Haig had gotten this nutty idea from seeing *The Exorcist*, which was about to hit theaters. The White House often got preview copies of films.)

Judge Sirica broke in. "Has anyone ever suggested who that sinister force might be?"

"No, your honor," Haig answered, as everyone laughed. Our team envisioned the famous Herblock political cartoons of Nixon with jowls and a five o'clock shadow.

After the hearing, Haig told reporters he now believed Rose had caused the entire gap, adding that it wasn't hard to understand how she thought an eighteen-and-a-half-minute erasure was only four minutes. "I've known women who think they've talked for five minutes and then have talked an hour," he said.

◼

It seemed to my team and me that the first step in solving the mystery of the eighteen-and-a-half-minute gap would be to figure out who had access to the June 20 tape and when. But the White House records, which we'd subpoenaed and received, were not reliable as to the whereabouts of the tape in the four months between July, when Alexander Butterfield revealed the White House bugging system, and November 26, when Judge Sirica took custody of the tapes.

After the taping system was dismantled following But-terfield's testimony, Haig took control of access to the hundreds of reels stored in a file cabinet safe in the Secret Service office at the Executive Office Building. Haig put one of his own aides, John Bennett, a retired Army major general, in charge, though Haig kept the keys to the basement office and the combination of the safe for a period that coincided with the week after our July 23 subpoena. Haig didn't give the keys to Bennett until mid-September. At any point during that period, Haig or the president, or the two men acting together, could have removed the tape from the safe, listened to it, and erased the damning conversation about Watergate.

Rose Mary Woods and Steve Bull also had ample opportunity to tamper with the June 20 tape. They took it to Camp David for the weekend of September 29–30. After that, Rose stored the tape in her office safe until October 4 even though she had no need for it after October 1. She again took it out of her safe for a trip with Nixon to Key Biscayne, from October 4 through October 7. She stayed in a villa near the presidential compound and kept the tape, along with the others, locked in a safe brought in by the Secret Service. At one point in the middle of the night, she summoned Bull to open the safe for her, and the next morning asked him to deliver an envelope to the president. Rose said she couldn't recall what the envelope contained. Bull said it felt like a sheaf of papers. Could it have been a reel of tape or a transcript? When Rose returned to the White House, the tapes went back into her own office safe, to which she alone had the combination.

We knew that Nixon had listened to a random snippet of the June 20 tape and had pressed some buttons on Rose's Sony machine while he and Rose were together in her cabin at Camp David. We didn't know whether this was the only time he heard the tape. Nixon's past behavior suggested he may also have listened to a larger segment earlier. We knew that before the public acknowledgment of the taping system and in advance of John Dean's testimony at the Ervin hearings, the president had spent an entire day listening to his conversations with Dean and making notes. There is even a recording of Nixon doing nothing but *listening* to the Dean tapes.

Soon, we also knew that whoever erased the tape didn't do it by accident. That was the verdict of a court-appointed panel of six technical experts who found that the gap was caused by at least five separate, deliberate erasures and not by a single accidental pressing of a wrong button. The panel also determined that the erasure had been done on a Uher 5000 like the one Rose got on October 1, though not necessarily on her particular machine. The Secret Service had four Uhers. James McCord also happened to have had an Uher set up in the Howard Johnson's hotel room across the street from the Watergate office building, to record conversations at the Democratic National Committee headquarters.

These facts added to the mystery we were trying to solve. It meant the gap could have been created on any of the White House Uhers before Rose got her new machine on October 1. Since there were no records of who used the Secret Service's Uhers or of when they did so, it was possible that the president, with the help of the Secret Service, used a Uher in the Lincoln Sitting Room of the residence—where he liked to spend time in the evenings and where his movements weren't tracked, as they were in the West Wing—to erase the tape. In any case, the empty hum was there when Nixon's lawyers listened to the recording on November 14.

In my mind, no possibility was off the table. Perhaps it was true that the erasure had started with an accident by

Rose. Often, a lying witness will build on a kernel of truth to concoct their lie. Or perhaps Nixon and Rose erased the tape together and then came up with the story about "the accident" to explain it. Or maybe Rose knowingly or unwittingly erased over an earlier erasure by Nixon himself.

The more I thought about Nixon and Rose, the more they reminded me of a Mafia boss and his capo. Like the gangsters I encountered prosecuting organized crime cases, they didn't have to speak at all about their crimes and the need to cover them up. Rose instinctively understood what Nixon wanted. The White House omertà functioned as tacitly and effectively as the mob's code of silence. Nixon would not have had to tell Rose to erase the tape. She would have known it had to be done, as surely as she knew never to talk about it.

As theories about the eighteen-and-a-half-minute gap piled up, so did the wild discrepancies in the witnesses' accounts and the discord among Nixon's lawyers. Our sources told us that the president was unhappy with Buzhardt's handling of the tapes case, a rumor confirmed when Nixon's press secretary, Ron Ziegler, announced that Buzhardt would soon be replaced by John J. Sullivan, another law school classmate of Nixon's, who'd also served with him in the Navy. After a week in Washington, however, Sullivan returned to his native Illinois, where he would soon be appointed to fill a vacancy on the state's appellate court. Buzhardt was reinstated. At a press conference after Sullivan's departure, Gerald Warren, Ziegler's deputy, announced, "Buzhardt is indeed in charge."

It wasn't hard to understand why Nixon was unhappy. After all, Buzhardt was the public face of the steady drip, drip of embarrassing revelations about the tapes, the messenger of the bad news that two tapes were missing and a third had a gap. He had failed to prevent the hearings from being disastrous for the White House. Most significantly, he hadn't kept the tapes private.

The first outsiders to hear them were Judge Sirica and his clerk, D. Todd Christofferson. On a cold morning in December 1973, they listened to the tapes on a Uher recorder borrowed from the White House, in a windowless room that had been swept for bugs. In a further precaution to avoid the tapes being overheard, Sirica insisted they use headphones. Since the recorder had only one port, a technical expert was brought in to create a splitter cable that could accommodate two headphone sets.

Then, at long last, the following Saturday, our turn came. After having copies made of the tapes, with passages of a personal or national security nature removed (under court supervision), the White House handed them over to us. Carl Feldbaum, dressed in weekend-casual pink bell-bottom pants, went to the White House to pick up the tapes and brought them to K Street in a cardboard box. Rick set up an old reel-to-reel player on top of a pile of papers on the desk in his office, and six of us crowded around.

"Which one should we listen to first?" Rick asked.

The unanimous choice was March 21, 1973, the conversation that John Dean had told us was particularly damaging to the president. We disabled the Record button to avoid our own "accidental" erasure, and pressed Play. The tape was scratchier and more difficult to hear in many places than we had expected. We listened for several minutes, and then we heard Dean telling Nixon that the Watergate cover-up had caused "a cancer on the presidency," and that keeping the burglars quiet would cost $1 million over two years.

"We could get that, and maybe we could get it in cash," Nixon said as clear as a bell.

Rick and I exchanged a knowing glance. It was exactly as Dean had testified under oath. The president had discussed paying hush money to the Watergate burglars. That was obstruction of justice, a federal crime. It was devastating to listen to it. I had been raised to respect and admire the president and the presidency. I felt a disconnection from the world I'd grown up in at actually hearing the president of the United States plan criminal conduct.

At the same time, I felt immense relief that the tape matched Dean's testimony word for word. If it had deviated even slightly, his credibility would be shot; our case would be in the gutter. Instead, we were on our way to proving that the most powerful man in the world was a crook.

"Leon has to hear this," Carl said, as he dashed out the door.

A minute later, he returned with the special prosecutor. As we played the tape for Leon, he turned white. His entire body deflated as if someone had punched him in the stomach. I thought he might be having a heart attack. Before I had a chance to ask him if he was all right, Leon turned on his heel and disappeared into his own office down the hall. He closed the door and didn't come out for a very long time.

12

TO INDICT OR NOT

A few days earlier, on December 6, 1973, Gerald Ford, the amiable House minority leader from Michigan, was sworn in as Nixon's new vice president, replacing the disgraced Spiro Agnew, who had resigned in October in the face of bribery and kickback charges. In his speech after taking the oath of office, Ford enthusiastically pledged his full support and loyalty to Nixon, which Rick and I thought a big mistake—even before hearing the "cancer on the presidency" conversation. We felt that Ford ought to have distanced himself from the entire Watergate mess to protect his own political career.

Remarkably, soon after, Rick and I encountered the new vice president at the glitziest social event of the season, the gala fund-raiser for the National Symphony Orchestra at the Shoreham Hotel. We'd been invited, and we decided to go together. When we arrived, the party was well underway, with women in long gowns and men in white tie jammed to a standstill in the grand ballroom. As the Peter Duchin Orchestra swung into a lively rendition of Cole Porter's "Anything Goes," I scanned the crowd and spotted Ford.

"I dare you to ask him if he listened to the March 21 tape," Rick said with a mischievous glint in his eye. I never backed down from one of Rick's challenges, so despite my usual shyness, I pushed my way through the crowd of politicians, lawyers, foreign dignitaries, and White House functionaries. There was Rose Mary Woods in a glittering sequined gown, twirling across the parquet with her escort, PR man Robert Gray, as if Watergate wasn't happening and she hadn't just spent several grueling days on the witness stand. Elliot Richardson, seemingly recovered from the Saturday Night Massacre, talked to Senator Birch Bayh of Indiana, and the dashing Israeli defense minister, Moshe Dayan, his black eye patch giving him an International Man of Mystery air, conferred with his nation's ambassador. They all seemed to know one another, and they laughed lightly as they sipped cocktails and discussed their work and holiday plans. Didn't they realize the government was falling apart around them?

"Congratulations, Mr. Vice President," I said when I'd reached Ford's side.

He shook my hand and smiled broadly. Then he asked me to dance. As the orchestra played "Come Fly with Me," Ford spun me around the ballroom. It felt surreal, as if I'd been dropped into someone else's life. When the dance ended, I found Rick again. "Well, Jilly Bean, did you tell him to keep the fuck away from Nixon?" Rick asked, his voice dripping with sarcasm.

We were sure that if Ford knew what we knew, he wouldn't have been so quick to defend the president. Of course, I would never have said any of this to the vice president's face, dare or no dare. I considered answering yes, to kid the great kidder. In the end, though, I told Rick no.

■

As the holidays approached, all the president's tapes, not just the one from March 21, were much on my mind, especially the June 20 reel with the mysterious gap. It had recently made another trip out of town, to a redbrick loft on West 131st Street in Manhattan. Accompanied by US marshals, the tape arrived at the Federal Scientific Corporation with Rose's Uher 5000 machine, headphones, desk lamp, IBM Selectric typewriter, and twenty color photographs showing the placement of equipment in her office.

As Carl Feldbaum from our staff and Richard Hauser from the president's legal team looked on, a group of court-appointed electronics experts subjected the tape to a process called developing. This involved covering the tape with a magnetic fluid that allowed the experts to look for its "signature quartet" of key markings: four tiny lines, each one just half a millimeter high. The ones they found on this tape indicated deliberate erasures. They also discovered multiple different "starts" to the erasing, concluding that the gap was the result of at least five and perhaps nine separate actions. Most likely, the tape was erased, rewound, and erased again.

The experts also rejected the theory that Rose's desk lamp and electric typewriter had caused the shrill buzz on the erased part of the tape. They attributed this high-pitched sound to any number of factors, including a defective component on the Uher recorder itself, interference from the electric power line to which the recorder was attached, and the movement of a human hand near the machine. Most disappointingly, though, the panel was unable to retrieve any conversation from the eighteen and a half blank minutes.

After the electronics experts issued their report, Leon ordered an FBI investigation of the suspicious gap. It was clear now that someone in the White House had deliber-

ately destroyed subpoenaed evidence, and the special prosecutor vowed to discover the culprit. We sent Angie Lano to
Camp David to examine all the typewriters at the presidential
retreat and compare them to Rose's IBM Selectric. By analyz-
ing the typewriter markings on Rose's transcripts we could
see how far she'd typed on the Camp David machines and
what she'd typed at the White House. It turned out that Rose
had told the truth about at least one thing: the point at which
she stopped transcribing the June 20 tape during the weekend
at Camp David and picked it up again in her office on Monday morning.

Although Rose remained the prime suspect in the erasure, Angie's investigations narrowed in on two additional
suspects: Al Haig and Steve Bull. Both men had motive—to
protect the president—and opportunity—access to the tape
before it was turned over to Judge Sirica. Angie wanted to
polygraph all three suspects: Rose, Bull, and Haig. At first,
Rose agreed. Then, after a story about her impending lie
detector test appeared in Jack Anderson's syndicated column,
Charles Rhyne accused us of leaking the news and canceled it.
(I suspected Rhyne himself of the leak so he'd have an excuse
to pull Rose out.) Haig would never make himself available to
the FBI. Bull did sit for an interview with the FBI and agreed
to take a polygraph. But his lawyer, thinking it was a bad idea,
stalled, and the FBI never followed up.

My theory of the gap placed Nixon as the prime suspect.
This was my reasoning: the June 20 tape was the first on our
list of subpoenaed conversations. If Nixon did indeed review
the tapes to determine what was on them, as I believe he
would have, it made sense that he would have started with
the first one we'd requested. I envisioned Nixon listening to
that one, discovering how damaging the conversation with

Haldeman was, and erasing it. Since Nixon was too inept to set up and work the machine himself—John Dean said the president had trouble taking the top off a fountain pen—he must have had help. His most likely accomplice was Rose. Nixon continued listening to more tapes and discovered that they were just as damaging. He realized that he couldn't keep erasing subpoenaed material, so he adopted the total stonewall approach. The only solution he saw was to prevent the tapes from ever becoming public.

◼

The second tapes hearing concluded toward the end of February 1974, and we sent our mountain of evidence—court testimony and the reports from the FBI and the electronics experts—to the Watergate grand jury. The jurors had already met more than one hundred times. Two jurors had lost their jobs because they missed so much work. A third juror, a night custodian at George Washington University, quit the panel because she had no time to care for her eleven children.

We also sent witnesses to the grand jury, but not Rose. We had decided not to indict her even though it was obvious she had lied; it was impossible to believe her "stretch" scenario, and the experts' testimony confirmed that the gap hadn't been caused by just one continuous "accident." However, since we couldn't prove how the erasure had happened, it was almost impossible to make a case for perjury against Rose. Moreover, we didn't want to be diverted from the bigger crimes we were pursuing. There also was the sympathy factor. We thought a trial jury would feel sorry for Rose because the White House had treated her so shabbily. It was hard not to see her as a victim whose chief crime had been her loyalty to Nixon.

The same wasn't true of the president's former White House and campaign aides, and we were fast moving toward indicting many of them on charges of conspiracy to obstruct justice. We had plenty of evidence against Bob Haldeman, John Ehrlichman, John Mitchell, Robert Mardian (a top Justice Department and CREEP official), and Kenneth Parkinson (an outside counsel for CREEP).

I wanted the president indicted as well. The evidence overwhelmingly justified indicting him for obstruction of justice, and I fervently believed it was wrong to prosecute Nixon's subordinates while letting Le Grand Fromage, as Rick called the president, go free. Leon, however, adamantly opposed indicting Nixon. He thought it was improper and irresponsible to indict a sitting president because the law in this regard had never been tested, and the nation would suffer devastating trauma while the complicated legal issues were sorted out. Leon recognized that Nixon had violated federal law but thought the correct way to deal with his crimes was through the impeachment process, though none was underway when we had this debate.

I wondered what Archie Cox would have advised. There's no wording in the Constitution that says a sitting president can't be indicted or that impeachment is the *only* way to get rid of a corrupt chief executive. The question was left open as to whether the best way to deal with a criminal president is through a criminal legal process or a political one.

Impeachment, as I understood the intention of the Founding Fathers, was created so that if a president ran amok, damaging the country and threatening national security—whether or not, in doing so, he committed a defined crime—Americans still had a way to get rid of him without waiting for the next election. But if a president *had* violated the law—which clearly

Nixon had—I believed he also could be indicted. Impeachment was an additional remedy, not the only one. After all,
there was precedent for indicting a vice president, so why not
a president? In 1804, a grand jury indicted Vice President
Aaron Burr for murdering Alexander Hamilton in a duel.
And just a few months earlier, Nixon's vice president, Spiro
Agnew, had been charged by a grand jury with a felony count
of tax evasion; as part of a plea deal, he pleaded no contest
and resigned.

None of this, however, swayed Leon. A ferocious battle
of wills ensued, pitting the aging special prosecutor against
many of his youthful staff, including me. He saw us as a band
of renegades who were too young and too zealous for our
own—and the nation's—good. We had airtight evidence of
criminality against the president; it was there in the tapes,
the heap of documents, the testimony of witnesses, the volu-
minous notes of White House aides like Bob Haldeman, and
the meticulously kept White House daily logs, which tracked
every waking moment of the president's life.

This evidence was the basis of a 128-page document
drawn up by Philip Lacovara, counsel to the Watergate special prosecutor, detailing Nixon's criminal culpability. Only
eight copies were made—one each for Rick, me, and the other
members of our trial team. No one who read it could come
away without a sense of our solid case against the president.

The grand jury also was on our side. On January 30, 1974,
the foreman, Vladimir Pregelj, wrote a three-page letter to the
president on behalf of the panel, which a court officer delivered to the White House. "Because the jury is eager to have
before it all relevant evidence respecting the involvement
or non-involvement of any persons in the activities under
investigation," the letter read, "and because we believe that

you should be offered and would wish to have an opportunity to present to us your knowledge of these activities, I am hereby requesting you on behalf of the Grand Jury to appear before it—at the White House or such other place as would be appropriate—to testify as other witnesses on matters that are subject of our investigation."

The letter closed with a request that "inasmuch as we are in the closing stages of our investigation, we would appreciate an early response."

I can only imagine the litany of obscenities with which Nixon greeted Pregelj's letter.

Needless to say, the president did not appear.

I marveled at the grand jury's devotion to truth and justice. The jurors' outrage over the immorality in the White House was palpable. "Is 'proper' an obsolete word these days?" a juror asked in frustration one afternoon. They'd worked long and hard studying and discussing the evidence, once deliberating until midnight, only to find that the courthouse cleaning crew had locked them into their windowless tenth-floor room. They had to pound on the door to alert the janitor to let them out.

But Leon wouldn't budge in his decision *not* to indict Nixon. Our battle with him over the issue escalated when four lawyers on our staff—Jerry Goldman, George Frampton, Peter Rient, and Carl Feldbaum—gave Leon a memo outlining their views as to why the president had to be brought to justice. The key evidence they cited was the March 21 "cancer on the presidency" tape that we'd recently listened to and that had shocked us all, Leon included. On that date, the memo concluded, Nixon joined the conspiracy to obstruct justice concocted by his closest aides—first by urging that $1 million in hush money be paid to the families of the Watergate burglars, and second, by approving new strategies to continue the cover-up so that damaging evidence against the White House wouldn't leak out.

Leon regarded the memo as a mutiny. Why would the lawyers make such a formal presentation, except to undermine his authority? On February 13, Leon asked to see Rick and me in his office. The special prosecutor was sitting behind his desk with the group's memo in front of him. The metallic drapes were open slightly, showing a slice of the gray wintry day outside.

Anger flashed in Leon's eyes as he stabbed the memo with his index finger. "I know you're behind this," he said to Rick.

"You're wrong," Rick answered. The veins in his temples throbbed, as he struggled to speak in a level tone. "I declined to be part of it because I wanted to keep an open mind so we'd have a chance to compromise."

Leon shot Rick a murderous look. He'd already decided Rick was guilty, and nothing was going to change his mind. It was inevitable, I thought, that their relationship would be charged with competitiveness; they were both alphas who brooked little interference with their strategies and goals. Leon's suspicions extended beyond Rick to most of the staff. The special prosecutor still didn't trust us—in part, I believed, because he knew we didn't fully trust *him*. Leon knew he could never replace Archie Cox in our hearts and minds, so he hadn't bothered trying.

The sterility of his office reflected his emotional coolness toward the staff. He hadn't hung a single picture on the walls, which remained as bare as the day Archie left. Nor were there any family photographs or any other personal mementos on Leon's desk. He treated me warmly, but with everyone else he remained distant and remote until the day he returned to

Texas, leaving what he surely considered all the snooty Ivy League brats behind.

Leon grabbed the memo, fluttering the pages, and waved it in Rick's face. "You're fomenting disunity to undermine my authority!" he shouted.

"That's ridiculous!" Rick shouted back.

"I won't tolerate disloyalty," Leon thundered.

This could have gone on for the rest of the day. Neither man was going to back down, and each of them wanted the last word. I watched in frustration as Leon and Rick raged at each other, knowing there was nothing I—or anyone else—could do to end the conflict. They were in a fever of anger, and it had to run its course.

I knew that neither Rick nor I had been part of writing the memo, yet I understood Leon's concern. He didn't want anything done that could look as if we were out to get the president, especially at a time when much of our damning evidence against the White House had not yet been made public. Leon feared giving Nixon an excuse to accuse us again of conducting a witch hunt. He needed to make sure that the American people saw our actions as fair. He also worried that going after Nixon too aggressively would jeopardize our case against his aides. If Nixon was indicted, he very likely would take the case to the Supreme Court on the issue of constitutionality. Though I believed the law was solidly on our side, there was no guarantee what the court would do. Moreover, such a case might take a great deal of time, likely delaying the trial of the president's men.

Tensions in the office remained high. In an attempt to mend relations, I invited the Jaworskis and the entire cover-up task force to dinner at my house on the last Saturday in February. Leon's driver got lost, so he and his wife arrived late, almost missing the cocktail hour. Over a catered dinner, the conversation flowed naturally, and everyone seemed to relax. During the dessert course—an English trifle I'd made from a law school classmate's recipe—Leon nodded off. At his age, he no longer had the stamina for long hours. He often dozed midafternoon in the office; clearly, he was exhausted.

Earlier in the evening, Rick had taken Leon aside and removed a sheaf of papers from his jacket pocket—our team's suggested revisions to the statement the special prosecutor would be making to the grand jury. The memo was addressed to Leon from Rick alone, in case Leon exploded at its content—as we feared he might. Rick had volunteered to take the heat and shield the rest of us if it came to that. I was sure that this precaution wasn't necessary, although the memo's suggestion that the grand jury vote on the list of unindicted co-conspirators was a novel approach. Grand jury approval of such a list is not required. In fact, none of us had ever heard of it being sought. Rick presented the idea to Leon as a way for him to have cover for the eventual disclosure of the named unindicted co-conspirators. That action would have the stamp of approval of the grand jurors, and wouldn't rest solely on Leon. My chest tightened as I watched the papers pass hands. Leon wordlessly stashed them in his own jacket pocket, and the two men chatted cordially for a few minutes. I sighed, relieved that they hadn't come to blows in the middle of my living room.

The dinner had been a success in bringing us all closer together. Leon thanked me for the evening and said he and his wife had to be going. I walked the couple to the door and stood on the stoop as the government car that brought them lurched from the curb and slipped quietly into the cold blue night.

13

THE ROAD MAP

After the dinner party at my house, we reached a compromise with Leon. He would appear before the grand jury to explain why it shouldn't indict the president, and at the same time, he would let us include Nixon as an unnamed "unindicted co-conspirator" in our case against his top aides. When this designation became public it would mark the president as a central figure in the cover-up, the behind-the-curtain evil Wizard of Watergate, and provide the legal grounds to introduce all the tapes as evidence against his co-conspirators. Though Nixon's name would not appear in the indictment, everyone would know whom we meant. Before trial, the president would be identified with the other co-conspirators in evidence we would turn over to the defense counsel. During the trial, Nixon's role in the conspiracy would be fully revealed.

Our team had arrived at this approach and designated Rick to present it to Leon in the papers he passed him at my dinner party. Leon, much to our surprise, had accepted it as an alternative to an outright indictment of the president.

Leon broke the news to the grand jury on a cold winter morning. All indictments had to be signed by him, and he would not sign an indictment against Nixon, he explained. The jurors listened with grim expressions as Leon spoke, but they accepted his decision.

Soon afterward, though, our press office got a call from the *Washington Post*. Apparently, Carl Bernstein had heard from a source that the grand jury had taken a straw poll and unanimously voted to indict Nixon. According to the source, the nineteen jurors present when the vote was taken were so convinced of Nixon's guilt that they each raised two hands— as if the vote were thirty-eight to zero.

We knew nothing about this in the prosecutor's office. John Barker, our deputy press officer, tracked down the *Post*'s publisher, Katharine Graham, in Connecticut, where she was giving a speech. "It's not true," Barker told her. Barker explained that not only would it be irresponsible to run the story, it also would be dangerous to the nation. If the public thought the grand jury had taken a vote, the informal poll might likely be interpreted as a prelude to a *real* vote to indict. And if Nixon thought he was going to be indicted, there was no telling what desperate measures he'd take to hold on to power. "You have to kill the story," Barker insisted.

Graham sounded stricken. "But my boys will be so disappointed," she said, referring to Bernstein and his reporting partner, Bob Woodward. She shook her head and kept repeating, "My boys, my boys."

In the end, the *Post* did not run the story, perhaps because they couldn't corroborate it. We were so sure it wasn't true that we never even asked the grand jurors if it was. Instead, we told them about the call from the *Post* and reminded them that they were never to discuss their work outside court.

We heard of no additional grand jury leaks, but years later, I learned that the straw vote story was, in fact, true, when Elayne Edlund, one of the jurors, told a reporter from ABC's *20/20* that after hearing the Watergate tapes, the grand jury had indeed voted to indict Nixon. The episode took place during one of their private sessions to evaluate evidence when no prosecutors were present. "There were nineteen people in the grand jury room that particular day," she said, "and we all raised our hands about wanting an indictment—all of us. And some of us raised both hands."

◼

As far as Nixon's top aides were concerned, there was little disagreement on whom to indict; they came to be known as the Watergate Seven. The first three were familiar names by then: John Mitchell, Bob Haldeman, and John Ehrlichman. Equally infamous was Charles W. Colson, a special counsel to the president and the architect of Nixon's notorious enemies list, an inventory of politicians, Democratic donors, and journalists targeted for retribution by the administration. Also included were Robert Mardian, a CREEP official and former assistant attorney general; Gordon C. Strachan, a thirty-year-old assistant to Haldeman; and Kenneth W. Parkinson, an outside counsel hired to defend CREEP after the break-in but who ended up playing an active role in paying hush money and in the cover-up.

Rick and I pushed vigorously to also include William O. Bittman, a partner at a prestigious Washington firm and the lawyer for E. Howard Hunt, who had been convicted for his role in the Watergate burglary. Bittman had participated in the White House hush money scheme: the $75,000 in cash that CREEP had promised Hunt as partial payment for the burglars' silence was delivered to Bittman in a brown paper bag placed in a phone booth in the lobby of his office building. By taking the cash and distributing it, Bittman had joined the conspiracy.

I was certain that indicting Bittman was the correct and just action. Leon, however, was firmly opposed. Rick and I also recognized that adding an aggressive criminal defense lawyer as a defendant could have unforeseen consequences, so in the end we conceded. Bittman went free.

◼

My colleagues and I were now working sixteen-hour days, seven days a week, preparing to deliver our recommendations on indictments to the grand jury. In addition to constructing a meticulous timeline, we had to review every piece of evidence and every word of grand jury and court testimony. The deluge of papers in our office overwhelmed us. We were holding ourselves to a standard of proof way beyond the normal measure of reasonable doubt. If you're going to take on the president's men, you'd better be close to 100 percent sure you can get a jury to convict them.

By early February, the House of Representatives had begun an impeachment inquiry against Nixon. Only once before in America had the House considered impeaching a president, more than a century earlier, in 1868, when Congress accused Andrew Johnson of abusing the powers of his office. Johnson was impeached, though he was acquitted of all charges in the Senate. He remained in office but failed to be nominated by his party for a second term.

We weren't about to let Nixon get away with *his* crimes. In addition to naming the president as an unindicted co-conspirator, we used what was then an obscure exception to the federal rule of grand jury secrecy to request court permission to give the House the evidence we had compiled against him. It was a virtual road map to impeachment, as I had called it in a conversation with Jim Doyle. The label stuck.

On the last Thursday in February, I worked late with George Frampton painstakingly packaging the Road Map and the supporting evidence, including tape transcripts and copies of the actual tapes themselves, White House calendars, Bob Haldeman's notes, and other documents. On Friday morning, before we departed for court to deliver the briefcase to the grand jury, George affixed an orange anti-Nixon bumper sticker that read, "Say Good-bye, Dick," to the side of the bulging case. Ian had given it to me in a rare show of interest in my work. It got a good laugh from the task force, but before we left for court, George removed the sticker and threw it away.

The Road Map was a straightforward, politically and legally neutral document without conclusion. It had a short introduction declaring that the grand jury "has heard evidence . . . bearing on matters that are within the primary jurisdiction of the House of Representatives Committee on the Judiciary in its present investigation to determine whether sufficient grounds exist . . . to impeach Richard M. Nixon, President of the United States," and that "It is the Grand Jury's strong and unanimous recommendation to the Court . . . that [this] evidence be transmitted forthwith to the House."

In sixty-two spare pages, the Road Map designated four avenues of investigation for the House to pursue: the $75,000 payment to Howard Hunt; the president's own ersatz "investigation" of Watergate; material bearing on events leading up to March 1973; and Nixon's false public statements about Watergate.

Within each section, the Road Map referenced and attached witness testimony, transcripts of tapes, and the tapes themselves, making it easy for committee members to find all the evidence they needed to reach a decision. For example, the first item stated that "On or about March 16, 1973, E. Howard Hunt . . . demanded approximately $120,000." Hunt, the Road Map noted, tried to put some muscle behind the demand by asking a CREEP lawyer to send a message to John Dean, reminding him that Hunt "had done some 'seamy things' for the White House and that, if [he] were not paid soon, Hunt would have to 'review his options.'"

With its overwhelmingly damning evidence, the Road Map would become the foundation for the Judiciary Committee's deliberations and drafting of articles of impeachment against Nixon.

◾

As the only woman lawyer on the Watergate trial team, it cheered me to see several women in prominent roles during the impeachment proceedings. The committee itself featured two extraordinary Democratic congresswomen, both freshmen—Barbara Jordan, of Texas, and Elizabeth Holtzman, of New York, who became stars in their own right through the televised proceedings.

Barbara Jordan grew up poor in the Jim Crow South and in 1972 became the first black person elected to Congress from Texas since Reconstruction. A tall, imposing woman who wore fashionable clothes in vivid colors and carried a copy of the Constitution in her purse, Jordan had a Churchillian command of English and spoke in a rich, ringing voice—how God would sound if God were a woman of color.

Jordan had been a star debater at the all-black Texas

Southern University, then went on to get her law degree at Boston University. She soon became involved in local politics in her home city of Houston, directing a voter drive in support of the Kennedy-Johnson ticket in 1960.

After a six-year stint in the Texas State Senate, Jordan was elected to Congress in 1972 and soon won a seat on the House Judiciary Committee with the help of her mentor and friend, former president Lyndon B. Johnson. Throughout the impeachment proceedings, Jordan made clear her chief concern: that Nixon had abused the Constitution for political ends. Arguing for the president's removal from office, Jordan delivered a stirring speech in which she drew on her personal experiences of injustice: "I felt somehow for many years that George Washington and Alexander Hamilton just left me out by mistake," she said, her basso resounding through the House chamber. "But through the process of amendment, interpretation and court decision, I have finally been included in 'We, the people.' . . . My faith in the Constitution is whole, it is complete, it is total, and I'm not going to sit here and be an idle spectator to the diminution, the subversion of the Constitution."

In a bright orange dress, she was the glowing sun in a universe of gray suits, lecturing the congressmen on constitutional law. She compared Nixon's actions with the standards of impeachment laid down by James Madison in 1788 at the Virginia convention for the ratification of the Constitution, and she cited the writings of Joseph Story, an early Supreme Court justice, whose commentaries are still held up as a standard interpretation of the Constitution. Richard Nixon, Jordan intoned, was a "president swollen with power and grown tyrannical," and, therefore, she insisted, "he must be removed from office."

Elizabeth Holtzman matched Barbara Jordan in toughness and passion. The daughter of Jewish immigrants who had settled in Brooklyn—her father was a trial attorney and her mother a professor of Russian—Holtzman showed an early talent for politics. In high school, she ran for student body vice president on a ticket with her twin brother, Robert, who ran for president. Their "Win with the Twins" campaign triumphed, and it seemed that the entire school turned out for their victory celebration at the Holtzman home.

Holtzman went on to Radcliffe College, where she majored in American history and literature, and she stayed to attend Harvard Law School, one of only 15 women in a class of 539. She spent a couple of years in private practice in New York and then became Mayor John Lindsay's liaison with the Department of Parks, Recreation, and Cultural Affairs. Frustrated by the inefficient bureaucracy of city government, she decided to enter elective politics, challenging the longtime congressman Emanuel Celler, who had first been elected during the presidency of Warren Harding. Celler had taken his reelection so completely for granted, Holtzman charged, that he didn't even bother to keep an office in Brooklyn.

Holtzman, meanwhile, threw herself into meeting voters and shaking hands on street corners and in laundromats, grocery stores, community meetings, and senior centers. Celler dismissed her as "a political nonentity," a "toothpick trying to topple the Washington monument." Against all odds, the toothpick prevailed. Holtzman won the primary by six hundred votes and then took the general election too. She was thirty-one when she was sworn in: the youngest woman ever to serve in Congress up to that time.

Holtzman first drew attention for a widely publicized court case against the Nixon administration, claiming that the US bombing of Cambodia was unconstitutional. She was the lead plaintiff and fought the case all the way to the Supreme Court, which ultimately ruled against her. The legal battle raised Holtzman's profile and showed her courage and determination, but Watergate made her famous.

She stood out, as I did, for her youth and gender and found herself the subject of intense media attention. Her slim figure and long brown hair led reporters to call her the Mary Tyler Moore of Congress. Photographers snapped her picture as she walked down the street, and pedestrians stopped her to exclaim, "You're Liz Holtzman! I saw you on TV!"

The public didn't see the hard work behind her moments in the spotlight. "I had to grapple with the impeachment clause in the Constitution. What is a 'high crime and misdemeanor'? We didn't study that in law school," Holtzman said in an interview for a House oral history project. "We had to learn that," she added, "and then go back and study ancient British legal history," where the arcane phrase originated.

When the Nixon tapes were first played for the House Judiciary Committee, Holtzman had the same reaction as I did to the revelation of Nixon's character: shock followed by deep sadness and distress. "I came to realize that Richard Nixon had an unremitting disregard for basic constitutional rights, that wire-tapping and bugging political opponents was a way of life for him," she told Madeleine Edmondson and Alden Duer Cohen in *The Women of Watergate.*

Liz Holtzman and Barbara Jordan shared my fears about the damage Nixon had done to American democracy. "Richard Nixon was given a sacred trust," Holtzman said. "Enormous power was given to him to use for the public interest. Instead, he used it to subvert the laws, to harm the people in this country, and for personal gain. This was an extraordinary wrong, and it helped to undermine the confidence of people in the system of government, which is not helpful to the health of the country."

In addition to Jordan and Holtzman, among the House lawyers investigating the charges against the president was a twenty-six-year-old blonde named Hillary Rodham, whom reporters dubbed "the Jill Wine Volner of the Impeachment Committee."

□

Throughout the first months of 1974, the calls for Nixon's removal from office grew louder. The mood of the nation was caught by a man wearing a Nixon mask and prison stripes who stood on Pennsylvania Avenue in front of the White House every day with a sign reading "Honk for Impeachment." A riotous screech of horns from cars, taxis, buses, trucks, and even police cars continued into the summer.

On K Street, we felt stressed to the breaking point by the gravity of the decisions we were making. At no time did we miss Archie Cox more than in the lead-up to returning indictments against Nixon's men. We craved assurance that we were doing the right thing, and only Archie could have provided it. Leon remained aloof from us, our dealings with him marred by mutual wariness.

One afternoon over a late lunch with Jim Doyle, I vented my frustrations with Leon. I didn't realize my voice had risen several decibels until I noticed Carl Bernstein standing nearby, listening to every word. At least, I thought he was listening. Carl never wrote anything about what he might or might not have heard. If he had, that would have been the end of my job.

◼

Throughout Watergate, my stolen moments with Kurt were about my only opportunity to relax, and on the rare days when I got a lunch break, I sometimes spent it with him. One day, Kurt picked me up at K Street and we headed to my house. As we drove down 20th Street past my town house on the way to turn into the garage, I was shocked to see Ian on the stoop in his camel military-style coat with his key in the front door lock, his back to the street. I'd never known Ian to come home in the middle of the day. *Why is he there?* I wondered. "Don't stop. Keep driving," I said to Kurt, my voice strained and my heart beating hard. If we'd arrived a few minutes earlier or later, we would have been busted. When it came to covering up my misdeeds, I had better luck than Nixon.

14

INDICTMENT

It was indictment day, March 1, 1974, and the Watergate grand jury was dressed to kill—the men in their Sunday best suits and the women in stylish outfits, many topped by church hats, colorful confections embellished with ribbons, feathers, and veils. Twenty-one jurors (two were absent) filled the first three rows on the left side of Judge Sirica's small wood-paneled courtroom on the second floor, four floors below the large ceremonial courtroom where most of the Watergate drama had played out. With the solemnity of a Baptist deacon, foreman Vladimir Pregelj rose from his front-row seat and handed Sirica a black briefcase. Inside was the fifty-page indictment against the Watergate Seven and, in a sealed envelope, our Road Map with the grand jury's recommendation that it be given to the House Judiciary Committee investigating impeachment charges against Nixon.

Sirica donned his glasses and pulled the envelope from the briefcase. The room was so still that Jim Doyle sitting in the back row could hear the blade of Sirica's letter opener slicing the envelope's flap. The judge read the letter to himself with a grave expression. Then, removing his glasses, he looked out at the crowd of spectators. "The court will, at the conclusion of these proceedings this morning, reseal the envelope that I opened," Sirica said. "It will be held in custody of this court in a safe place until further order of this court."

Rick heaved a second briefcase onto the judge's bench, where it sat for the rest of the hearing, heavy with historic meaning. This one was reddish brown, faux leather, and locked. Inside were the Road Map's supporting documents, including copies of the seven tapes we'd wrested from the White House. "All the material which is made reference to in the document you just read" was there, Rick said. He paused before adding that Sirica would find the key to unlock our case in a separate envelope in the grand jury's black case.

The judge pounded his gavel and with a swish of black robe, exited the courtroom.

Our press staff had made four hundred copies of the indictment. In the middle of the job, our photocopying machines had broken down, forcing the staff to use machines belonging to the National Endowment of the Arts on another floor of our K Street building. Some of the copies had been distributed to the regular Watergate reporters as they entered court that morning. The rest were stacked up in our press office on K Street, available to be picked up later by interested journalists.

The indictment was the culmination of nine months of gestation—of relentless work, thought, and investigation. We had labored to write and rewrite it until it was perfectly formed. It spelled out our case against the president's men and told the story of the cover-up in clear, straightforward language that the public—and a trial jury—could understand. Although the indictment referenced eighteen unindicted co-conspirators, including Nixon, it did not name any of them. The grand jury minutes recording their names were locked inside the safe in Leon's office and would remain Washington's best-kept secret for many months. Not even Judge Sirica knew who they were.

The seven men named in the indictment were former officials of the Nixon White House, his 1972 re-election campaign, or both. All were accused of a massive conspiracy "by deceit, craft, trickery, and dishonest means." Forty-five overt acts to block the burglary trial and the Watergate cover-up investigation were spelled out, including destroying documents; lying to the FBI, the grand jury, and the Senate Watergate Committee; offering "leniency and executive clemency" to the original Watergate defendants; and paying those original defendants more than $400,000 in hush money. The cover-up conspiracy began, the grand jury charged, within hours of the break-in and continued "up to and including the date of the filing of" the indictment.

In addition, all but Mardian were charged with a separate count of obstruction of justice, and Mitchell, Haldeman, Ehrlichman, and Strachan were accused of multiple counts of lying to the FBI, the grand jury, the Senate, and others.

▪

Most devastating for Nixon was the indictment's perjury charge against Haldeman, for lying to the Ervin Committee about the now famous March 21, 1973, meeting between the president and John Dean, which Haldeman joined in the last minutes. The jurors had listened to a copy of the tape, as Dean warned Nixon that there was "a cancer on the presidency" and that the burglars were demanding a million dollars in hush money. They heard Nixon respond, "There is no problem" in raising the money, "We could get that, and we can get it in cash." They did *not* hear Nixon add, "*but it would be wrong*," as Haldeman had testified to the Ervin Committee. Haldeman "well knew" those words "were false," the indictment charged.

As the world would soon learn from accounts of the indictment in the press, the cover-up involved a series of elaborate schemes. Hours after the burglars were caught, John Mitchell told Robert Mardian to tell G. Gordon Liddy, who hadn't yet been arrested, to contact Attorney General Richard Kleindienst about getting the Watergate burglars released from jail before they talked and linked the break-in to CREEP and the White House. Liddy tracked Kleindienst to the locker room at the Burning Tree Golf Club, an exclusive men's golf club in Bethesda, Maryland, where Nixon and other high-ranking political leaders were members. It was here that Liddy made the request.

The indictment continued: the next day, Gordon Strachan, acting on the instructions of his boss, Bob Haldeman, destroyed documents relating to the break-in and bugging of the Democratic Party headquarters. A day later, on June 19, Ehrlichman told Dean to tell Liddy to tell Howard Hunt, the break-in's coordinator and recruiter, to leave the United States. That same day, Mitchell also told Jeb Magruder to destroy documents relating to the break-in, and Magruder complied.

The indictment detailed how the president's men scrambled to find money to silence the burglars. Mitchell and Mardian discussed with Dean a plan to ask the CIA to "provide covert funds for the assistance of persons involved in the Watergate break-in," a scheme Ehrlichman approved two days later. As time went on, the hush money arrangements grew more and more tangled, trapping a gaggle of men in a web of lies, including a former CREEP fund-raiser and Nixon's personal attorney, Herbert W. Kalmbach, whom Ehrlichman enlisted to raise the funds and distribute them to the convicted men and their families.

In a scenario that could have been lifted from a Howard Hunt spy novel, Anthony Ulasewicz, a former New York police investigator whom the White House had called in previously to conduct some political spying, secured most of the money from secret CREEP stashes through Kalmbach, who got it from Mitchell's aide Frederick C. LaRue. The players in this shabby episode used code names. Kalmbach and LaRue, for example, were both "Bradford," and Ulasewicz was "Rivers." Ulasewicz, who looked and sounded more like a mafioso than a White House employee, toted the hush money in paper bags, which he dead-dropped on top of phone booths, on a shelf in a lobby of a Howard Johnson's motel, and in storage lockers at National Airport. To ensure that he always had enough change for the endless phone calls he made to Kalmbach about their sordid activities, Ulasewicz carried a bus driver's coin dispenser. (Kalmbach and LaRue later served short prison terms for their role in the cover-up; Ulasewicz was never charged for his activities as a Watergate bagman but later served a year of probation after being convicted of filing false income tax returns: he had failed to report his White House undercover pay.)

Over time, the burglars' money demands increased, and the cover-up intensified. Nixon's special counsel Charles Colson played a particularly duplicitous role. He recorded his conversation with Hunt in which the break-in architect discussed payments to the burglars; Colson gave the tape to Dean, who played it for Haldeman and Ehrlichman at Camp

David. Colson then took the tape to New York to play it for Mitchell.

As the trial of the burglars approached in December 1972, they demanded more and more hush money. According to the indictment, CREEP attorney Kenneth Parkinson gave Dean "a list of anticipated expenses" of the Watergate burglars during their trial. The grand jury also charged that Haldeman approved using $350,000 in cash he controlled for these expenses. Strachan gave the money to LaRue in two payments, and LaRue delivered it in four installments to Hunt's lawyer, William O. Bittman. Hunt and the four men he'd recruited for the burglary pleaded guilty during the trial, and a jury convicted McCord and Liddy. Hunt's demands for money for himself and the others continued as they awaited sentencing.

The charges relied heavily on information provided by our chief witness, John Dean. With respect to many of the forty-five acts of criminal conduct cited, Dean was the *only* government witness. With respect to others, the only witness was mine, Jeb Magruder. Both men had pleaded guilty to one count each of conspiracy and were awaiting sentencing by Judge Sirica. They were still cooperating with us, as the threat of long jail terms hung over them if they didn't tell us everything they knew.

The indictments were "an occasion for sorrow mingled with pride," wrote the *New York Times* in an editorial the next day. Not since the bribery scandals of the Harding administration "half a century ago has the office of the Presidency been brought to such ignominy," wrote the newspaper. "But the citizens of this republic can take pride in the fact that wrongdoing at the very highest levels of government can still be exposed and the alleged offenders brought before the bar of justice. . . . It is a time of shame and a time of hope."

■

On K Street, Leon and the entire Watergate task force took the next week off. Many of us went out of town. Leon returned to his ranch in Texas. Ian and I traveled to Eleuthera in the Bahamas.

We checked into a small, thatch-roofed cabin on a stretch of pink beach. Salty ocean smells filled the air, and a hot sun shimmered on the gentle sea. My relationship with Ian hadn't changed—there was still no romance between us, and I continued to feel psychologically abused. But after nearly nine years of marriage, we'd learned how to enjoy vacations together. Away from Washington in this peaceful, exotic setting, I started to relax. Being with Ian was better than being alone. He was a companion, someone to stroll with along Eleuthera's brilliant coral reefs, to lounge with on the beach, and to dine with on the terrace under a starlit sky.

I began to feel restored mentally and physically, but there was no relief for my general malaise. Something was missing from my life that I couldn't ignore now that I was away from work. Oddly, I found myself thinking not only of Kurt, but also of my high school boyfriend Michael Banks, who had written to me recently after seeing my picture in the *New York Times*. It was the first time Michael and I had been in touch in a decade, and his words brought back memories of a happier, simpler time.

We'd started dating my junior year at Niles Township High, when Michael was a senior. In the fall of 1959, he went off to Florida State University in Tallahassee on a swimming scholarship, but we continued to see each other on vacations, and he returned in the spring to attend my senior prom with me. We saw each other during summers throughout our college years, and though we never officially broke up, we drifted apart, pulled to opposite ends of the map by travel and school.

In his letter, Michael told me he'd done graduate work at the University of Wisconsin and Cambridge University and had taught school in Chicago to avoid being drafted. He had recently returned from a sojourn in Ireland, where he had lived with a girlfriend and written poetry. He'd been married briefly years earlier, but was now single and had just opened an antiques business in the Chicago suburbs. I wrote him back, thanking him for being in touch. That prompted him to write again. Michael's second letter was more intimate. He asked whether I was happy, and he reminded me of the close romance we'd shared, of what could have been if we'd stayed together. I threw the letter away and didn't respond. I wasn't about to tell Michael or anyone else about the sorry state of my life with Ian. By refusing to admit that my marriage was a sham, I felt I could keep it in a dimension outside reality. I wouldn't have to spend my life being an unhappily married woman. I could focus my emotions more productively—on the very important job of taking down a corrupt president.

So I pushed away all thoughts about Michael. When I returned to K Street after six days of R and R, there was no time to think of anything but work, as my colleagues and I prepared to take the Watergate Seven to trial. We were in good shape; we had enough evidence to convict them. Still, you can never have *too* much evidence. We knew there were more White House tapes that would strengthen our case, and we acted to secure them, relying on John Dean's astonishing memory to help us identify the conversations that would be most useful to us. We pinpointed sixty-four tapes involving Nixon and Dean and three of the men named in our indictment: Haldeman, Ehrlichman, and Colson.

On April 16, at our request, Sirica issued a trial subpoena directing Nixon to turn over the sixty-four tapes. Nixon refused. Instead, he issued his own version of their contents, 1,254 pages of transcripts that were so heavily redacted as to render them meaningless. We were sure that the president's versions would turn out to be misleading. The Government Printing Office ran off 45,000 copies, which were quickly bought up by the media and the public. Journalists acted out the juicier conversations on the TV news, as did Americans across the nation who had a grand time at parties that spring inserting their own profanities where Nixon's "expletives" had been deleted.

Humor was one way to beat back frustration and fury over White House corruption. That spring I took part in a "Counter-Gridiron" carnival to protest the exclusion of women from the prestigious Gridiron Club, a by-invitation-only organization for top journalists. Our event, which raised money for reporters jailed for refusing to reveal their sources, was held in tents on the grounds of Mount Vernon College on the same night as the official white-tie Gridiron dinner at the Statler-Hilton. While a group of luminaries including Judge Sirica and Vice President Ford listened to the Gridiron's traditional lampoon of political leaders at the Statler-Hilton, many of the nation's leading journalists attended the event at Mount Vernon College. I sold kisses in a booth with Dan Rather. John Mitchell's estranged wife, Martha, famous for her indiscreet calls to reporters, sold phone calls: for a small fee, she would dial any number of your choice and introduce herself in her buttery Arkansas drawl. Close by, Elliot Richardson sold prints of a doodle he had made for the event, an owl atop the scales of justice surrounded by a female symbol. Later in the evening, I bought one. As I handed it to the former attorney general to autograph, he looked hard at me and said, "I know you. I lost my job because of you." We both laughed.

◼

Why the White House tapes still existed at all was a mystery to me. I wasn't the only person who wondered why Nixon hadn't had a bonfire on the South Lawn as soon as Alexander Butterfield announced their existence during the Ervin hearings. Surely that would have been easier than waging the protracted battles that followed. The president claimed that he wanted the tapes so he'd have an accurate record when he sat down to write his memoirs. I was sure he never imagined he'd have to turn them over.

Of course, it was lucky for us he hadn't burned them, as it was for the House Judiciary Committee. We heard that the committee's investigation was relying heavily on our Road Map, which included seven of the first tapes we had requested. The committee's lawyers, John Doar and Albert Jenner, met with Leon several times in May to delve deeper into our evidence and to seek our advice on where to concentrate their inquiry. Each of the thirty-eight members of the committee was given a "statement of evidence" book prepared by the committee staff when they met in closed-door sessions. These evidence books, which contained thousands of pages of facts, were read aloud during the Judiciary Committee's meetings, and then locked in each congressman's office safe at night.

Mastering the Watergate materials was a herculean task for the Judiciary Committee, as it had been for us. "Trying to absorb the issues," Elizabeth Holtzman later recalled, "was like being in quicksand. There was no bottom. No matter where you looked, you were in muck all the way down."

In listening to the tapes, the committee members were particularly shocked to hear Nixon's utter lack of concern for how Watergate affected the nation. "Never once in those tapes, did the president or his associates say, 'What's the right thing to do? What was good for the country?'" Holtzman later recalled. "They acted with such total disregard for the office of the Presidency and for the American people that at times all I wanted to do was take off the headphones and leave."

On May 20, less than a month after Nixon released the redacted transcripts, Judge Sirica ordered the president to turn over the sixty-four tapes we had requested for the trial. Once again, Nixon refused. Bypassing the Court of Appeals, Leon asked the Supreme Court to hold a special session during their summer recess to hear the case, and the high tribunal agreed.

On Monday morning, July 8, I arrived at the Supreme Court with Rick and the rest of the trial team. Leon came in a separate car with his wife, Jeannette, and their son, Joseph, himself a trial lawyer in Texas. For the occasion, I'd applied and been admitted to the Supreme Court bar, an important moment in a lawyer's life that requires taking an oath to conduct oneself "uprightly and according to law and . . . support the Constitution of the United States."

The massive, pillared courthouse, stark white under the scorching sun, rose up from a grand marble plaza. The crowd swarming the steps had begun gathering two days earlier. The police had allowed them to camp out on the Capitol lawn across the street, where they'd formed a committee that issued its own tickets to the proceedings, which they persuaded the courthouse guards to honor. Only 136 of 400 available seats were set aside for the public, with an additional 27 seats to be given out on a rotating five-minute basis during the arguments. The rest of the seats were reserved for lawyers, members of Congress, and reporters.

As we mounted the steps, the crowd applauded. Someone shouted, "Go, America!" Then another voice yelled, "Shut up, that's partisan."

Actually, not so. The comment related to an essential quality of the Supreme Court—scrupulous fairness. As the words carved into the façade above the marble columns announced, "Equal Justice Under Law."

Inside the cavernous, high-ceilinged courtroom, I was surprised to see Bob Haldeman, his crew cut grown out into a poufy TV newsman coif, sitting next to Jeannette Jaworski. Also present were five members of the House Judiciary Committee.

Promptly at ten, the towering red velvet drapes behind the immense, polished bench parted, and the nine justices took their places. Four of them had been nominated by Nixon: Chief Justice Warren E. Burger, along with Lewis F. Powell Jr., Harry A. Blackmun, and William H. Rehnquist. One had been nominated by Lyndon Johnson: Thurgood Marshall (the court's first African American); one by John Kennedy: Byron White; two by Dwight Eisenhower: Potter Stewart and William J. Brennan; and one by Franklin Roosevelt: William O. Douglas.

Rehnquist stayed only a minute to announce a decision in another matter and then left, recusing himself from the Nixon case because he had once worked at the Justice Department under John Mitchell, now a Watergate defendant.

Leon, who had declined to wear a morning coat—the traditional garb for (male) lawyers arguing before the Supreme

Court—looked elegant in a crisp navy suit, his silver hair glistening from a recent blue rinse administered by his barber. Speaking in a soft Texas drawl, he focused his nearly hour-long statement on Nixon's contention that his White House records were protected by executive privilege and that he could not be forced to surrender them for evidence in a criminal investigation.

"Now, the president may be right in how he reads the Constitution," Leon said. "But he may also be wrong. And if he is wrong, who is there to tell him so? And if there is no one, then the president, of course, is free to pursue his course of erroneous interpretations.

"In our view, this nation's constitutional form of government is in serious jeopardy if the president—any president—is to say that the Constitution means what he says it does, and that there is no one, not even the Supreme Court, to tell him otherwise."

In response, James D. St. Clair, Nixon's Boston-based chief counsel, argued for a broad interpretation of executive privilege. Nixon had a right to keep his confidential conversations private, even if they concerned criminal activity, he told the justices, to preserve "candor in discussions between the president and his aides."

Justice Powell interrupted to ask, "What public interest is there in preserving secrecy with respect to a criminal conspiracy?"

"The answer, sir," St. Clair said, "is that a criminal conspiracy is criminal only after it's proven to be criminal."

In the briefs submitted to the Supreme Court, we revealed that the Watergate grand jury had named Nixon an unindicted co-conspirator in the criminal case against his aides. St. Clair asked the court to strike Nixon from the indictment, but the justices questioned whether the request was relevant to the issue of the tapes subpoena at all. Leon insisted that it was. He told the justices that Nixon had to be part of the indictment "in order to prove this conspiracy and in order to provide all of the links in the conspiracy." If Nixon had not been named a co-conspirator, his taped conversations would be hearsay and not admissible in the trial of the Watergate Seven. The president's role, Leon argued, made our right to the tapes absolute.

When the oral argument was over and we were standing outside blinking against the white-hot sun, I felt relieved and optimistic. Our briefs were as strong as possible. Leon and Phil Lacovara, who had written most of our brief and delivered the summation, had argued well—much more compellingly than St. Clair, in my view and that of most of the press. As we made our way down the endless marble steps of the plaza, a crowd shouting Leon's name followed us. A few people were knocked down in the crush.

In the coming days, as we awaited the Supreme Court's decision, Leon grew depressed. This was partly a result of the inevitable letdown after the intense pressure of arguing before the nation's highest tribunal. He also missed his family. His wife and son had returned to Texas, where the rest of the Jaworski children and grandchildren lived. But on top of those factors, Leon was hurt by some criticism of his Supreme Court performance. Mostly, the papers had praised him, but he'd seized on the one or two negative remarks and couldn't forget them.

I thought Leon had done fine, though his talent was mainly as a trial lawyer, which requires charm and force of personality in communicating with a jury and winning them over to your side. Arguing before judges is a different, more cerebral game, drawing on the cooler powers of the intellect. This was Phil Lacovara's strength. The logic of his Supreme Court brief was razor sharp, and his brilliant rebuttal to St. Clair's summation, most observers agreed, was the outstanding presentation of the case.

Leon moped around the office and left early every day. Then he stopped coming to K Street at all, and my colleagues and I grew concerned. One afternoon, I went over to the Jefferson Hotel, where Leon had been living since becoming special prosecutor, and met him in the hotel restaurant. He looked tired and old. The furrows in his brow seemed to have deepened, and there were dark circles under his eyes. We settled at a corner table and ordered coffee. I completely understood how he felt. I, too, am hypersensitive to anything negative said about me; the slightest offhand comment hurts me to the quick. I told Leon this and pointed out to him all the good press he'd gotten. "You're doing a terrific job. You've kept us on track; everything is going well," I said.

Leon shook his head. "I just don't know," he replied. A waiter poured us each a cup of coffee. As Leon took a sip, I noticed his hand shook slightly. "I'm thinking of resigning," he said in a glum tone.

No matter how rough things had gotten in the previous year, Leon had never before mentioned quitting.

"That's ridiculous," I said. "We're going to win this case. That's what you need to focus on."

Leon assured me that I'd cheered him up, but in the next couple of weeks he failed to return to K Street, spending most of his time holed up at the hotel, where Carl Feldbaum twice a day brought him the letters and telegrams of support that flowed in from around the nation. Carl also was a balm to him. He told Leon how much the staff respected his courage in showing up alone to take up the special prosecutor's post after Archie had been fired, not bringing a single lawyer from his firm in Houston, or even his personal secretary.

■

Under questioning by White House reporters, Nixon's deputy press secretary, Gerald L. Warren, refused to assure Americans that the president would abide by the Supreme Court's ruling, if it went against him. I didn't put it past the president to behave like a dictator in a banana republic. It was possible that Nixon would *never* produce the tapes. What would happen then? Armed guards protected the White House. We couldn't just walk up to the front door and knock. And we couldn't break in. The special prosecutor's office didn't have a plumbers unit.

Around this time, my brother, Stevie, a senior at the University of Illinois, sent me a copy of the popular comic book *The Incredible Hulk*, which featured Rick and me as the superhero duo June Volper and Ben Vincent. I liked my pen-and-ink counterpart. June Volper had supreme self-confidence and exquisite judgment in all matters, not to mention beautifully drawn hair that never wilted, even in the muggiest Washington summer.

She and Ben Vincent managed to sneak into the White House, which had been overrun by humanoid monsters hellbent on destroying democracy. "Whatever we've stumbled on, it makes the Pentagon Papers look like nickel and dime shoplifting," Ben said to June in one frame. All hope rested with them, two young people "who saw the truth and were not afraid to follow it."

If only real White House villains could be crushed as easily as comic-book monsters.

15

EXIT THE KING

Time passed at a glacial pace as the country awaited the Supreme Court's decision. Then, on the morning of July 24, two weeks after the justices had heard arguments in the case, I looked up from my desk to see George Frampton standing in the doorway grinning.

"We won! It was unanimous!" he announced.

The nation's highest tribunal had just ordered Nixon to turn over the sixty-four White House tapes. Later, as I read the opinion written by Chief Justice Warren Burger, I felt almost dizzy with relief. The court had rejected every one of Nixon's arguments. Executive privilege did not exempt the president from honoring our subpoena. He had to obey the law like everyone else. The needs of a criminal investigation trumped claims of executive privilege.

The next two weeks passed in a blur of events so momentous and swift they seemed disconnected from reality. Only Washington's summer heat was familiar. During the day, the temperature didn't fall much below ninety. Under the blazing sun, the sidewalks burned, and the flowers in the parkways wilted.

Nixon was in San Clemente when news of the decision broke, and it took him several hours to respond. Finally, at seven p.m., James St. Clair announced that the president would comply with the court's order. With the memory of the missing tapes and the eighteen-and-a-half-minute gap fresh in our minds, we weren't going to count on the White House's word. The next day, Leon went to court and obtained from Judge Sirica an order for Nixon to produce the tapes in three batches over ten days. The tapes we were most eager to get held conversations involving Nixon, Haldeman, and Ehrlichman starting on June 20, 1972, three days after the Watergate break-in.

The same day the Supreme Court decision was handed down, the House Judiciary Committee began televised impeachment hearings, which I watched sporadically with a group of my colleagues on the black-and-white TV in our office. The proceedings weren't as dramatic as the Ervin hearings. There were no surprise witnesses or stunning disclosures as in Dean's opening statement or Alexander Butterfield's revelation of the White House taping system.

The two women on the committee whom I so admired continued to perform powerfully. Remarks by Elizabeth Holtzman and Barbara Jordan were highlights of the session on July 25, and their sincerity and integrity moved me deeply. With her glorious voice resonating in her fifteen-minute opening statement, Jordan passionately defended the Constitution, which had originally left out people like her—blacks and women.

As her twin brother and her mother looked on from the spectator section, Elizabeth Holtzman gave a straightforward recounting of the facts of Nixon's involvement in Watergate, "using every opportunity," she recalled, "to describe the extensiveness of evidence against him."

Three days after the Supreme Court's ruling, the House Judiciary Committee voted 27–11 to recommend impeaching Nixon on charges that he had obstructed justice in the Watergate case. The bipartisan majority vote, the first impeachment recommendation against a president in more than a century, included the votes of three conservative Southern Democrats (James R. Mann of South Carolina, Walter Flowers of Alabama, and Ray Thorton of Arkansas), and six Republicans. Three of those Republicans (Lawrence Hogan of Maryland, M. Caldwell Butler of Virginia, and William S. Cohen of Maine) hailed from states where Nixon was so popular that supporting his impeachment threatened their careers.

As the congressmen solemnly cast their votes, there was no joy in the committee room. After voting "Aye," the committee chairman, Peter Rodino, a Democrat from New Jersey whose strong leadership enabled the bipartisan vote, went back to his office and wept. "I don't feel good about it," said Representative Tom Railsback, a Republican from Illinois who also voted "Aye." Even such ardent Nixon opponents as Elizabeth Holtzman found voting for impeachment a wrenching experience. She later explained the unexpected sadness that overwhelmed her. "I had to judge. I couldn't turn away from it," she recalled. "Richard Nixon was contemptible, but I . . . realized the enormous difference between voicing a personal opinion and issuing a formal judgment of condemnation."

Two more articles of impeachment were quickly passed. Article II, which was adopted by a 28–10 vote, charged Nixon with a "persistent effort to abuse his authority in violation of his constitutional oath" to faithfully execute the duties of his office and "uphold and defend the nation's laws." Article III, which passed 21–17, with two Republicans and two Southern Democrats who had voted for the first two articles switching sides, charged Nixon with obstructing Congress and impeding the impeachment process by defying the subpoena for the tapes and withholding other evidence.

Committee approval of any of these articles of impeachment would suffice for an impeachment vote on the House floor. It looked certain now that all three would pass the full House. The case would then go to a trial in the Senate, where a two-thirds vote would be required to remove Nixon from office. Nixon's support was quickly vanishing. In a little more than a year and a half, he'd gone from winning a landslide victory, carrying forty-nine states with a margin of 18 million popular votes, the largest in American history, to an approval rating of 24 percent. In the end, the citizenry had been persuaded by the facts revealed in the public hearings, which were indisputable. Just as important, the public had also observed the rigorous fairness of the House Judiciary Committee proceedings.

At the White House, rumors swirled that Pat Nixon had started packing. The president, though, hadn't given up. He knew he would lose an impeachment vote in the House, but he thought he had a good chance of being acquitted in a Senate trial. All he needed to stay in office were 34 of 100 votes. Alexander Haig and James St. Clair urged him to resign as a preferable alternative. But Nixon held firm.

◼

In the middle of this crazy, hot summer, Jim Neal returned. Leaving his family and law practice behind in Nashville, he moved back to Washington temporarily to take over the trial team for the upcoming prosecution of the Watergate Seven. He reclaimed the corner office that had stayed vacant in his absence, and once again the pungent odor of cigar smoke floated through the ninth-floor hallways at K Street.

Also that summer, the first of the Watergate memoirs was published—*An American Life: One Man's Road to Watergate*—by my witness, Jeb Magruder. In May, Judge Sirica had sentenced Magruder to between ten months and four years for his role in Watergate. Afterward, Magruder stood on the courthouse steps to talk to reporters. He said ambition had been his undoing. "I was able to lose the beliefs I'd been brought up with," said Magruder. "This has bothered me for the past year, and I'm sure it will be some time before I have that sorted out in my own mind."

My eyes traveled over the crowd gathered on the sidewalk, settling on a familiar-looking tall, dark-haired man, the novelist Philip Roth. Three years earlier, well before Watergate, he had published *Our Gang*, a send-up of the Nixon administration. Now the truth had outstripped his fiction. Roth, who was on assignment for *Esquire*, narrowed his eyes at Magruder, and I wondered whether he shared my disbelief in the former White House aide's sincerity.

Magruder knew he'd done something stupid and illegal, but he never accepted that he'd actually behaved in a corrupt way. I heard him express remorse only about having been caught, never about having committed crimes. His chief emotion at being sent to prison was anger at Nixon, whom he now hated more than the president's most rabid political enemies did. In his book, which I had read in manuscript and cleared for publication, Magruder tried to sound contrite, but, as one reviewer noted, his conscience didn't seem bothered much by Nixonian dirty tricks such as "sending fake telegrams" or "writing memos on how to put the screws" to prominent media figures. Following his sentencing, Magruder was sent to the minimum-security federal prison at Allenwood, Pennsylvania, as his book climbed the best-seller lists alongside Roth's latest novel, *My Life as a Man*, and Carl Bernstein and Bob Woodward's account of their Watergate investigation, *All the President's Men*.

John Dean, our chief witness, also was working on a book, though *Blind Ambition* would not be published for two more years. On August 2, Judge Sirica sentenced the former White House counsel to between one and four years in prison, but Dean had yet to begin serving his sentence and was at K Street nearly every day. We gave him an empty office, where he sat, dressed in a suit and tie, available if anyone had a question for him. The trial team relied heavily on Dean's astounding memory. I recall him making only one error in his testimony at trial: he said that a meeting had occurred at the Mayflower Hotel, when it actually took place at the Mayflower Coffee Shop in the Statler Hotel a few blocks away.

Nearly a week after Sirica's order, we still hadn't received a single White House tape from the batch that the Supreme Court had ordered to be turned over to us. We believed that Jeb Magruder and John Dean had given accurate testimony about the nefarious activities that were the basis of our case against the Watergate Seven and that the tapes would prove beyond a shadow of doubt that our witnesses were to be believed.

As we awaited the arrival of the tapes, top White House officials were listening to them with a growing sense of disaster. One recording, from June 23, 1972, would soon be seared into American history as the smoking gun that ended the Nixon presidency. It recorded the president and Bob Haldeman scheming to thwart the FBI investigation into the hundred-dollar bills found on the Watergate burglars when they were arrested. (The bills were traceable to a campaign check that had been deposited into a Florida bank account belonging to one of the burglars.) Nixon and Haldeman discussed a plan to lie to the CIA director, Richard Helms, and his deputy, General Vernon Walters, about national security being at risk if the burglars' cash was investigated. On these grounds, they hoped to persuade the CIA officials to tell the acting director of the FBI, L. Patrick Gray, not to follow the money—because the money trail would reveal that CREEP had paid the burglars. The tape proved that Nixon was directly involved in the cover-up from the start, a clear and obvious obstruction of justice.

We later learned that when Haig and St. Clair listened to the tape, they realized its devastating implications and suggested to Nixon that he resign. The president listened to the tape, too, and in a remark that took self-delusion to an entirely new level, pronounced it "not so bad." He thought if he released a transcript himself—rather than if we released it—the public might judge him less harshly.

The transcript the White House gave to the press on the afternoon of August 5 was a shock—as much to us as to anyone else. We had subpoenaed the June 23 tape because the conversation we sought was one of the first after the Watergate break-in. We did not know exactly what was on it since we had no cooperating witness who was part of it. Though Nixon had a history of releasing severely redacted transcripts from which the worst parts had been removed, in this case—when we later got the tape and listened to it—the transcript closely tracked the tape.

Nixon still expected his hard-core supporters to stay with him. But when the ten Republican congressmen who had voted against every article of impeachment read the June 23 transcript, they said they now favored removing Nixon from office. Even such conservative stalwarts as Senator John G. Tower, a Republican from Texas, fell away. "I suppose there is a certain amount of immorality that almost all politicians will tolerate," Tower said. "But there is also a threshold, and that is the president's problem." Nixon had crossed the threshold into criminality, and there was no going back.

On August 7, three of the leading Republicans in Congress—former presidential candidate Senator Barry Goldwater of Arizona, Senate Minority Leader Hugh Scott of Pennsylvania, and House Minority Leader John Rhodes of Arizona—visited Nixon in the Oval Office. "You've only got fifteen Senate supporters left," Goldwater told the president, and in a comment attributed to him in many accounts of the meeting, added, "I'm not one of them." Finally, the reality sank in. Nixon knew he was doomed and decided to resign.

Until that moment, Rose Mary Woods thought he would stay and fight. Even as Nixon was meeting with Goldwater, Scott, and Rhodes, she was wandering the East Wing insisting to staffers that the president would remain in office. Now it was over. Nixon couldn't bear to tell his wife and daughters himself, so he sent Rose to break the news to them in the White House solarium, where the family had gathered late in the afternoon. "Your father has decided to resign," Rose said, in perhaps the most painful sentence she ever uttered.

A few minutes later, the president appeared. "We're moving back to California," he said matter-of-factly. Julie and Tricia burst into tears. Pat and Rose remained dry-eyed.

Nixon told the nation in a televised speech the following evening, and the next day, August 9, his resignation became effective.

I watched Nixon leave the White House for the last time on the black-and-white TV in our office, surrounded by my colleagues and the task force secretaries and press staff. In what became a famous image of American iconography, he stood in the door of the presidential helicopter and raised his arms in a double V sign. Then he disappeared inside with his wife. A moment later, the propeller spun, the helicopter lifted, and Nixon was gone.

As the now ex-president headed to the plane that would take him and Pat to their home in San Clemente, Leon was on his way to Dulles Airport to catch a flight to Texas for a weekend with his family. The intern who had been assigned to drive him returned to the office with a story that summed up for me the deep difference between Leon and Archie. Sitting in the front seat of a black Chevy Nova (which replaced the government's old Rambler) Leon turned to the young man, a college student.

"Did you watch the president's resignation speech?" he asked.

"Yes, sir," the intern answered.

"Well, let me ask you something else," Leon said with an impish twinkle.

"What has two wings and a crooked dick?"

"I have no idea, sir."

Leon smiled wickedly. "Air Force One."

If it had been Archie in the car, the intern would likely have heard a meditation on the Constitution instead.

◼

With Nixon's resignation, Gerald Ford became president. Since Nixon was no longer a sitting president, the debate about whether to indict and prosecute him raged anew at K Street.

Rick and I argued vociferously for amending the indictment to include Nixon. Earlier, while Nixon was in office, Leon had insisted that indicting him would be too disruptive to his ability to govern. Obviously, that was no longer the case, but Leon remained unpersuaded. The other young lawyers on the task force agreed with us, though Jim Neal, senior to Rick and me by fourteen years, sided with Leon. It's worth noting that Leon didn't base his decision on a sense that Nixon had suffered enough, a feeling prevalent among some Americans. Rather, he worried that indicting the disgraced former president would delay the trial of his aides.

"So what?" I told Leon one afternoon. On the wall behind him hung a huge white bedsheet emblazoned in red paint with the words "Nixon: No Amnesty," and the peace symbol. It had arrived that morning in the mail from a man in Ohio, and the secretaries had tacked it up on Leon's office wall without consulting him. "We'll make sure Mitchell, Haldeman, and the rest get tried no matter when it is," I said. "If it's a long time from now, and we take other jobs, we'll come back."

Leon regarded me with a steely glare. It was the kind of hard look I'd often seen him give Rick. "Absolutely not," he said.

As I left his office, Leon rose from his seat and tore the bedsheet from the wall.

◼

We did not give up. Nor did Leon relent. I thought his stubbornness on the issue had something to do with his eagerness to get back to Texas. Any delay that might be caused by an indictment of Nixon would keep the special prosecutor stuck indefinitely in DC. But on September 8, as we were still arguing the point, President Ford pardoned Nixon on all counts, mooting our debate. Phil Lacovara and George Frampton researched the legal issues surrounding presidential pardons, searching for a way that Ford's action might be challenged in court, but nothing turned up. A pardon is forever.

During the spring, the legal staff had made some headway in our relationship with Leon, but that was lost in this latest battle. The tensions that had always been there because of the difference in our ages and sensibilities resurfaced and caused new strains. Leon spent less and less time in Washington, returning often to Texas for long sojourns on his ranch. When he was in the office, he avoided communicating directly with us, relying on Jim Neal to fill us in on anything we needed to know.

There was no time, though, to nurse grievances. The trial was scheduled to begin in a few weeks, and we were overwhelmed by work. There were myriad witnesses to interview and re-interview, complicated legal papers to formulate and file, and sixty-four tapes now in our hands to listen to and analyze. It goes without saying that the White House transcripts were mostly worthless; we had to prepare our own. This job was accomplished by a group of FBI employees recruited from offices around the nation. They were young women in their twenties, chosen for their expertise in transcribing conversations from wiretaps. Angie Lano set them up with typewriters at tables in the FBI's Washington field office, and he reported that many of them had tears streaming down their faces as they worked. The gutter level and criminality of the Oval Office conversations horrified and saddened them, as they had so many of us. These young women from the heartland had expected the president and his men to conduct themselves with dignity and honor.

After the typists finished each transcript, they turned

it over to us, and we compared it with the underlying tape, checking for accuracy and completeness. As I listened to the group of recordings I'd been assigned, I understood why it had taken Rose Mary Woods so long to transcribe even one sentence. The tapes were as scratchy and difficult to decipher as she had said.

When the job was completed, we went to court to testify that the transcripts prepared by the FBI typists represented a correct record of the presidential conversations we would introduce as evidence during trial. It was the first time I'd been on the other end of a cross-examination as a witness, and it terrified me, though I wasn't sure why. I knew and respected the defendants' lawyers, two of whom had worked in the Justice Department organized-crime section. The hearing was a standard, pro forma proceeding, narrowly focused on the tapes and transcripts. And yet I found it frightening to be sworn in, to promise that the testimony I was about to give was the truth, the whole truth, and nothing but the truth. Suddenly, I was unsure of the transcripts I'd approved. Could I trust my ears? Had I really heard the words correctly? It was like being in third grade and facing the teacher as she asked who took Tommy's coat.

As I trembled in the same witness box where Rose had sat just a few months earlier as I grilled her on the eighteen-and-a-half-minute gap, a sudden wave of guilt hit me. I felt an abiding empathy for her, for how hard it must have been for her to answer my questions and keep her composure. With the best intentions, I had exposed her to national ridicule and won accolades from my colleagues and the press. It was a moment of glory for me, but for Rose a lasting curse.

16

THE TRIAL

If Bob Haldeman's lawyer, John Wilson, was trying to unsettle me, he didn't succeed. It was the first day of jury selection in the Watergate trial, and with the prospective jurors out of the courtroom, we were discussing a female candidate whom the bald, rotund seventy-four-year-old Wilson found particularly attractive. With a sly look in his eye, Wilson mused aloud that if we chose the young woman to sit on the jury, she'd be "competition for Jill." I wasn't about to let Wilson get away with this chauvinist remark. "Mr. Wilson," I said in as stern a tone as I could muster, "I expect you to treat me as you would any lawyer in this case. I'd appreciate your never making another comment like that again." He never did.

I no longer recall if the woman whose looks so impressed Wilson made it onto the panel. I do remember, though, that it took two weeks to choose the nine women and three men who would sit on our jury. The group of mostly African Americans included a retired secretary, a loan specialist for the Department of Agriculture, a variety-store counter girl, and a logistics coordinator at George Washington University.

The foreman was a retired policeman for the National Park Service and a registered Republican.

By the time the trial started on October 1, 1974, the Watergate Seven had dropped to Five. Charles Colson had pleaded guilty in June to obstruction of justice in the prosecution of Daniel Ellsberg for leaking the Pentagon Papers, and as part of a plea bargain, all Watergate cover-up charges against him were dropped. Colson was now serving a one-to-three-year sentence at Maxwell Correctional Facility in Alabama. And the day before jury selection began, Gordon Strachan was granted a separate trial as a result of legal complications from the immunity he'd been granted for his grand jury testimony. Later, the obstruction of justice charges against Strachan for destroying reports he received from wiretaps at the Democratic Party headquarters were dropped.

Leon showed up for the first day of jury selection looking elegant as ever, in an expensive suit and with freshly blued hair. During the morning, one of the prospective jurors, a dotty-looking woman wearing a red hat, approached him and said, "Mr. Jaworski, I think you're the finest man in America." Sirica dismissed her.

Leon never made another appearance in the courtroom either, and two weeks later he resigned as special prosecutor. I knew how much Leon missed his family and his ranch, how he couldn't wait to move out of his small suite at the Jefferson Hotel and get back to the open lands and big skies of Texas. After Nixon's resignation and with the office's main case now underway, he felt that his job in Washington was done. Though we'd had our fights with Leon—notably over his refusal to indict Nixon—in the end, he had stood up for what was right and resisted the White House's stonewalling. Leon was leaving us in good shape, with his and Archie's very capable deputy Henry Ruth taking over as special prosecutor and Jim Neal, one of the nation's best trial attorneys, as our team leader.

Archie had brilliantly organized the office and set the tone of honoring the Constitution and adhering to the highest principles of justice, but Leon brought a different skill, a trial lawyer's strategic combativeness, at a crucial time. Leon wasn't going to let Nixon get the better of him. His doggedness was as important to the phase of the case he oversaw as Archie's high-mindedness had been at the start of our work.

■

The night after Leon announced his resignation, Sunday, October 13, the ginkgo trees on my street, as if shocked by the news, dropped their yellow leaves in one swoosh. In the morning, the glorious fan-shaped foliage blanketed the sidewalk and cars. A day earlier, the street had been a cathedral of gold; now nothing but bare brown branches stretched against the slate sky.

At the courthouse the next morning, I found the usual media circus—TV crews, reporters, photographers, network trucks, crowds of onlookers, and a police car standing nearby in case things got out of hand. So far, there had been only one ugly incident: on the first day of jury selection, a man had spat on John Ehrlichman as he entered the courthouse.

The trial was held in Judge Sirica's regular courtroom on the second floor. It was smaller and more intimate than the ceremonial courtroom, and more conducive, I thought, to the jury focusing on the proceedings and paying attention to the nuances of testimony.

There were five defense tables arranged in front of Judge Sirica's bench and to his left, one for each of the defendants and their lawyers. The prosecutors—myself, Rick, Jim Neal, and a revolving cast of members of our task force—sat to his right, just inches from the jury. John Ehrlichman's seat was so close to my place at the prosecution table that I could see the faces he doodled on a legal pad, mostly of witnesses. Ehrlichman had lost a lot of weight, and his suits sagged in despair on his body. John Mitchell, too, had changed. He looked worn out and sickly, so ashen, in fact, that a courtroom artist whose daily drawings illustrated newspaper stories about the trial used gray chalk for his skin tone. Of the big three defendants, only Haldeman looked fit, with a new, longer haircut and fashionable sideburns stretching to the bottoms of his ears.

The four wives of the defendants—Jo Haldeman, Pamela Parkinson, Dorothy Mardian, and Jeanne Ehrlichman—and one estranged wife, Martha Mitchell, sat in the first two rows of the spectator section behind the defense tables. They were well coiffed and stylishly dressed, and they stood out, sad and isolated, like widows at a funeral.

◼

For his opening statement, Rick wore a pin-striped suit, his signature attire when he wanted to look powerful. (When he wanted to look less intimidating, he wore a blazer, but no reporter ever noted that.) Standing at the lectern, he gave a detailed account of the cover-up, which started soon after the five burglars, one of whom, James McCord, was the security director of CREEP, were arrested for the break-in. "In the hours following, the word went out across the US, notifying high White House officials and Nixon campaign officials of the crime," Rick said. Gordon Liddy, who had not yet been arrested, called Jeb Magruder in California, who told John Mitchell and Robert Mardian. Magruder then broke the news in calls to Bob Haldeman, who was in Florida with Nixon, and John Dean, who was returning from a trip to the Philippines.

"Within two weeks of the arrests," Rick told the jury, "a massive, covert, secret operation" was set into motion by the conspirators to accumulate and deliver cash, which over an eight-month period totaled more than $400,000, to the Watergate burglars, the very people who the conspirators were saying at the same time were off on a lark of their own. Rick said we would show that this money was collected by the conspirators from the coffers of CREEP, from additional campaign contributions, and from a secret White House fund under Haldeman's control.

Rick's opening highlighted Nixon as one of the central conspirators, and he quoted the president's words on the many tapes we would use as evidence. Rick cited a tape recording where the president and some of his co-conspirators discussed "drawing wagons around the White House" and sacrificing some of their associates to the prosecution to save themselves. "Give the investigators an hors d'oeuvre, maybe they won't come back for the main course" was how Rick characterized their attitude.

John Dean, our first and chief witness, was on the stand for nearly two weeks. Federal marshals escorted him to and from court every day from Fort Holabird in Baltimore, where he had begun serving his sentence on September 3. He was always impeccably groomed, but the stress and humiliation of incarceration and the separation from his wife had taken their toll. He'd lost weight, and his face looked tense and pale.

In their opening statements, several of the defense lawyers stressed that Dean was a convicted felon, suggesting to the jury that nothing he said was to be believed. Jim Neal met that difficult truth head on. He started his questioning of Dean by asking him his current occupation. "I'm presently serving a prison term at Fort Holabird in Maryland," Dean said in the same flat monotone he'd used during his Senate testimony.

"For what crime?" Neal asked.

"Conspiracy to obstruct justice."

On cross, Haldeman's attorney John Wilson stressed that Dean had done terrible things and had been a major part of the cover-up. Before the original burglars went to trial, Wilson noted, Dean removed two incriminating notebooks from Howard Hunt's safe at the White House and shredded them, a blatant obstruction of justice.

We'd announced this ourselves in a press release months earlier, at the time of Dean's guilty plea, but this was the first time Dean admitted it publicly. Now Wilson asked Dean whether he had told prosecutors that he had destroyed evidence in any of his first five discussions with them.

"No sir, I did not," Dean said. A stricken expression crossed his face. The shame of what he had done was still with him.

Wilson gave the jury a knowing look, as if to say, *Why should you believe Dean now?*

During the first recess, after the jury left, Dean rushed toward his wife, Mo, who was standing now in front of the bar, her lovely face as unreadable as ever and her posture stiff, with her arms pressed into her sides. Dean reached out to her for an embrace, but she drew back, avoiding his touch.

My heart broke for Dean. Later in the week, though, when Mo delivered fresh shirts to her husband in the suite of rooms on the top floor of the courthouse where we'd set up offices for the duration of the trial, I realized I'd misinterpreted her coldness. Now, seeing the couple smiling and holding hands,

I felt the love and affection between them. Mo's icy demeanor in public, it seemed, was a defensive device to get through the disaster of Watergate with her health and sanity intact.

Mo was in court every day, sitting on the opposite side of the aisle from the defendants' spouses and family members, and never once showed a crack in her mask of cool detachment, not even while listening to her husband say some damaging things on the White House tapes. We began playing a sampling of the tapes during the second day of Dean's testimony. No sooner was the jury seated than we trundled out several grocery carts full of stereo headsets wrapped in white plastic and distributed them to the judge, jurors, lawyers, and spectators. A tape player installed on a table in a corner of the courtroom had wires radiating out to junction boxes set up around the courtroom so everyone could listen to the tapes through the individual headphones.

The marshals distributed transcripts of the September 15, 1972, tape to the jurors, who followed along as they heard Dean reporting to Haldeman and Nixon about the state of the cover-up. "Well, the whole thing is a can of worms as you know," Nixon said. "And the people who worked [on it] are awfully embarrassed. And uh, the uh, but the way you've handled it seems to me very skillful—just putting your fingers in the dike, and the leaks that have sprung here and there." Dean promised Nixon that "fifty-four days from now [election day], not a thing will come crashing down to our surprise."

In the next weeks, the jury and spectators heard more than twenty hours of White House tapes. They heard the treachery, the scheming, the profanity, the contempt for political opponents that marked Nixon's conversations with his closest aides and that gave the lie to the defendants' denials. They heard how the lies were compounded by more lies, how the cover-up expanded as the president became more desperate to hold on to power and more incoherent in his conversations as he felt it slipping away. They heard about stashes of cash in White House safes to pay off the Watergate burglars, and offers to grant them clemency if they kept their mouths shut. They heard the June 23, 1972, "smoking gun" tape and the March 21, 1973, "cancer on the presidency" tape.

I believed that Nixon's unfiltered admissions on the tapes were far better for our case than any live testimony from the former president himself could have been. But the defendants wanted Nixon to appear, perhaps hoping that his presence would highlight for the jury the injustice of the boss going free while his lieutenants stood trial. The ex-president had recently undergone an operation in California to remove a blood clot in his leg, and after three cardiovascular specialists appointed by the court examined him, they pronounced him unfit to travel until mid-February. Sirica did not want to delay the trial to get Nixon's testimony, so the case proceeded without him.

After Dean's testimony, which proved devastating to their clients, the defense lawyers stepped up their efforts to catch Sirica in errors. With an acquittal looking less and less likely, a mistrial seemed their best hope to save the president's men from prison. As we knew from the burglary trial, Sirica didn't always observe judicial norms—for instance, he had jumped in to question witnesses—and his decisions often presented a risk that they'd be reversed on appeal. So we took a cautious approach; unless we were 100 percent sure that, say, a motion to strike testimony would be upheld on appeal, we wouldn't ask.

Sirica knew himself and his tendency to interrupt during the questioning of witnesses, so he bent over backward to be scrupulously fair to the defense. Sometimes, though, he couldn't help himself. At one point during the cross-examination of John Dean, Sirica asked the defense lawyer doing the cross if he was trying to make Dean "look like a liar." The judge immediately regretted the remark, and quickly added, "I think all you defense lawyers have done a pretty good job."

Sirica's words hung in the air like a bubble of judicial error. We asked him to make a statement to the jury to try to undo the damage, and after a break he told the panel that they were "the sole judges" of the case. "Thus, I have expressed no opinion regarding this witness or his testimony," he said, promising not to express any more such opinions going forward.

The incident occurred during Dean's eighth and final day on the stand. Next up was my witness, Jeb Magruder. I'd worked hard to have him well prepared mentally and emotionally. Magruder had been incarcerated since June at Allenwood prison, which is about three hours by car from Washington. On the weekend before the trial began, I'd had him transferred to the DC jail so we could get an early start preparing for his testimony.

Two marshals brought him to my office, but before I even had a chance to say hello, he collapsed in the chair opposite my desk. His entire body crumpled, and the color drained from his face.

"Jeb, are you all right?" I asked.

He burst into tears. His head fell on my desk, and his shoulders shook violently as he sobbed.

"Jeb, what is it? How can I help?" I asked him.

But he was sobbing so hard he couldn't talk.

At Allenwood, Magruder slept in a motel-like room and encountered mostly white-collar criminals. I wondered whether something horrible had happened to him during his one night in a gritty urban jail with violent inmates—if he had been assaulted, or, more horrifically, raped. If so, I suspected he'd never admit it to me or any other woman. I left Jeb alone in my office to find Tony Passaretti, the short, gray-haired IRS investigator whom we'd borrowed from the US attorney's office in New York to summarize all the hush money payments. Tony had a warm, caring manner, and he and his wife, Judy, were parent figures to me and the rest of the young staff, often inviting us to their home for delicious pasta dinners. I asked Tony to talk to Magruder.

"I don't know what's wrong," I said, "but I can't interview him. He's not going to be able to testify. He's a mess."

I waited in Tony's office. Ten minutes passed, and Tony returned.

"What's wrong?" I asked.

"Jeb couldn't sleep in the DC jail," Tony said, shaking his head. "The lights were on all night long, and so was the television. The boy didn't get a wink of shut-eye."

I arranged to have Magruder transferred to Fort Holabird, a minimum-security facility where he could serve his sentence during the trial and, I hoped, get enough sleep to be clearheaded for his testimony. Now Magruder was close enough to come more often to my courthouse office, where I let him share picnic lunches alone with his pretty wife, Gail. They had four children together and seemed to have the kind of strong, loving bond that would withstand the sorrow and stress of Watergate. They always spoke calmly and fondly to one another, so I was surprised years later when they divorced.

My opinion of Magruder wasn't helped by his hysteria over his sleepless night in jail. Not only was he a liar, he was emotionally weak. He comported himself well enough on the witness stand, however. Much of his testimony echoed his statements at the Ervin hearings, though through my work with him he was able to recall some new information that was damning to John Mitchell. Magruder testified that he had discussed with the former attorney general the idea of bugging George McGovern's hotel room in Miami during the 1972 Democratic Convention. He also testified that as the cover-up collapsed, he gave Mitchell a "laundry list" of things he would need if he were sent to prison, including money and help finding a job after he'd served his sentence. Mitchell approved all the items on the list, Magruder said, adding that Mitchell "asked me to continue to hold, not to break, in effect, and the conditions would be met."

◼

Day by day the evidence against the defendants mounted. Throughout October and November, we told the full story of the cover-up, from the White House's misuse of the CIA to try to thwart the FBI investigations to the trail of hush money paid to the burglars. Much of this had come out before— during the Ervin hearings and the House impeachment inquiry, and in the endless stories in the press. But now we laid it out in all its undeniable criminality. Moreover, the jury was hearing actual recordings of the defendants engaged in illegal activity.

We rested our case on Monday, November 25. On Thanksgiving, three days later, the jury, which had been sequestered for two months at the Midtown Motor Inn at

12th and K Streets, would be treated to a banquet with their families (and a coterie of federal marshals to guarantee there was no discussion of the case) at the Shoreham Hotel. For us it was mostly a working holiday.

On Tuesday, before the holiday recess, the defense began its case. In divvying up the five defendants to cross-examine, we decided I would take the least implicated among them, Kenneth Parkinson, and the one reputed to have the worst temper, Robert Mardian. Parkinson was a lawyer hired by CREEP five days after the break-in to handle legal problems arising from the burglary. Robert Mardian, as an assistant attorney general under John Mitchell, had prosecuted Vietnam draft dodgers and represented Nixon in his unsuccessful fight to keep the *Washington Post* from publishing the Pentagon Papers. As an aide to Mitchell at CREEP, Mardian had been an integral part of the cover-up.

Unlike the others, Parkinson was not a bad man. He was new to politics and was way over his head in dealing with his "clients." He got caught up in something he knew was illegal. He had broken the law, and for that he deserved to be indicted and prosecuted, but his role in the cover-up was more limited than that of Mitchell, Haldeman, Ehrlichman, and Mardian.

These assignments made perfect sense. Jim Neal was the head of the trial team, so it was logical that he would take the biggest fish, John Mitchell. And Rick's aggressive courtroom style was better suited than my calm persistence to cross-examining the snarling White House German shepherds, Haldeman and Ehrlichman. But Parkinson was a sympathetic character, and his cross required a gentler touch. With Parkinson, Rick's brash forcefulness might have looked like bullying to the jury.

In the case of Mardian, there was a strategic reason for my being assigned to him. Unlike the accident of timing that resulted in my questioning Rose Mary Woods during the tapes hearings, this assignment was well planned. A key player in covering up the plumbers' activities, Mardian was known to be a hot-tempered, nasty guy whom "no one liked," according to John Dean. We thought it possible that he would lose his temper on the witness stand, and if he yelled at me, we reasoned, the jury would be far more outraged than if he yelled at Rick or Jim. We also considered the possibility that the strategy might backfire for two reasons: Mardian might be too chauvinistic to yell at a woman, and second, I'd have to be careful to question him sharply enough to elicit his rage, but not so harshly as to be perceived as an aggressive bitch. We decided it was worth the gamble, and it paid off.

In court, no sooner had I asked Mardian a couple of questions than he was screaming at me. "What do you want me to say? Yes? Yes?" he shouted sarcastically. The veins in his temples pulsed as the jury stared at him with expressions of disgust. Then Judge Sirica ruined it all by butting in. "Now, Mr. Mardian," Sirica warned, "you never gain arguing with a woman."

I stood numb at the podium. My face turned white, and I could hardly swallow. This was as bad as when Sirica had interrupted me during my cross-examination of Rose Mary Woods to say, "We can't have two ladies arguing in the courtroom." The defense attorneys compounded Sirica's meddling by immediately calling for a break, which destroyed any chance I had to further exploit Mardian's temper. As soon as Sirica left the bench, the defense lawyers rushed toward Mardian, ordering him to "get ahold of yourself. You're kill-ing yourself. The jury hates you. You can't act this way toward Jill."

I believe Sirica would have stopped Rick, too, from enraging Mardian. With Rick, though, Sirica would not have used sexist language. To be fair, the judge wasn't used to dealing with women lawyers; the percentage of lawyers who were women had not changed much since I was in law school, and only a small fraction of the women in law were litigators. During the trial, there was only one other female lawyer in the courtroom. Judy Denny, in her first job out of law school, was assigned to the data entry team for the special prosecutor's office, where her legal training was not being used at all. She spoke to Rick and me about that, and I was proud to mentor her and help her to have a small role in the courtroom, where she appeared briefly, handing documents to Jim Neal during his cross-examination of John Mitchell.

Also, there was a female law student in court: Bob Haldeman's daughter, Susan, who had taken a leave of absence to assist in her father's defense. She sat near him every day, taking notes, and I recall how uncomfortable I felt seeing the stricken look on her face as she listened to the devastating testimony about her father's deep involvement in the cover-up, not to mention his own voice uttering incriminating words on the tapes.

In presenting their cases, the defense attorneys tried to portray their clients as victims of a White House conspiracy to have them take the blame for Watergate. All five men took the stand and gave testimony that was marked by evasions and denials. At one point, Ehrlichman cried when describing how he asked Nixon to one day tell his children about why the former aide resigned. Mostly, though, I saw them as their usual arrogant, unrepentant selves. Not even the parade of character witnesses who appeared on their behalf (Mitchell's chief character witness was a former maid) could dispel the aura of gloom that hung over the defendants.

For me, the highlight of the trial was Jim Neal's stirring summation on December 29. The courtroom fell silent as he approached the lectern. Wearing one of the two identical suits he alternated throughout the trial so the jury would think him a man of modest means, he pushed his glasses onto his forehead. His shining blue eyes looked into the faces of the jurors as he spoke in a voice rich with the round, slow tones of his native Tennessee. Oration had been bred into his bones. To entertain him when he was a child, his father, a tobacco and strawberry farmer, had taken him to the local courthouse to hear country lawyers argue cases, and Jim had internalized the cadences of formal speech. The prosecutors weren't casting "stones with joy or happiness," Jim said. "But to keep society going, stones must be cast. People must be called to account" if government officials commit crimes, if they "cover up" their mistakes or "strike foul blows or assault the temples of justice."

He urged the jurors to concentrate on one word, *why*, which he pronounced in two syllables as *wah-eye*. "Why were documents destroyed? Why was the CIA used to obstruct the FBI's investigation of Watergate? Why was a cover story for the burglary funds developed? Why were veiled, camouflaged offers of clemency made without using that word? And why was nearly a half million dollars paid for seven people caught wiretapping and burglarizing Democratic National Headquarters? Why?"

Jim spoke eloquently of the tapes containing "conspiratorial conversations" that "tragically have happened in the hallowed halls of the White House of the United States, where once strode such giants as Jefferson, Jackson, Lincoln, the two Roosevelts, Eisenhower, Kennedy. Can you compare the White House, perhaps when Jefferson was drafting his second inaugural or Lincoln was writing 'with malice toward none, charity for all,' with the tapes you've heard in this courtroom?"

The case went to the jury on December 30, after three months of testimony from seventy-eight witnesses that generated more than a thousand pages of transcripts. Two days later, the first day of the new year, the jurors asked to have Sirica's instructions regarding perjury read to them. In mid-afternoon, they requested a list of all documentary evidence introduced. By 4:30, they'd reached a verdict.

The jurors, unsmiling and staring straight ahead, filed into their box in Courtroom Two. I felt my pulse racing. Judge Sirica looked toward the defense tables. "Would the defendants please rise," he said.

There was a scrape of chairs, and the five men and their lawyers were on their feet.

The jury foreman, John A. Hoffar, handed a manila envelope to the court clerk, who removed five white pages and passed them to Sirica. The judge read each page silently and returned them to the clerk, who read the names of the defendants and the verdicts against them, starting with John Mitchell: guilty on all six counts. It was the same for Haldeman, Ehrlichman, and Mardian—guilty, guilty, guilty on all counts. When he read Parkinson's name, though, he said, "Not guilty."

The defendants, with the exception of Mardian, who

slumped in his seat, took the verdicts stoically. Mardian's wife, Dorothy, stuck her tongue out at the jury and gave a Bronx cheer. "We'll get you," she shouted as they filed out, and then to us, gathering up our papers at the prosecution table, "We'll get you, too!"

Jo Haldeman congratulated Pamela Parkinson, whispering, "I'm so happy for you," as her daughter Susan fled the courtroom in tears. I, too, felt that Parkinson had been justly acquitted. I felt sorry for him, and I assumed the jury did, too. I was not unhappy that he wouldn't be going to jail.

◼

Though Martha Mitchell—"the Mouth of the South," as reporters dubbed her—was recently separated from her husband, she attended the trial regularly. During the weekend of the break-in, Martha had been detained by the FBI against her will in a California hotel room to prevent her from talking to the press. She called herself "a political prisoner" and said she'd been given injections in her butt by a security official. After the verdicts were read, Martha approached her ex-husband and reached out to comfort him, but he pushed her away with a violent jerk of his hand.

I felt relieved, totally exhausted, and a little sad that this great adventure was ending. As the defendants left the courthouse, reporters shouted questions and poked microphones in front of them. "I know I'm totally innocent," Haldeman said as he moved quickly down the steps. When asked if he was going to take a vacation now, Mitchell answered, "Yeah, I'm going to the moon."

Only Ehrlichman stopped for a lengthy chat with the press. Watergate "had been a tragedy from beginning to end," he said, adding that he had known he wouldn't get a fair trial in the District of Columbia and "nothing that has happened today has changed my mind."

As he spoke, a fierce wind whipped the air and a cavalcade of clouds passed overhead, black and ominous. The storm, though, had already come, the storm against him and the rest of the president's men.

17

AFTER WATERGATE

I sat in the anchorman's chair in the fluorescent glare of an ABC News set as cameras whirred around me. The network had brought me in for a screen test for a job as an on-air legal correspondent, one of the many opportunities that opened up to me at the end of the trial. The producer had asked me to write two scripts, one autobiographical, which I read in my best imitation of Howard K. Smith, the news anchor whose desk I now sat behind. I felt the test wasn't going well. As I heard myself reading my five-minute script, I knew it was not conversational enough. It sounded too much like a newspaper story meant to be read silently, not spoken to a television audience. Also, talking about myself made me self-conscious. I sounded stiff and awkward. The producer asked if I wanted a retake and gave me a few minutes to rewrite the script on the spot. My second take with the revised material was a big improvement.

I did even better with the second part of the tryout. The producer let me choose any topic I wanted for this segment, so I wrote a news report on the Equal Rights Amendment, a subject I felt passionately about. In 1975 the ERA was close to becoming law—it needed the votes of just four more states for ratification as a constitutional amendment—but it had come under assault from Phyllis Schlafly, the conservative activist who campaigned to halt it with outrageous stories about unisex bathrooms, the end of alimony, and a military draft for women. An ABC camera crew filmed me speaking into a microphone on the steps of the Supreme Court: "Equal citizenship status of men and women should be a fundamental tenet of the Constitution, like free speech," I said, mimicking the authoritative tone of newscasters.

I shined enough at the screen test that ABC continued talking to me about joining the network, and I seriously considered pursuing a career in television news. The on-air reporters I met at the Watergate trial, like their print counterparts, had fast-paced jobs that placed them at the center of important events, aspects of journalism that appealed to me.

Now that the trial was over, I got a chance to see a few of them socially, including Art Buchwald, the famous humor columnist for the *Washington Post*. On a dare from Rick the day after Buchwald mentioned me in one of his syndicated columns, I asked our secretary, Susan Kaslow, to get him on the line, and a moment later Buchwald and I were chatting on the phone. At the end of the conversation, he asked me to lunch. Rick, standing nearby, mouthed, "Me too."

"Can I bring my trial partner Rick Ben-Veniste?" I asked.

"Of course," Buchwald said.

A few days later, Rick and I met Buchwald at Sans Souci on 17th Street, just blocks from the White House. A favorite lunch spot for the powerful—only tourists went there for dinner—Sans Souci served classic French cuisine, including foie gras and *canard à l'orange flambé*, a rich departure from the takeout sandwiches we were used to on K Street.

Sans Souci's maître d', Paul DeLisle, kept track of Washington's ever changing status hierarchy and seated diners accordingly. When Rick and I arrived, the diplomatic Frenchman showed us to a table near the front (prime dining real estate) where the portly, balding Buchwald sat on a green leather banquette next to a middle-aged woman with wavy gray hair and the haughty air of a society grande dame. She was Mary McGrory, the legendary *Washington Star* columnist, whom I had met during the Watergate trial, which she covered brilliantly in stories that won her the Pulitzer Prize for commentary. I no longer recall what Buchwald talked about at lunch, though we laughed a lot. I do vividly remember McGrory telling me that her house had been broken into, as mine had been. Like me, she suspected the plumbers. "At first I thought it was an ordinary burglary," she said. "But the second time, I knew better."

"My house was burglarized twice, too!" I said. "One time to plant a bug, and one time to remove it."

McGrory, the only woman on Nixon's infamous enemies list, peered at me imperiously over the top of her glasses. "Well, my dear," she said, "I was broken into *three* times."

◼

On February 21, 1975, Judge Sirica sentenced John Mitchell, Bob Haldeman, and John Ehrlichman each to between thirty months and three years in prison. The sentences were stiff for first-time white-collar offenders and more severe than the sentences Sirica had given John Dean and Jeb Magruder, who had pleaded guilty. Robert Mardian, who had played a lesser role in the scandal than his co-defendants, received a sentence of ten months to three years.

"It could have been worse," Mitchell told a reporter after the sentencing. The judge, he said, "could have sentenced me to life with Martha Mitchell."

If he'd known what was in store for his ex-wife, Mitchell might not have been so snarky. Martha would soon be diagnosed with multiple myeloma, a blood cancer that would kill her less than a year and a half later. Even before her devastating illness, Martha's life was in shambles. The Mitchells had once "had everything," Martha told a reporter. "Now, we have nothing."

They were hardly the only ones whose lives had been wrecked by Watergate. The scandal left in its wake a host of ruined careers and bank accounts, and it brought humiliation and grief to many families. Among the sufferers was Rose Mary Woods. By all accounts, she had become increasingly bitter, tense, and unhappy following Nixon's resignation. She no longer had access to the West Wing and spent her days at the Executive Office Building, where she preserved Nixon's office exactly as he'd left it, down to the crumpled papers in the wastebasket and the half-smoked cigar in his ashtray.

Then, in February 1975, that office was dismantled, and Rose was shunted across the street to a government-owned town house at 716 Jackson Place. Spiro Agnew had been exiled here to sort his papers after he resigned the vice presidency in disgrace. Rose now sat all day answering mail for Nixon that had been sent over from the White House. The windows were mirrored so no one on the outside could see in, though Rose could look out onto leafy Lafayette Square. All of the ex-president's papers, letters, and telegrams, even those addressed to Rose herself, had been frozen by the courts, and she could not read or forward any of Nixon's mail to San Clemente.

We heard that she talked to Nixon on the phone every day. I never understood why she didn't move to San Clemente herself to be with the Boss and Pat. Though Rose loved her apartment in the Watergate and had many close friends in DC, none were as close to her as the Nixons. At the insistence of her friend and frequent escort, Robert Gray, she still went out two or three times a week to dinners and parties, but her heart didn't seem to be in it. Washington's top hostesses had dropped her like a hot coal when she lost her perch close to power. It wasn't much fun being a B-lister at B-list events. Perhaps Rose hoped to find a new job. She no longer was a government employee. Nixon still paid her $36,000 salary, but he was also shouldering huge legal bills, and who knew how long he could continue to support her.

Maxine Cheshire, the *Washington Post* society columnist, reported that a friend of Rose's was surprised to see the former White House secretary walking home from the Executive Office Building one day instead of taking a taxi. When the friend asked Rose about it, she said, "This is what you do when you're between jobs."

I wondered what kind of job Rose would want or could get. Born three years before women had the right to vote, she was now fifty-seven and had been employed by Nixon for most of her working life. Perhaps she could find employment with another politician or in the private sector, but it seemed her opportunities were limited.

Unlike Rose, I had many options in addition to ABC. Several law firms expressed an interest in hiring me, including Fried, Frank, Harris, Shriver and Kampelman, a prestigious

New York–based firm that had a Washington office. I was torn between accepting the position and pursuing a career in broadcast journalism. Though I'd never set out to be a lawyer, I'd discovered I was good at it, and I liked it. Also, the job was high-paying, but so was TV news, and explaining legal issues to the public might be more fun and stimulating than writing court briefs.

At Fried, Frank I'd be one of only a handful of women lawyers. The firm had a single woman partner, Patricia Harris, an elegant, groundbreaking African American attorney who during an era of deep feminist stirring in the early 1970s seemed to have it all—a lucrative career, a happy marriage, and engagement with the most important issues of the day. She had been a Justice Department attorney under Robert Kennedy, and President John Kennedy had appointed her to co-chair the National Women's Committee for Civil Rights. She remained active in social justice causes and Democratic politics throughout her career.

Harris (no relation to Fried, Frank's founding partner Sam Harris) was known for her intelligence, wit, and style. She wore a lot of soft, pale Ultrasuede, the epitome of seventies chic, and in a sharp reversal of the norm, employed an attractive male secretary who sported shirts unbuttoned to mid-chest. I remember seeing a beautiful photograph of Harris in *Vogue*, taken by the society photographer Lord Snowdon, the husband of Britain's Princess Margaret. Harris seemed to be that rare woman who had reached the top of her profession while not sacrificing her femininity or personal life.

Time was running out. I had to make a decision. I sought advice from Jim Doyle, our press officer at the special prosecutor's office. He asked me to answer without thinking, "Who do you want to be? Barbara Walters or Pat Harris?"

I answered without hesitation. "Pat Harris."

"Then don't take the job at ABC."

Doyle's astute question clarified things for me: I wanted to make news, not report it. Soon after this conversation, I accepted Fried, Frank's offer.

◼

I resigned from the Watergate task force in May, though the special prosecutor's office hadn't yet gone out of business. There were still briefs to file in the appeals of the five defendants, the deposition of Nixon to take in his (ultimately unsuccessful) lawsuit to gain custody of his presidential tapes, and other legal loose ends to tie up. Eventually, Henry Ruth resigned and was replaced by Charles Ruff, my mentor and former boss at the Justice Department. The K Street office was dismantled and what staff remained were moved to a cramped suite of rooms with ugly green walls and jammed with file cabinets, across the street from the spanking-new FBI headquarters.

I'd planned to take the summer off to recharge my batteries before starting at Fried, Frank. In a rested and relaxed state of mind, I also thought I'd have more clarity about my personal life, which was still in chaos. I was grateful for my career, which I owed in part to my miserable marriage. Had I been happy with Ian, I might not have worked so hard and been so ambitious. And now that I was on the fast track, I didn't want to get off. At the same time, I yearned to be loved and to love someone totally in return. I wanted to have it all, like Pat Harris.

I still found deep solace in Kurt's company, and I used this interlude to spend more time with him. But I did not want to be a mistress forever, and I wasn't sure that either Kurt or

I wanted to marry the other. Our relationship had been conducted in secret, and it was impossible to know whether I'd feel the same about him if I were free to be with him openly.

That summer, though, I did try to slow down. In defiance of my lifelong lack of athletic interest or ability, I took tennis lessons at the Hilton Hotel Pool and Tennis Club. I had fun, but after a few sessions, the pro told me to quit. Since I didn't understand how a ball bounced, he said, I'd never get it over the net. Instead, I swam at the pool and lounged on the deck reading. One afternoon, another member of the club introduced me to his friend Dustin Hoffman, who was in town filming the movie version of *All the President's Men*. He was portraying Carl Bernstein to Robert Redford's Bob Woodward. Hoffman knew I'd been a Watergate prosecutor. He said everything related to the scandal fascinated him, and he wanted to know more about my work. I was having a Watergate party at my house and somehow found the courage to invite him, saying he would have a chance to talk to Rick and the other members of the task force, as well as defense attorneys and members of the press who had covered the trial. To my amazement, he accepted. On the evening of the party, Hoffman showed up at the same moment as Mary McGrory and introduced himself to her on my stoop. When I opened the door, McGrory, ever the skeptical journalist, nodded toward him and asked me, "Who is this person, *really*?"

My guests were delighted to meet Hoffman—except Phil Lacovara's wife, Madeline, who mistook the actor's friendliness for inappropriate flirting and ignored him. Later, Dustin's friend, who accompanied him to the party, asked Madeline why she had been rude to Hoffman.

"Dustin Hoffman?" she exclaimed. "I thought that was Carl Bernstein hitting on me."

▣

After several weeks of lounging and reading, I felt my energy returning. It was also nice to have more time with Kurt, but I hadn't come any closer to addressing the disaster of my marriage or making a decision to leave Ian. My solution to the disorder in my personal life was to do what I'd always done and throw myself into work.

I was supposed to start at Fried, Frank after Labor Day, but when the firm called in August to say they had an assignment for me and wanted me earlier, I jumped at the chance. I was returning to Watergate, physically at least, as the firm's office sat in the curving complex of buildings made famous by the scandal, though on the opposite end from where the burglary had occurred. Fried, Frank's reception rooms had long expanses of cool, pale carpeting, polished chrome surfaces, and tasteful modern art. My own office had a panoramic view of the Potomac River and Theodore Roosevelt Island. The glorious vista was consolation for the long hours I spent on my first assignment—a civil case stemming from the collapse of a twenty-six-story apartment building under construction in nearby Fairfax, Virginia. The accident killed fourteen workers and injured thirty-four others. It occurred when a subcontractor prematurely removed shoring from newly poured concrete pillars surrounding steel reinforcing rods. We represented the owner of the building.

I'd just been involved in one of the most momentous events in American history. I'd helped take down a criminal president, and I was only thirty-two years old. Now I was a lowly associate slogging through construction documents and books on cement, going home at night to a husband who ignored and belittled me. Many afternoons, overcome with sadness, I closed my door, slumped at my desk, and cried. It didn't make me feel better. It just made me think about Watergate and how much I missed the trial team and the feeling I had of excitement and high purpose. I wouldn't be happy until I had that feeling again.

18

NO FEAR OF FLYING

Two years later, I was standing on an Army training platform three stories off the ground, wearing fatigues, boots, and a helmet, a parachute strapped to my back, ready to jump. I shouted my name into the air, but not loud enough for anyone below to hear. I thought it was unladylike to yell, though I knew I wouldn't get the signal to jump until they heard me on the ground. I tried again. Still, nothing. On the third try, I screamed my name as if my hair was on fire, and finally, a voice shouted back from below—"Go!"

I stepped off the platform, the parachute opened, and I floated slowly, feeling free from the job I'd just left and, for the moment, from the husband I hadn't. A few months earlier, I'd left Fried, Frank to accept President Jimmy Carter's offer to serve as general counsel of the US Army, the first woman to hold the position. It was 1977, and my hiring coincided with the integration of women into America's military academies, basic training, and many previously all-male field units, including jump teams. I wanted to share something of female paratroopers' experience—and thus today's practice jump at Fort Benning, Georgia.

Within moments, the force of the wind filled my canopy and jerked my body backward. At the same time the chute's struts tightened and knocked my helmet off. I watched it tumble away, violating the first rule of jumping: never look down. If you do, you tend to stiffen up as you see the earth fast approaching, causing injury on landing. Fortunately, I hit the ground with only minor pulled muscles. I insisted on a second jump to prove I could manage it without incident, and this time my helmet stayed on, sort of. It had slipped down my forehead, cut my nose, and covered my eyes. I couldn't have seen the ground if I'd tried.

The helmets were all built for men, and women are not just small men. As soon as I got back to the Pentagon, I recommended new helmets designed especially for women. I also made sure military women had boots made to fit them and—for the mothers-to-be—maternity uniforms. No one had thought of this before. The Pentagon was as much a man's world as Watergate, with sexism firmly embedded in the culture. I saw this the day I arrived, when I was introduced to Army Chief of Staff Bernie Rogers, a handsome, white-haired general straight out of Central Casting, with a square jaw and a row of medals clattering on his chest.

"You're too cute to be general counsel," Rogers said to me with a grin.

"And too smart not to be good at it," I replied.

During my tenure, I pushed hard to change the atmosphere and institutions that disrespected Army women and kept them down, often enlisting a "front man" for my proposals to make them more salable within the Pentagon. In 1978,

I worked on legislation that abolished the Women's Army Corps, the female auxiliary branch that had been converted to active-duty status in World War II and had remained the only branch where women could enlist. The legislation also made female soldiers part of the Regular Army, which opened the Army's top jobs to qualified women who had previously been ineligible as WACs. I also observed tests to determine how units in the field would function with women in their ranks. At the time, women, unlike men, had to be high school graduates to join the Army, so educationally they were better prepared to solve problems than their male counterparts. I watched an all-male unit construct a gigantic tent by clambering over the metal substructure, lugging the heavy camouflage canvas behind them. It took forever and would have exposed the men to enemy fire if they had tried to do it this way during actual combat. And the men were exhausted by the time they were done. I then watched a group of women soldiers do the job in a fraction of the time by throwing ropes attached to grommets in the canvas over the substructure, catching it on the other side, and easily pulling the canvas into place. Brains trumped brawn in this instance and many others.

I'd been tapped for the general counsel job by Secretary of the Army Clifford Alexander, through connections I'd made during Watergate (Mitzi Wertheim, the wife of one of the Watergate defense lawyers, was part of the Carter transition team) and campaigning for Jimmy Carter in his run against President Ford in 1976. I was offered other opportunities in the Carter administration, but Cliff's brilliance and extensive experience at high levels of government convinced me I wanted to work for him. Also, the transition team's description of the job responsibilities left no doubt that Army general counsel was the job I wanted.

Soon after I was ensconced at the Pentagon, President Carter decided to withdraw American troops from South Korea, but military intelligence resisted, claiming that new-found intelligence showed that North Korean troop strength had increased. I was sent to Korea to evaluate the facts on the ground. I reviewed photographic evidence and, after ejector seat training, flew in an Army intelligence plane that swooped low over North Korean military facilities, where I saw for myself vast evidence of the North's military power. Our troops stayed.

At home, soldiers saluted me when I passed by in my Pentagon car with a flag waving from the hood, signaling my four-star rank, the same as General Rogers, but reporters often focused on my gender when interviewing me, asking me questions they would never ask a man. While working on the contract for the development of a new tank, the Abrams M1, I flew to New York to talk about it on ABC's *Good Morning America*. It was my first time on television, screen tests aside. Near the end of the interview, I was feeling good about my mastery of the technical details when David Hartman, one of the hosts, said, "Just one last question, Jill. Are you planning to have children?"

"Well, David," I said, trying to hide my chagrin, "it's interesting you should ask that question because it shows how many choices women have nowadays."

If I'd met Hartman's impertinence with a personal reply, I might have answered, "Definitely not with my current husband."

Ian and I were still married, but our unhappy story was coming to an end. Like Isadora Wing, the heroine of Erica

Jong's runaway bestseller, *Fear of Flying*, which came out
during Watergate and tapped a nerve among my generation
of women trying to find our place in an age of rapid social
change, I'd finally faced my fears about divorce.

I was helped in this process by Dr. Gene Gordon, whom
I'd started seeing while I was still at Fried, Frank. At the end
of our first session, he said the lack of sex in my marriage
wasn't normal and wasn't my fault. "I'm a trial lawyer, and
you've only heard my side of the story," I protested.

"You could be Clarence Darrow," Dr. Gordon replied.
"But I'm a good psychiatrist and I'm telling you the problem is
your husband's, not yours."

I told Dr. Gordon that I had stayed married because Ian
was working to solve our problems by seeing a psychiatrist
of his own. Dr. Gordon doubted that Ian was getting help,
but it took me two years of therapy to develop the confidence
and courage to admit he might be right. One winter morning, before leaving home for the daily eight a.m. Army senior
staff meeting, I searched the desk Ian and I shared in the
basement of our town house for some evidence that Ian was
in therapy—an appointment on his calendar or a cancelled
check to his doctor—but found none. I marched back upstairs
and confronted Ian as he dressed for work in our bedroom.
The cheerful yellow-and-white wallpaper and romantic floral-
print linens belied the misery of our marriage.

"You're not seeing a doctor, are you?" I demanded.

Ian's shoulders slumped, and he dropped into a chair,
averting his eyes. "No," he answered in a flat tone.

"Then we're done. I want you out of the house," I told
him. I felt sad and angry, mostly at myself for not ending our
marriage sooner.

Ian moved into the guest room that night, saying he

needed time to find a place to live. At his request, we saw a marriage counselor who confirmed my decision to divorce. "I've seldom seen anyone treat their spouse as dismissively as your husband treats you," the counselor told me. "He has interrupted you and insulted you every time you spoke. Sometimes, a marriage gets so bent out of shape that it can never be put back together. I think you are in that situation."

Months later, Ian moved out. By then I felt accepted enough at the Pentagon to announce our pending divorce. Army attitudes about relations between men and women, at least on the surface, were traditional in the extreme, starting at the top. Generals tended to marry their high school sweethearts and stay married. Wives worked to enhance their husbands' careers and entertained frequently, following rules of etiquette that seemed lifted from a turn-of-the-century manual by Emily Post.

I saw this firsthand at a dinner for top Pentagon officials and their spouses at the beautiful home of General Rogers and his wife, Ann, at Fort McNair. After dinner, I walked into the living room with another guest, General Max Thurman, who years later would go on to lead the US invasion of Panama that resulted in the arrest of its leader, Manuel Noriega, on charges of drug trafficking and money laundering. We were in the middle of a lively conversation when I felt a tap on my shoulder and turned to see Ann Rogers. "We're in there," she whispered, pointing to another room where the wives had gathered. No one had warned me that cigars and cognac in the living room were for men only. I looked at General Thurman and spoke firmly. "If you get into trouble," I said, "I'll talk to someone else or stand in the corner, but I'm not leaving."

General Thurman smiled as he signaled the server and gave a command: "Bring this woman a cognac and a cigar!"

He became a good friend, and with other Pentagon officials, including General Edward "Shy" Meyer, gave me confidence that I could reveal my separation without being viewed as a dangerous divorcée. The gum-chewing, backpack-wearing General Meyer often showed up unannounced in my office, put his feet on my desk, and sought my advice. He valued my counsel and didn't care a whit about my marital status or gender.

Now I was free to be with Kurt openly. By this time, though, my relationship with him had suffered a major trauma. During one of our afternoon trysts while I was still married, I saw another woman's dresses and makeup at Kurt's Georgetown town house. He had been seeing a Justice Department paralegal behind my back, and he had allowed the woman to move in with him. I was so tired of being deceived. Was I choosing the wrong partners, or did all men have cheating hearts? I knew Kurt had a right to date. I was married, and he was single. We had never promised to be exclusive lovers. But his actually living with someone else and hiding it from me felt like a cruel betrayal.

Kurt's affair with the paralegal soon ended, but his deception continued to trouble me. To make him jealous, as soon as my separation was public I began dating other men, including a speechwriter for President Carter, a French vineyard owner, and Representative Pete McCloskey from California. (Pete, my first and only Republican, was very liberal and had run a primary challenge against Nixon in 1972.) It was fun and exciting, but also confusing, because Kurt's powerful hold over me hadn't abated. If he called while a date was at my house, I'd get rid of the man, hop in my car, and drive to Kurt's place.

During this time, I came across a holiday card from my high school boyfriend, Michael Banks, in a drawer in the dressing room connected to my office, where I'd stashed it. The card had arrived more than a year earlier, when I was in the throes of separating from Ian and wasn't ready to answer it. Now I was ready. I was scheduled to be in Chicago for meetings with the Army Recruiting Command at Fort Sheridan and planned to stay for my parents' fortieth wedding anniversary, and I thought it might be nice to see Michael when I was in town. I wrote him a very prim note, not knowing his relationship status, suggesting we get together. Twenty-four hours after I mailed the note from the Pentagon, Michael called me. We hadn't seen each other in fifteen years, and we talked for several hours, catching up on each other's lives and reminiscing. It was an easy conversation, full of fond memories and laughter. At the end, Michael invited me to a black-tie dinner in Chicago that was being held the weekend I'd be in town.

I landed at O'Hare, where an Army helicopter met me for a short flight to Meigs Field on Chicago's downtown lakefront, near the Army Recruiting Command on Michigan Avenue. After my meetings there, I returned to Meigs for a helicopter ride to Fort Sheridan and more meetings. The trip north followed Chicago's lakefront and many scenes of my childhood: the totem pole at Waveland Park, around which I'd ridden my tricycle; the rock garden where I'd climbed with my friends; the tennis courts where I'd watched my father play on summer afternoons, the beaches where I jumped with glee in the waves.

We landed at Fort Sheridan and I worked the rest of the day. A black Army sedan with my four-star flag waving from the hood drove me to a college friend's home to change into a long halter dress of lilac Ultrasuede, by Halston, for my date with Michael. He arrived in a tuxedo, looking as handsome as I remembered him. We headed to the University

Club downtown for the dinner, one of many held around the world, by Oxford and Cambridge Universities to celebrate their annual boat race. Michael was a Cambridge alum, and during the cocktail hour he introduced me to his friends. Afterward, we sat down for dinner in the club's elegant wood-paneled ballroom. No sooner had the soup been served than we looked at each other and silently agreed we wanted to be alone. We politely excused ourselves and went to Michael's apartment. The next evening, Michael joined me at my parents' anniversary party at Biggs, a romantic Northside restaurant in a Gilded Age mansion. On Sunday before my flight home, we walked through Lincoln Park with Michael's Dalmatian, Ivan, as snow swirled around us.

We had made plans for Michael to visit me the following weekend in Washington, but on Monday he called to say he was flying to DC that night. I broke my date with Kurt, telling him, "I think I'm going to marry Michael."

"Nonsense," Kurt said. "You're going to marry *me*!" That was the first I'd heard him mention marriage, and now it was too late. I was in love with Michael.

We didn't want a commuter marriage. Michael had a successful business in Asian and primitive antiques on the North Shore of Chicago, and I thought it would be harder for him to develop a new client base in Washington than it would be for me to join a Chicago law firm. I left the Pentagon in the fall of 1979, put the 20th Street town house on the market, and made plans to leave town. I spent my last Sunday in DC with Rick Ben-Veniste, walking around the cobblestone streets of Georgetown, talking. Rick had taken a job at Melrod, Redman & Gartlan, a real estate and banking law firm, and he was dating Mary Travers, the blond singer in the world-famous folk group Peter, Paul and Mary. It turned out that Mary and

I wore the same size shoe; she gave me a pair of very high-heeled over-the-knee boots that, she said, hurt her feet.

For the first time, Rick and I confessed to each other our moments of self-doubt during Watergate. I told Rick that I often felt like a fraud. Psychologists call this feeling "impostor syndrome," the sense that you are unprepared and don't fit into the role you've taken on. Rick amazed me by admitting that he, too, had those feelings, which experts say are common among high achievers and creative artists. In our case, the sense that we were impostors was exacerbated by our youth and relative inexperience. At a very young age, we'd been thrown into a role with enormous responsibility, and though everyone around us assured us we were doing excellent work, we both wondered, *Am I good enough?*

When we parted at the end of the day, Rick and I promised to stay in touch. "Good luck, Jilly Bean," he said, using his favorite nickname for me. No one else would ever call me that.

■

Michael and I were married on January 12, 1980, in the stately but crumbling nineteenth-century home we'd bought and were planning to restore in Evanston. We chose that date because Judge Abner Mikva would be in Chicago that day, and we wanted him to preside. While working for the Army, I'd gotten to know Judge Mikva, then a Democratic congressman from Evanston and one of the nation's leading liberal politicians. He and I worked together on legislation to end the Army's long-standing practice of sending surplus weapons to the National Rifle Association. When the bill passed, Ab became Enemy Number One of the NRA, which spent $1 million trying to block his confirmation as a federal judge.

In Chicago, I joined Jenner & Block, one of the city's most prestigious law firms, as a litigation partner. I knew the senior partner, Albert "Bert" Jenner, from Watergate, where he had served as special counsel to the Republicans on the House Judiciary Committee during the impeachment hearings. I also knew three other partners through my appointment as a government representative to the American Bar Association Litigation Section, including one woman, Joan Hall. What I didn't know was that gender bias and sexual harassment were rife at the firm. Female associates were rated negatively for being "harsh" or "bitchy," while male associates were praised as "assertive" for the same behavior. At Jenner & Block, I also experienced my first unwanted sexual overture, during an out-of-town trip for a case with a senior partner. After I rebuffed his advance, he withheld assignments from me.

Luckily I was saved by an offer from the Illinois attorney general, Neil Hartigan, to become the state's first solicitor general; I was then promoted to be the state's first female deputy attorney general. I supervised all appellate cases in Illinois and argued before the state and US Supreme Courts in cases that involved important issues—disability, civil rights, senior rights, and criminal justice. While there, I was honored to receive a fellowship from the European Economic Community that allowed me an extraordinary opportunity to meet European leaders, such as Simone Veil, who was the first president of the European Parliament, and members of the British Supreme Court. I also observed the trial of Klaus Barbie, the SS and Gestapo officer known as the "Butcher of Lyon" for having personally tortured French prisoners in Lyon, France. This was better than the junior year abroad I wished I'd had.

The sense of purpose I had in the attorney general's office—reminiscent of my days as a Watergate assistant special prosecutor—was enhanced by my happy home life. My marriage to Michael had opened up a new world of people and experiences. One night, Michael brought a client and his wife home for dinner. The client, David Leake, had worked in the Peace Corps with the Kadazans, an indigenous head-hunting tribe in north Borneo; there he'd met Ann, the daughter of the Kadazan chief. The couple had been married in a Western-style ceremony, but they gave us an intriguing description of traditional tribal weddings. Michael and I, who share a love of adventure, expressed an interest in visiting this remote part of the world. Since we were newlyweds, David suggested we might want to make the trip the occasion for a second wedding ceremony. "If you're willing to pay for a feast, the tribe would adopt you and marry you, too," David said.

And so we found ourselves in March 1982 in Borneo's state of Sabah, home of the Kadazans. We stayed in a traditional thatched-roof longhouse with no plumbing and with human skulls hanging from the rafters. It had a narrow shared living space lined with doors that opened to private sleeping areas for each family. For our wedding, Michael went bare-chested and wore shorts, a batik crown, and a sash. I wore the wedding outfit shared by all village brides: a black velvet vest and sarong skirt with five silver belts and a silver necklace, which I donned after my ritual shower from a spigot attached to a hand pump in a field of water buffalo. The marriage rites were sealed when Michael and I fed each other rice cooked in banana leaves, followed by a feast of roast pig and chicken. We danced the sumazau, the Bornean version of the electric slide, to a symphony of gongs borrowed from a local family. The sky turned orange, the same color as the enormous Rafflesia flowers surrounding the wedding lodge, and slowly faded to black. Everyone drank too much of the wickedly strong homemade wine called tapai, and we all fell asleep on the bamboo floor. Outside, flying squirrels stirred the trees as monkeys chattered back and forth.

When we returned to Chicago, Judge Mikva, who'd seen an item about our Borneo wedding in the press, sent me a note. "Wasn't the ceremony I performed good enough?" he asked with his tongue firmly in his cheek.

I'd traveled around the world to Korea and Borneo, but my personal journey represented a more dramatic quest. Since I'd last lived in Chicago, I'd become a lawyer, married and divorced, broken up with a lover, and married again. I'd had a front seat to the biggest political scandal in US history and a key role in taking down a corrupt and criminal president. I'd faced my fears, broken the chains that held me back, and come home to a life of fulfillment and joy.

I was exactly where I wanted to be.

EPILOGUE

As I write this, more than four decades after Watergate, I see history repeating itself with the presidency of Donald Trump. Like Nixon, Trump is corrupt, amoral, vindictive, paranoid, ruthless, and narcissistic. The election of both men involved scandalous cover-ups. Twitter called the criminal investigation of President Trump by special counsel Robert Mueller #WatergatewithRussianDressing. The hashtag couldn't be more apt. Now, as then, there's a sense that our country is spinning toward chaos, that our democratic institutions might not survive. Today the peril is worse than in the 1970s because Trump is more dangerous than Nixon. In the end, Nixon did comply with the Supreme Court order to turn over the tapes, while there are widespread fears that Trump will not respect the rule of law. Trump's stonewalling surpasses Nixon's, and he challenges Congress's oversight role—so essential to our constitutional framework of checks and balances—in unparalleled ways. Moreover, Trump has set the stage for continued foreign meddling by his refusal to acknowledge or penalize

Russia's interference in the 2016 presidential election, and (on the factual record available as of this writing) he appears to have committed impeachable offenses in his request that President Volodymyr Zelensky of Ukraine "do us a favor though" by announcing an investigation of former Vice President Joe Biden and his son before US military aid would be released. Trump wanted this announcement not to further US national security interests but to help his 2020 reelection by hurting Biden, the candidate he considered his leading political rival.

One of Trump's first Nixonian acts of obstruction of justice, in my view, occurred on May 9, 2017, just three and a half months into his term, when he fired FBI director James Comey in an effort to thwart the Bureau's investigation into Russian interference in the presidential election. Two days earlier I had taken a one-day crash course in opinion writing offered by the OpEd Project, an organization devoted to increasing female and minority voices in commentary forums. I used that training to write an op-ed deploring Comey's dismissal and comparing it to Watergate, which the *Chicago Tribune* published. Immediately, all three networks, CNN, and MSNBC called me about appearing on air to discuss it, but by then I was with my closest friends at an annual bridesmaids' reunion in rural Texas and nowhere near a television station. I was excited and agreed to appear when I returned home. Michael accompanied me to the studio, because we thought it would be his only chance to see TV news in the making. Soon I was doing shows on every network until MSNBC hired me to work exclusively for them as a legal analyst. Now I'm on TV regularly, trying to explain the Trump scandals, the convictions and guilty pleas of the president's former advisors, the revelations of fraud and hush money payouts, and the sexual abuse allegations against a Supreme Court nominee and the president himself. I also get to talk about the #MeToo movement and about subjects connected with my Pentagon experience, including Korea and sexual assault in the military. I'm often called on to draw parallels between Trump and Watergate. There's a hunger for more insight, more wisdom, and more perspective as the public tries to make sense of Trump's presidency.

With my work at MSNBC, I've come full circle—starting college with aspirations to become a journalist, then going to law school in order to get a good journalism job, and nearly fifty years later becoming a news commentator. Given my career arc since Watergate, television is the last place I thought I'd end up.

After the Army (where I'm proud to say my successor as general counsel was also a woman), Jenner & Block, and the Illinois attorney general's office, I was recruited by a search firm to be executive director of the American Bar Association, one of the world's largest professional organizations with more than 340,000 members. I was the first woman to hold the position—and the job produced another first for me, the first time I faced major public criticism.

It started during the final round of interviews. The outgoing ABA president, Eugene Thomas, opposed my appointment and tried to stop the vote to hire me by falsely claiming that I'd had a "messy divorce" that would embarrass the organization. Actually, my divorce from Ian was amicable. There was nothing about it to concern the ABA, as the search firm that brought me in reported to the board before its vote. But Thomas could not accept a woman as the ABA's chief executive, much less one like me, who was relatively young (I was forty-four at the time), Jewish, and by his standards, too liberal. He later made other untrue charges against me. One involved the death of Michael's and my Dalmatian Finnegan. After a technician at the animal hospital told me that Finnegan had died due to mistreatment by our veterinarian, I knew I had to do something. The technician said it wasn't the first time the vet was guilty of malpractice, and that if I didn't report it, he would. Concerned for the future well-being of other pets, my husband and I filed a complaint with the agency that licenses veterinarians. Thomas wrote a letter, with no supporting facts, claiming that I abused my "clout" as the former deputy attorney general to get that agency to appoint our lawyer in his place. Actually, I never had clout over that agency; it was under Republican control, and I had been appointed by the Democratic attorney general. After hearing the evidence against the veterinarian, the state panel found him guilty of malpractice, concluding that the dog's life likely would have been saved if he had received proper care. The state panel suspended the vet's license for forty-five days and placed him on a two-year probation.

But my experience at the ABA also included many wonderful times. I got to know many outstanding lawyers, and worked with a great staff. I created a new section that offered programs for government lawyers, which drew scores of new members to the organization who previously had seen no value in joining. More important, it opened my eyes to the possibility of a business career when I discovered I liked management.

In 1990 I left the ABA to move to Miami, where Michael was relocating his business. Almost as soon as we arrived, however, Michael realized that Chicago was a better home than Florida for a gallery selling Asian and primitive antiques, and when his lease expired we moved back. I used the year in Florida to learn golf, study Spanish, and think about what I wanted to do next and decided to pursue a career in business instead of returning to practice law. I landed at Motorola after my dear friend Christie Hefner introduced me to the CEO, George Fisher.

I loved my new job, which involved traveling the world from Pakistan to China, Singapore, South America, Russia, and Ukraine. I chaired the board of Motorola's telecom-operating company in St. Petersburg, where I met Vladimir Putin and had to cope with the assassination of the deputy mayor, who was a member of our board.

I could fill a separate volume with stories of the hurdles I faced dealing with the complexities of international business and being a woman in a nearly all-male world. There was gender bias at every turn, as well as racial discrimination. During one senior staff meeting of the cellular infrastructure group at Motorola, for instance, one of the few women in the room asked what steps were being taken to bring more diversity to the company. The president of the unit answered, "Well, we can't lower our standards just to have more women and blacks."

In 1999, Lloyd Ward, the incoming CEO of Maytag, at the time one of the few African Americans to head a major US corporation, recruited me to be a vice president of the company, doing the same international work I was doing at Motorola. I worked in Japan and Europe and again loved the job, but after two years, Ward was forced to resign and all his senior hires were asked to leave. At Maytag I suffered my second encounter with anti-Semitism. The first had occurred during a vacation when I was a child: my family and I were denied rooms at a hotel in Michigan because we were Jews. Maytag was planning a dinner to celebrate the outstanding financial results of the international operation, but the date they chose was the first night of Passover. Within minutes of the announcement, I asked that the date be changed, but the human resources department told me there was no other available time. After calling the restaurant and discovering this wasn't true, I checked back with HR. "The restaurant must have had some cancellations, because it's wide open now, and we could do it on any other night," I said.

But the HR representative wouldn't change the date. As they explained, "You're the only one"—that is, the only Jew.

I didn't have such problems at my next jobs, first as the CEO of Winning Workplaces, a nonprofit dedicated to helping small businesses be better places to work and more profitable through strong human resources practices. The founders, the Lehman family of Chicago, had owned Fel-Pro, a gasket manufacturer honored by *Fortune* magazine for its ground-breaking family-friendly policies. The mission of Winning Workplaces resonated with me, and I agreed to help their startup. I created a board, developed a product, and initiated sales. With all that done, I went on to be the chief officer of career and technical education for the Chicago Public Schools after being recommended for the job by another close friend, Roxanne Decyk. I worked with CEO Arne Duncan, who later became President Barack Obama's secretary of education. While there, in partnership with DeVry University, I created DeVry University Advantage Academy High School, where students graduate in four years with both a diploma and an associate's degree. The school has turned into a resounding success, with higher rates of graduation and four-year college attendance than the public school average. Working with a local bank, I developed a fully functioning bank branch inside a high school, run by the students, who learned skills invaluable for future employment. I also worked with the Chicago Architecture Foundation to publish a textbook that integrates architectural drawing expertise with writing, research, and other skills.

I retired at sixty-five and joined another wonderful friend,

Joan E. Steel, in doing consulting work and getting involved in charitable and civic activities, until MSNBC changed my life.

◼

I'm grateful to Watergate for opening up so many opportunities for a fascinating and varied career—and for having reunited me with Michael. Over the years, I've kept in touch with my colleagues from the special prosecutor's office, and I've attended our reunions every five years around October 20, the anniversary of the Saturday Night Massacre. Everyone from the office—lawyers, paralegals, secretaries, interns, security guards—is invited. One year we played a video of Archie Cox's last press conference on the day of his dismissal, and I was struck anew by his eloquence and integrity. I don't recall if Archie was present that year, though unlike Leon Jaworski, who never came, Archie showed up for several reunions before his death in 2004. Jim Neal also attended reunions until his death in 2010.

I attended Jim's funeral with Rick Ben-Veniste, who's now known as Richard and remains a close friend. Waiting for our planes at the Nashville airport after the service, Rick and I reminisced about Watergate and how far we'd traveled since then. He was now a partner at Mayer Brown, one of the nation's top global law firms, and was happily married to his second wife, Donna, who has also become a valued friend.

Rick said he was glad I'd found happiness with Michael. "I never understood why you stayed with Ian, he treated you so badly," he told me.

"Well, I had another relationship that made up for it," I said.

Rick was astounded. He never suspected that I was having an affair.

"With whom? Anyone I know?"

I was sure he did know Kurt, but I refused to divulge the name. Still, Rick kept asking me probing questions, trying to get me to reveal the name of my former lover, until it was time to board our planes.

I have kept in touch with Kurt over the years. In the mid-1980s, I suggested that he meet Susan Pearce, one of my Washington friends, who was working as a lawyer in Paris when Kurt was stationed in Rome for the Justice Department. My instincts were right. Susan was Kurt's soulmate and became his second wife. Kurt was in Rome in 1985 when the *Achille Lauro*, an Italian cruise ship, was hijacked by PLO terrorists who murdered and threw overboard a wheelchair-bound New Yorker named Leon Klinghoffer. The hijackers were arrested after their plane was forced down in Sicily and surrounded by armed troops from Italy and the United States. Kurt arranged a lineup and helped Klinghoffer's widow identify the men who had killed her husband. Overcome by grief, she ignored Kurt's advice not to engage with the suspects and spat on each of the men she identified.

Perhaps my most unlikely post-Watergate friendship is with John Dean. We became reacquainted in 2008, when he and I served on a panel about ethics at the St. Thomas Law School in Minneapolis, along with Charles Breyer, a former colleague from the special prosecutor's office, who is now a federal judge in San Francisco. During the lunch before the panel, I talked to John for the first time about our personal lives and learned that he had lived in Evanston as a child, and that we both love our dogs. Since then, we have kept in touch, and we now talk frequently about the parallels between today's scandals and Watergate, and how much worse off the country is now than in the 1970s.

I never saw Jeb Magruder again. He died in 2014, after spending his last years as a Presbyterian minister in Columbus, Ohio. A dissembler to the end, he changed his account of Watergate several times, telling interviewers at one point that it was *he* who had instructed Gordon Liddy to break into the Democratic Party headquarters, and, at another, that Nixon himself had ordered the burglary.

Nor did I ever see Rose Mary Woods after 1974, though I would have loved a chance to talk to her. The more I learned about Rose and her struggles, the more I respected her strength and deplored her treatment by the White House. I decided Rose was not the self-abnegating servant the press portrayed. She was as interested in power as any of the president's men. If Rose had been a man, she would not have been seen as a victim to be pitied. She would have been regarded like Jeb Magruder or John Dean, a striving Washington insider blinded by ambition.

If she had been a man, she also might have been the chief of staff instead of a secretary, given how much the president relied on her advice, as the tapes of their conversations clearly illustrate. She also might have enjoyed a second act as a speaker, writer, or political consultant. Instead, because she had come of age at a time when women lacked status in the working world, she had few options.

In 1994, Rose attended Nixon's state funeral at the Richard Nixon Presidential Library and Museum in Yorba Linda, California. By this time, she had left Washington and returned to Ohio, settling in a town house in Alliance, a few miles from Sebring, where she'd been born and raised. She went to mass every day, and occasionally she attended events sponsored by the local Republican Party.

Rose died in 2005 at age eighty-seven, and when I began

work on this book I decided to reach out to a few of her friends who I hoped might be open to talking to me. I wanted to portray Rose as those who loved her remembered her. I called Ed Cox, hoping he'd put me in touch with his wife, Tricia, Nixon's elder daughter. Like her sister, Julie, Tricia had been very close to Rose. As soon as I explained who I was, though, he hung up on me.

Soon afterward, I traveled to Alexandria, Virginia, where Sally Buikema, who'd worked with Rose as a White House appointments secretary, lived with her husband. The journalist Bob Woodward, whom I've gotten to know in the years since Watergate, had advised me to show up at her house, rather than call first. "It's harder for people to shut the door in your face than hang up on you," Bob said.

But that's exactly what happened. I arrived at the Buikemas' redbrick town house just as Sally's husband stepped through the front gate, followed by the couple's daughter. "My mother will never talk to you," the young woman snapped and stomped away, slamming the gate.

In 1997, several additional Nixon tapes were released by the National Archives, and I was fascinated to discover that Rose was much more deeply involved in the Watergate cover-up than we had known. Not only did she know about the hush money paid to the burglars, she actually kept some of it in the safe in her apartment, including about $100,000 supplied by Thomas Pappas, a wealthy Greek American industrialist and one of Nixon's chief campaign contributors. The tapes make clear that Pappas, who was never charged and who died in 1988, had supplied the funds "to keep people in place," as Bob Haldeman put it, referring to the money spent to silence the seven original Watergate defendants.

On March 21, 1973, right after Nixon told John Dean that

he would have no trouble getting $1 million in cash to pay the burglars, the president spoke with Rose in the Oval Office. The conversation was dark and mysterious and the references not always clear, though it was obvious that Rose was privy to Nixon's secrets and that Nixon and his loyal secretary were involved in some kind of financial intrigue.

> NIXON: We may have a need for substantial cash. . . . How much do you have?
>
> ROSE: I still have that hundred [thousand?]. I'm so worried. They called earlier, and I said it had been used for a special project, so that there'd be no record.
>
> NIXON: And you have some other as well?
>
> ROSE: Yes. I don't know. I would have to look. I'd have to get in the safe. I don't remember.
>
> NIXON: But it's a sum you can take. We may have to call on that. . . . We have to use it for certain purposes . . .
>
> ROSE: Nobody here knows I have it.
>
> NIXON: Well, I know, and nobody any place else knows.

Two weeks earlier, on March 7, Pappas had visited Nixon in the White House, and the president thanked him for helping out "on some of these things that . . . others are involved in." Nixon worried that Pappas would reveal to investigators the true reason for his gratitude, and he enlisted Rose's help to make sure that Pappas told the correct story. On a tape from June 6, 1973, he asked Rose to contact Pappas to ensure he wouldn't say anything that would be damaging to the president.

> NIXON: And, of course, I don't want to have anything indicating that I was thanking him for raising money

for the Watergate defendants. I think he's smart enough to know that, but you know, uh, you just never know.

ROSE: Well, I, I think he is too, but because of that fact, is it even safe for me to talk on the phone . . . ?

NIXON: No, don't talk on the phone. . . .

ROSE: I'll call his girl today and say as soon as he gets back into town, say I need to see him.

In the long decades since I cross-examined Rose Mary Woods about the eighteen-and-a-half-minute gap, that missing section in the tape from June 20, 1972, remains the most enduring mystery of Watergate.

Despite determined efforts by interviewers and researchers, we are no closer now than we were then to knowing the truth about who erased the tape, how it was done, or precisely what the missing minutes contained. In 1977, in Nixon's first televised interview after resigning, the journalist David Frost tried to pin down the former president as the culprit, but Nixon refused to admit erasing the tape. "So, you're asking us to take an awful lot on trust, aren't you?" Frost asked him.

Nixon demurred, saying that he had already testified to a grand jury that he had nothing to do with it. Moreover, he told Frost, his pardon by Gerald Ford wouldn't cover his lying under oath after his resignation, and he wasn't about to open himself up to a perjury charge.

Years later, when I began research for this book, I sought out Steve Bull, the former White House aide who had been in charge of marking the conversation in the June 20 tape that Rose transcribed. Bull told me that one day after he'd denied to a reporter that he'd caused the eighteen-and-a-half-minute gap, Alexander Haig told him, "You shouldn't be so quick to deny your culpability."

"What?" Bull said in a shocked, vehement tone.

Haig wouldn't elaborate and never brought it up again, but Bull thought the chief of staff was suggesting, albeit in a cryptic way, that Bull take the blame for the missing section of the June 20 tape. That made me wonder if Haig had approached Rose or anyone else with the same comment.

Today, Nixon's presidential tapes are preserved in a climate-controlled vault at the National Archives in Washington. Using the latest technology for restoring audio, experts have attempted over the years to recover those missing minutes of conversation between Nixon and Haldeman. Nothing has worked. In 2009, Phil Mellinger, an independent security expert, and a group of forensic scientists hired by the National Archives tried to unlock the mystery by studying the sheets of paper containing Haldeman's notes of the meeting. Mellinger suspected that the notes had been tampered with and speculated that at least a page corresponding to the gap was missing. The group used sophisticated CSI-type methods to study impressions of Haldeman's notes, but no new information was revealed.

■

I used to think Watergate was a never-to-be repeated perfect storm, the catastrophic joining of a flawed president, his amoral cronies, and lax campaign finance laws that allowed them to raise money without transparency and spend freely on illegal acts. I know better now.

Today, we are up against a deeper existential threat to democracy than we faced during Watergate, a peril exacerbated by a more complicated political, social, and cultural landscape than existed in the 1970s. The country is more divided now, and today's media is a minefield of fake news and shrill voices from a multiplicity of sources. During Watergate, three TV networks dominated the national news, and all reported the same facts. The public debated the meaning of those facts but didn't challenge their very existence. There was no Fox News to present an alternative universe to 40 percent of the population.

If Fox News had existed in 1973, America might have continually heard that Nixon's tapes were fabricated, that the CIA and FBI were awash in deep state corruption with the primary objective of removing a duly elected president. Perhaps I would have been accused of having secret motives to harass the Nixon administration. Rose Mary Woods might have appeared on Fox News to tell Sean Hannity that it was *I*, Jill Wine Volner, who had deleted the eighteen and a half minutes from the June 20, 1972, tape because the missing material actually exonerated Nixon, and I wanted him out.

Donald Trump is more dangerous than Richard Nixon, not only because he encouraged a foreign power to interfere in our national civic life, but also because he exceeds Nixon in hatefulness and venality. Trump incites the worst angels of our nature; he tells us to ignore what our hearts and minds and eyes tell us is the truth, and to believe only him. He has obliterated civil discourse and unleashed racism, misogyny, xenophobia, and disrespect for the rule of law and the separation of powers. He puts in peril the fundamental principles on which our nation was founded.

America survived Watergate because our institutions were strong at their core. Our leaders spoke to one another across the political divide and felt a responsibility to preserve democracy. It falls to us, once again, to stop this new threat to what has made America great.

A NOTE ON SOURCES

The Watergate Girl is a memoir that reflects my recollections and my interpretation of the events I experienced. In some instances, my memory differs from the memories of others, though I've tried not to contradict known facts. To supplement my recollection, I've relied heavily on public documents, including newspaper accounts, court transcripts, and audio recordings. I've also interviewed as many people as I could who were witness to the events described here.

The vast records of the Watergate Special Prosecution Force at the National Archives in Washington; the Rose Mary Woods Papers at the Richard Nixon Presidential Library and Museum in Yorba Linda, California; and the Watergate Special Prosecution Force Report have been invaluable. The *New York Times* and the *Washington Post* exhaustively covered the hearings on Nixon's presidential tapes and the trial of his associates and aides that began in October 1974, and I've relied on their accounts for details, atmospherics, and reported quotes.

Where possible, in recounting scenes and reconstructing

dialogue, I've drawn on documents such as court records, audio recordings, and contemporary news accounts. When this material hasn't been available, I've tried to capture the truth and spirit of the conversations, if not the exact words.

I've also drawn on the many memoirs, contemporary accounts, and histories of Watergate. In particular, I'm indebted to these books:

Richard Ben-Veniste, *The Emperor's New Clothes: Exploring the Truth from Watergate to 9/11* (New York: Thomas Dunne Books, 2009).

Richard Ben-Veniste and George Frampton Jr., *Stonewall: The Real Story of the Watergate Prosecution* (New York: Simon & Schuster, 1977).

Carl Bernstein and Bob Woodward, *All the President's Men* (New York: Simon & Schuster, 1974).

John W. Dean, *Blind Ambition: The White House Years* (New York: Simon & Schuster, 1976).

James Doyle, *Not Above the Law: The Battles of Watergate Prosecutors Cox and Jaworski* (New York: William Morrow, 1977).

Madeleine Edmondson and Alden Duer Cohen, *The Women of Watergate* (New York: Stein & Day, 1975).

Leon Jaworski, *The Right and the Power: The Prosecution of Watergate* (New York: Reader's Digest Press, 1976).

Stanley E. Kutler, *Abuse of Power: The New Nixon Tapes* (New York: Free Press, 1997).

Jeb Stuart Magruder, *An American Life: One Man's Road to Watergate* (New York: Atheneum, 1974).

John J. Sirica, *To Set the Record Straight: The Break-in, the Tapes, the Conspirators, the Pardon* (New York: Norton, 1979).

Bob Woodward, *The Last of the President's Men* (New York: Simon & Schuster, 2015).

Bob Woodward and Carl Bernstein, *The Final Days* (New York: Simon & Schuster, 1976).

ACKNOWLEDGMENTS

This book would not exist without the help of so many. My incredible lawyer, Steve Sheppard, introduced me to the best agent ever, Philippa "Flip" Brophy of Sterling Lord Literistic who believed in my story and brought it to Henry Holt and Company, where I was exceptionally lucky to have the superlative Paul Golob as my editor. He clearly got my book, seeing it as a combination of *Hidden Figures* and *All the President's Men*, a concept that immediately excited me and still does. I hope that, with his help, I have fulfilled his vision. Not only is he a man of great knowledge and intellect, but he was a delight to work with and his cuts, corrections, and rephrasing dramatically enhanced how the story reads. I have also had the support of Scottie Bowditch and Colleen Osborne at the Macmillan Speakers Bureau and the entire Holt team including Amy Einhorn, Maggie Richards, Pat Eisemann, Carolyn O'Keefe, Jason Liebman, Katy Robitzski, and the indefatigable Natalia Ruiz.

Thanks, too, to Flip for introducing me to Gioia Diliberto,

my indispensable partner in this project. She worked hand-in-hand with me to put my experiences on the page. Her contributions are enormous. I thank her especially for being willing to quibble with me over each and every word in this book and for pointing out to me the unnecessary throat-clearing and legalese in my early drafts. If this book comes alive and tells a compelling narrative, it is because of her. For that I am eternally grateful, as well as for what I know will be a lifelong friendship.

Also, without June Reinisch and Leonard Rosenbloom's persistence, I would never have even started to write this book. Their love and support enriches my life in so many ways, as does that of Civia Tamarkin, Christie Hefner, and Lorraine Mandel—they all read and reread my numerous drafts and offered incredible insights and improvements. Thanks, too, to Roxanne Decyk and Joan E. Steel, whose friendship helps me every day in every way, and to Lew Watts, a wonderful poet, who solved writerly problems for me.

Then there are all who gave generously of their time, knowledge, and friendship to make this book authentic, accurate, and, I hope, fun to read, especially Richard Ben-Veniste, John Dean, James Robenalt, James Doyle, Tim Naftali, Carl Feldbaum, George T. Frampton, Gerald "Jerry" Goldman, Susan Kaslow, Kurt Muellenberg, Maggie Fraser, John Barker, Phil and Madeline Lacovara, Stephen Bull, Alexander Butterfield, Suzanne Thevenet, Angelo Lano, Lawrence "Larry" Iason, Judy Denny, Don Loeb, Mitzi Wertheim, John Damgard, Elizabeth Holtzman, Pete McCloskey, Thomas Mallon, Scott Turow, Diane Dorfman, Richard Hauser, Lawrence Tribe, Geoff Stone, Ken Gormley, Diane Swonk, Patrick Anderson, John Hanrahan, Karen Scheinberg, Marty Wine, Steve Wine, Barbara Kosovske, Ivy Bouillerce, Jonathan Hilkevitch, Judy Pardonnet, Varda Goldman, and Nina Stillman. Special thanks to Pamela

Forbes Lieberman and Stu Lieberman, who always keep me informed of the latest breaking news and often give me great lines for this book and for television. Bob Woodward generously read an early draft and gave me tips on how to approach uncooperative witnesses as well as a lead to new information. Evanston Writers Meet Up started me on this path with their comments on my early outline eleven years ago for what became this book, and The Chicago Network HerStory attendees got me back on track to writing it when I had almost given up. Rita Dragonette was instrumental in my residence at Ragdale, where I was taken seriously as a writer and given the time to focus on writing. She also suggested I take an OpEd Project class that directly led to my reinvention as an MSNBC legal analyst and opinion writer. For that I am eternally grateful. I recommend that class (www.theopedproject.org) to all who have something to say about current events or issues of concern. As they say, "Whoever tells the story, writes history."

Enormous thanks are owed to everyone at MSNBC, where I can tell it as I see it. MSNBC has the most wonderful hosts, producers, bookers, camera operators, sound engineers, and hair and makeup pros. I'm grateful for all my fellow commentators, but especially my #SistersInLaw. You teach me so much every day. I'm honored to be part of the team. I would especially like to thank (in alphabetical order): Nick Akerman, Yelda Altalef, Jonathan Alter, Cynthia Alksne, Cynthia Anoniak, Meredith Bennett-Smith, Berit Berger, Natasha Bertrand, Michael Beschloss, Paul Butler, Jonathan Capehart, Danny Cevellos, Elizabeth Chmurak, Lily Corvo, Michelle Cumbo, Joanne Denyeau, Mieke Eoyang, Frank Figliuzzi, Kendis Gibson, Michelle Goldberg, Shannah Goldner, Eric Greenberg, David Gura, Chris Hayes, John Heilemann, Nancy Hirsch, Beryl Holness, David Cay Johnston,

Neal Katyal, Glenn Kirschner, Ron Klain, Sally Kohn, Steve Kornacki, Nicholas Kristof, Jessica Kurdali, Jillian Lazzaro, Stephen Lewis, Harry Littman, Richard Liu, Rachel Maddow, Ruth Marcus, Chris Matthews, Zerlina Maxwell, Kat McCullough, Barbara McQuade, Jon Meacham, Ari Melber, Craig Melvin, Matt Miller, Andrea Mitchell, Ayman Mohyeldin, Elena Nachmanoff, Malcolm Nance, Nkechi Nneji, Tim O'Brien, Lawrence O'Donnell, Justin Oliver, Richard Painter, Ariana Pekary, Karine Jean Pierre, Joy Reid, Carl Reiner, Phillippe Reines, Kelly Rice, Laura Roberts, Querry Robinson, Mimi Rocah, Chuck Rosenberg, Carly Rubel, Jennifer Rubin, Stephanie Ruhle, Marci Santiago, Diane Shamis, Rev. Al Sharpton, Michael Steele, Lawrence Tribe, Katy Tur (whose memoir inspired me), Joyce Vance, Yasmin Vassoughian, Ali Velshi, Nicolle Wallace, Michael Weiss, Maya Wiley, Brian Williams, Alex Witt, Dan Wolfman, Betsy Woodruff Swan, and everyone at NBC's Chicago Bureau, especially Nadine Comerford and David "Cowboy" Durham, as well as Debbie Davis, Chiquita Eubanks, Maria Blanco, Danielle Dettore, Matthew Winter, Mark Ringo, Sharon Pearson, John Kooistra, and Steve Lazzarro. Thank you all for making me look good.

Thanks also go to everyone at TV House in Chicago (Ted James, Mike Barnard, Kevin Vicks, Marcia Forbes, and Kelly LaBanco), Canadian Broadcasting Company, Australian Broadcasting Company, BBC Radio, and stations that had me on before I signed on with MSNBC, especially *Democracy Now!* (my first ever commentary, done while I was hiking in Arizona when the "Tuesday night massacre" occurred), NPR, Christiane Amanpour at CNN, Soledad O'Brien, and many at Sirius XM POTUS Radio. The list is not complete without highlighting Progressive Talk Radio where I have enjoyed talking with Stephanie Miller, the host who gave me a jingle that makes me dance. She also delighted me by putting me completely out of my comfort zone—on a comedy show stage with her, John Fugelsang, Margaret Cho, and my own Congressman, Rep. Jan Schakowsky (D-IL). Thanks also to Travis Bone and pup, Kathy Griffin, and everyone at Politicon, including the fans—it was an amazing experience for a news junkie like me.

I thank my professors and classmates at Columbia Law School, with special thanks to those who still enhance my life, including Rena Pokempner Gordon and her husband Mike Gordon, Lois Lempel Weinroth, and Judge Naomi Reice Buchwald—and Jane Bergner for her trifle recipe. I thank my Justice Department colleagues, especially Gerald "Gerry" McDowell, Phil Michael, and the late Charles "Chuck" Ruff, who accepted me as a friend and peer when I was the only woman in the room; all my Watergate colleagues; Secretary of the Army Clifford Alexander and Adele Logan Alexander; Attorney General Neil F. Hartigan; and my colleagues everywhere I've worked.

Thanks and recognition must be given for the help I received from Robert Reed at the National Archives and Records Administration and from Steve Greene, who helped my research there, and especially to the best fact-checker ever, Jack Cassidy. Despite their assistance and the time of all who shared their knowledge with me, if there are any errors of fact, they are all mine. Also, I'm grateful to Geoff Shell, who created and manages my website and helps with my social media.

I only wish my late parents were here to enjoy this book and receive my gratitude. They taught me that there were no limits—even for a girl. My Aunt Ethyle and all my other aunts, uncles, and cousins, too, are part of who I am today.

I cannot end the thanks without a shout out to my amazing cadre of Twitter (especially Kireau Kendrick who answers all my questions), Facebook, and Instagram followers who inform and inspire me every day and keep my #JillsPins collection clever and current. And I want to add a very humble thank you to former secretary of state Madeleine Albright for the thrill and honor she bestowed on me by sending an inscribed copy of her book *Read My Pins*. It is displayed prominently in my library, next to the well-worn copy I have long used as inspiration for #JillsPins. She is a role model as a leader, pin wearer, and brooch book writer.

No doubt I have omitted the names of many who should be included; I hope they will forgive my oversight.

Finally, I started with dedicating this book to my husband, Michael Banks, but he merits the last word as well. In fact, he deserves a medal for valor and heroism for endlessly reading every draft and for putting up with the hours I spent getting this done. His suggestions made the book so much better, just as his partnership, sense of humor and adventure, support, and love have enhanced my life.

INDEX

ABC News, 108, 147, 202–3, 206, 215
Achille Lauro hijacking, 232
Acker, Marjorie, 115
Agnew, Spiro, resignation of, 52, 134, 140, 205
Air Force One, 84, 180
Alexander, Clifford, 214
All the President's Men (Bernstein and Woodward), 177
All the President's Men (film), 209
American Life, An (Magruder), 176–77
American Bar Association, 90, 110, 222, 227–28
Anderson, Jack, 114, 137
anti-Communism, 11
anti-Semitism, 100–101, 103, 229–30
anti-war movement, 28, 30, 51, 66–67, 85
Assembly of Captive European Nations (ACEN), 11

Bailey, F. Lee, 98
Banks, Michael, 162–63, 218–21, 226
  marriage to Jill, 221, 223–24, 228, 231
Barbie, Klaus, 222
Barker, John, 146
Bayh, Birch, 135
Bay of Pigs invasion, 19, 66
Bennett, John, 129
Ben-Veniste, Donna, 231
Ben-Veniste, Richard, 42, 43, 52, 70, 73–78, 111, 132, 139, 157, 166, 209
  courtroom style of, 33, 91, 94, 126–27, 187, 195, 221
  Jaworski and, 91–94, 142–45
  personal life, 14–15, 220, 231
  Saturday Night Massacre and, 62–64
  Watergate trial, 184–201, 221
  work relationship with Wine-Banks, 15–16, 68, 77, 94, 125, 134–35, 171, 203, 220–21

Bernstein, Carl, 3, 10, 146, 154, 177, 209
Bittman, William O., 147–48, 161
Blind Ambition (Dean), 177
Blackmun, Harry, 17, 167
Bork, Robert, 62–63, 71, 88, 92
   firing of Cox, 62–63, 71–73
Boston Globe, 55
Bradlee, Ben, 35
Brennan, William J., 17, 167
Breyer, Charles, 64, 232
Brokaw, Tom, 108
Brown, Pat, 83
Buchwald, Art, 203–4
Buikema, Sally, 234
Bull, Stephen B., 76–77, 79, 80, 114, 129, 137, 236
Burger, Warren E., 167, 172
burglars, Watergate, 3, 6, 19–25, 27–30, 124, 187
   hush money demands, 22, 37, 40, 46, 132–33, 141–42, 147–48, 158–60, 177–78, 188, 191, 194, 198, 234–35
   trial, 3, 20–22, 26, 27, 37, 54, 158, 161, 191
Butler, M. Caldwell, 174
Butterfield, Alexander, 39–44, 79, 84–85, 109, 114, 128–29, 165, 173
Buzhardt, Fred, 46–47, 74, 93, 122, 126–27, 131

Camp David, 39, 44, 76, 79, 109, 117, 119, 129, 137, 160–61
Canzoneri, Tony, 126
Carr, Jesse, 8, 77, 80
Carter, Jimmy, 212–15, 218
CBS, 108, 126
Celler, Emanuel, 152
Central Intelligence Agency (CIA), 11, 19, 22, 159, 178, 194, 198, 238

Cheshire, Maxine, 206
Chicago, 7, 57, 60, 101–5, 163, 219–22, 228, 230
Chicago Architecture Foundation, 230
Chicago Public Schools, 230
Chicago Tribune, 226
China, 84, 228
Christofferson, D. Todd, 132
Chung, Connie, 108, 126
civil rights, 23, 66–67
Civil War, 23, 29
Clinton, Hillary Rodham, 154
CNN, 226
Coffin, William Sloane, Jr., 30
Cohen, William S., 174
Colson, Charles W., 147, 160–61, 164, 185
Columbia Law School, 8–11, 14, 18, 57–59, 67, 125
Comey, James, 226
Committee to Re-elect the President (CREEP), 3, 20–22, 26–30, 68, 139, 147, 150, 158–61, 178, 187, 188, 195
Congress, US, 21, 52, 225
   impeachment proceedings against Nixon, 148–50, 156, 165–66, 173–74
   women in, 150–54, 173
Connally, John, 90
Constitution, US, 23, 24, 46, 139, 150, 151, 153, 166, 168, 173, 186, 203
Cox, Archibald, 8–9, 69, 111, 117, 118, 231
   firing of, 61–73, 87
   Jaworski as replacement of, 88, 92, 139, 142, 154, 180, 186
   as Watergate special prosecutor, 8–9, 22–25, 35, 46–49, 53–56, 61
Cox, Edward, 42, 234

Cox, Phyllis, 24–25, 55
Cox, Tricia Nixon, 42, 82, 179, 234
Cuba, 19

Dayan, Moshe, 135
Dean, John, 27, 40–46, 111, 138,
    150, 173
  "cancer on the presidency"
    remark, 45, 132–33, 135, 141,
    158, 191
  Ervin Committee testimony,
    40–46, 53–54, 68, 130–33
  plea deal and prison sentence,
    40, 42–44, 53–54, 161, 177,
    188, 189, 204
  post-Watergate friendship with
    Wine-Banks, 232
  remorse of, 43–44
  role in Watergate scandal,
    28–29, 40–46, 53–54, 68, 74,
    132–33, 158–61, 177, 188–92
  tapes and, 45, 74–76, 132–33,
    158, 163–64, 188, 190–91, 234
Dean, Maureen, 41, 42, 188, 189–90
Decyk, Roxanne, 230
DeLisle, Paul, 204
Democratic National Committee,
    1, 3, 5–6, 9–10, 19, 130
  headquarters break-in, see
    Watergate break-in and
    cover-up
Democratic National Convention
    (1972), 28, 194
Denny, Judy, 197
DeVry University Advantage
    Academy High School, 230
Dickerson, Nancy, 10, 202
Doar, John, 165
Donaldson, Sam, 108
Douglas, William O., 167
Doyle, James, 24, 55, 68, 127, 149,
    154, 207–8
Duncan, Arne, 230

Edlund, Elayne, 147
Egypt, 51
Ehrlichman, Jeanne, 187
Ehrlichman, John, 42, 139, 187,
    200–201
  indictment of, 139, 147, 158–61
  resignation of, 40, 197
  role in Watergate scandal, 45,
    112–13, 117, 158–61, 164
  tapes and, 79, 112, 117–18, 158,
    164, 173
  trial, 184–201, 204
Eighteen-and-a-half-minute gap,
    2–5, 93, 107, 109, 111–20,
    127–131, 136–138, 173, 236–37
Eisenhower, Dwight, 36, 41, 82–83,
    167
Ellsberg, Daniel, 114, 185
Equal Rights Amendment (ERA),
    203
Ervin, Sam, 23, 31, 46
Ervin Committee, 22, 23–25, 29,
    39, 51, 75, 79, 165, 173, 194
  Dean testimony, 40–46, 53–54,
    68, 130–33
  Haldeman testimony, 41,
    158–59
  Magruder testimony, 30–38
Esquire, 90, 176
European Economic Community,
    222
Executive Office Building, 3, 39,
    40, 45, 74–76, 83, 112–14, 118,
    129, 205, 206
executive privilege, 45, 46, 48, 168,
    172

Fear of Flying (Jong), 215–16
Federal Bureau of Investigation
    (FBI), 67, 177–78, 194, 198,
    200, 208, 226, 238
  false statements given to, 22,
    37, 158

Federal Bureau of Investigation
   (FBI) (*cont'd*)
   Saturday Night Massacre and,
      61–63
   phone taps investigated by, 5,
      123–24
   tapes investigated by, 136–38
   tapes transcribed by, 182–83
Feldbaum, Carl, 18, 19, 24, 64, 71,
      73, 132, 133, 136, 141, 170
Feminine Mystique, The (Friedan),
      58
feminism, 58, 203
Fisher, George, 228
Flowers, Walter, 174
Ford, Gerald, 52, 134, 214
   becomes president, 180–81
   Nixon pardoned by, 181–82,
      236
   as vice president, 52, 134–35,
      164
Fox News, 238
Frampton, George, 17, 27, 39, 40,
      53, 61, 62, 111, 141, 149, 172,
      182
Fraser, Maggie, 99–100
Free Europe Committee, 11
Fried, Frank, Harris, Shriver and
      Kampelman, 206–8, 210, 212
Friendly, Henry, 94–95
Frost, David, 236

Garment, Leonard, 69–70, 93, 113,
      122
Gemstone plan, 28–30
Germany, 97
   Nazi, 89–90, 92, 100–101, 103,
      222
Gideon's Trumpet (Lewis), 10, 108
Goldman, Jerry, 17, 111, 141
Goldwater, Barry, 29, 179
Good Morning America, 215
Gordon, Gene, 216

Gordon, Rena, 95
Graham, Katharine, 84, 146
grand jury, Watergate, 47–49, 63,
      75, 91, 122–23, 138–55
   indictments, 138–44, 145–55,
      156–61, 168–69, 180–82
   leaks, 146–47
   straw vote on Nixon indictment,
      146–47
Gray, Robert, 85, 206
Gridiron dinner, 164–65
Griswold, Erwin, 19

Haig, Alexander, 76, 87, 88, 91, 110,
      117, 118, 175, 178, 236–37
   "devil theory" of, 128
   tapes and, 129, 137
Haldeman, H. R. "Bob," 29, 32, 76,
      83, 139, 167, 181, 187
   Ervin Committee testimony, 41,
      158–59
   indictment of, 139, 147, 158–61
   notes of, 45, 113–14, 140, 149,
      237
   resignation of, 40, 82
   role in Watergate scandal, 4,
      40, 41, 45, 93, 107, 112–18,
      158–59, 164, 177–78, 187–88,
      197, 234, 237
   tapes and, 4, 40, 79, 93, 107, 109,
      112–18, 138, 158–59, 164, 173,
      177–78, 237
   trial, 184–201, 204
Haldeman, Jo, 187, 200
Haldeman, Susan, 197, 200
Hall, Joan, 222
Hamilton, Alexander, 140, 151
Hannity, Sean, 238
Hanrahan, John, 35
Harding, Warren G., 23, 152, 161
Harris, Patricia, 207–8
Hartigan, Neil, 222
Hartman, David, 215

Harvard Law School, 17, 18, 22, 152
Hauser, Richard, 136
Haynsworth, Clement F., 18
Hefner, Christie, 228
Helms, Richard, 178
Heymann, Philip, 16
Hoffa, Jimmy, 15
Hoffar, John A., 199
Hoffman, Abbie, 28
Hoffman, Dustin, 209
Hogan, Lawrence, 174
Holtzman, Elizabeth, 150, 152–54, 166, 173–74
House Judiciary Committee, 148–51, 153, 167, 222
impeachment proceedings and vote, 148–50, 156, 165–66, 173–74, 194
House of Representatives, US, 148, 175
Hunt, Dorothy, 22
Hunt, E. Howard, 19, 20, 22, 147, 149–50, 159–61, 189

Iason, Larry, 17–18
impeachment, 139–40
House inquiry and hearings, 148–50, 156, 165–66, 173–74, 194
public opinion on, 154
Road Map, 148–50, 156–57, 165
women in prominent roles during, 150–54
imposter syndrome, 221
indictments, Watergate, 138–44, 145–55, 156–71
lawyers' memo on, 141–44
Nixon and, 139–47, 168–69, 180–82
Nixon as unindicted co-conspirator, 145–46, 148, 157–58, 168–69

public opinion on, 146
Watergate Seven, 147–48, 156–61
Iota Alpha Pi, 10, 106
Israel, 51
ITT Corporation, 9, 114

Jaworski, Jeannette, 166, 167, 169
Jaworski, Leon, 87–96, 231
leadership style of, 142–43, 186
refusal to indict Nixon, 139–46, 180–82, 185
resignation of, 185–86
Supreme Court performance, 167–70
as Watergate special prosecutor, 87–89, 111, 133, 136, 139–44, 154, 165–70, 180–82, 185
Jenner, Albert, 165, 222
Jenner & Block, 222, 227
Jews, 57, 101–6, 152
persecution of, 100–101, 103, 229
Johnson, Andrew, 148
Johnson, Lyndon B., 51, 90, 92, 151, 167
Jordan, Barbara, 150–52, 154, 173
journalism, 10–11, 202–4, 207
women in, 10, 58, 202–4, 226–27
Justice Department, 8, 11–12, 13, 27, 52, 64, 88, 97, 183
firing of Cox, 62–73

Kalmbach, Herbert W., 160
Kaslow, Susan, 203
Kennedy, John F., 10, 35, 66, 83, 151, 167, 207
assassination of, 10, 52, 90
Kennedy, Robert, 207
Kent State shooting, 66
Key Biscayne, Florida, 32, 33, 44, 76, 84, 129
Keyes, Paul, 86

King, Martin Luther, Jr., 10, 66
    "I Have a Dream" speech, 10,
      66–67
Kleindienst, Richard, 159
Klinghoffer, Leon, 232

Lacovara, Madeline, 209
Lacovara, Phil, 18, 47, 73–74, 140,
    169, 170, 182, 209
Ladies' Home Journal, 84
Lano, Angie, 123–24, 137, 182
LaRue, Frederick C., 160, 161
Laugh-In (TV show), 86
Leake, David, 223
Leventhal, Harold, 18
Lewis, Anthony, 10, 108–9
Liddy, G. Gordon, 20–21, 27–30,
    159, 161, 187, 232
    Gemstone Plan, 28–30
Lincoln Sitting Room, 39, 130
Lindsay, John, 152
Los Angeles Times, 84

Madison, James, 151
Magruder, Gail, 31, 193
Magruder, Jeb Stuart, 26–38, 40,
    54, 111, 233
    book deal, 36, 38, 176
    Ervin Committee testimony,
      30–38
    Gemstone plan, 28–30
    plea deal and prison sentence,
      26–38, 161, 176–77, 192–93, 204
    role in Watergate scandal,
      26–38, 42–43, 159, 176–77,
      187, 192–94, 232
    Watergate trial testimony,
      192–94
Mann, James R., 174
Marbury v. Madison, 24
Mardian, Dorothy, 187, 199–200
Mardian, Robert, 139, 147, 158,
    159, 187, 195–97, 199, 204–5

Marshall, Thurgood, 19, 167
Marshall Plan, 82
Maytag, 229
McCarthyism, 66
McCloskey, Pete, 218
McCord, James W., Jr., 19–21, 29,
    43, 54, 68, 130, 16, 187
McGovern, George, 194
McGrory, Mary, 204, 209
McRae, Edna, 104–5
Mellinger, Phil, 237
#MeToo movement, 227
Meyer, Edward "Shy," 218
Mikva, Abner, 221, 224
Miranda warning, 111, 112
Mitchell, John, 27, 42, 85, 164, 167,
    181, 187, 197
    indictment of, 139, 147, 158–61
    role in Watergate scandal,
      28–32, 34, 74, 76, 158–61, 187,
      194, 195
    trial, 184–201, 204–5
Mitchell, Martha, 164, 187, 200,
    205
Montoya, Joseph, 31
Moorer, Thomas, 85
Motorola, 229
MSNBC, 226–27, 230
Muellenberg, Kurt, 97–101, 106,
    110, 155, 162, 208–9, 210, 218,
    220, 232
Mueller, Robert, 225
Muskie, Edmund, 9

National Archives, 234, 236–37
National Rifle Association (NRA),
    221
National Security Agency (NSA),
    109
National Women's Committee for
    Civil Rights, 207
Nazism, 89–90, 92, 100–101, 103,
    222

NBC, 108
Neal, Jim, 15, 18, 26–27, 40–47,
  68, 69, 92, 175–76, 181, 182,
  186, 231
  courtroom style of, 198–99
  Watergate trial, 186–99
Newsweek, 122
New York, 56–58, 152
New York Post, 82
New York Times, 10, 48, 66, 82, 88,
  90, 108, 125, 161, 162
Nixon, Julie, 84, 179, 234
Nixon, Pat, 81, 84, 113, 175, 179,
  180, 206
Nixon, Richard M., 44, 81, 83–84,
  191, 218
  death of, 233
  impeachment proceedings
    against, 52, 148–50, 156,
    165–66, 194
  indictment debate over, 139–46,
    180–82, 185
  interview with David Frost,
    236
  library, 42, 233
  1968 campaign, 27, 29, 42
  pardoned by Ford, 181–82, 236
  public opinion on, 3, 50–51, 66,
    143, 175
  reelection campaign, 9, 20–22,
    26–30, 33, 68, 158
  resignation of, 179–80
  role in Watergate scandal, 3–4,
    32, 40, 44–46, 107–20, 129–38,
    141–42, 145–50, 153–54,
    174–75, 178, 188–91, 232–37
  Saturday Night Massacre, 61–73,
    87, 231
  speeches of, 50, 82–83, 85–86,
    107, 179–80
  tapes and, 3–4, 46–51, 54–56,
    69–70, 138, 164–74, 177, 208,
    225
  Trump comparison, 225–26,
    237–38
  unindicted co-conspirator
    status, 145–46, 148, 157–58,
    168–69
  Vietnam War policy, 84, 85, 153
  Woods and, 4–5, 76–77, 81–86,
    110, 117–19, 122, 129, 131, 138,
    179, 205–6, 233–36
Noriega, Manuel, 217
North Korea, 215, 226
Nuremberg trials, 89–90, 92

Obama, Barack, 230
O'Brien, Lawrence, 20
Oliver, R. Spencer, 20
OpEd Project, 226
organized crime, 8–9, 72, 98
Our Gang (Roth), 176
Oval Office, 3, 39, 83, 179, 182, 234

Palestine Liberation Organization,
  232
Panama, 217
Pappas, Thomas, 234, 235
Parkinson, Kenneth, 139, 147, 161,
  195, 199–200
Parkinson, Pamela, 187, 200
Passaretti, Tony, 193
Pearce, Susan, 232
Pentagon, 213, 215, 217, 218, 219,
  227
Pentagon Papers, 9, 114, 185, 195
Petersen, Henry, 71–73, 77
Philadelphia Inquirer, 125
"plumbers" unit, 9, 28, 124
polygraphs, 137
Powell, Lewis F., Jr., 167, 168
Powers, Samuel J., 78–79, 118
Pregelj, Vladimir, 47, 140–41, 156
presidential elections, 9
  of 1952, 82
  of 1968, 27, 29, 42

presidential elections (*cont'd*)
  of 1972, 9, 20, 28, 158
  of 1976, 214
  of 2016, 225
press, 1, 55, 84, 153, 237
  fake news, 237–38
  on grand jury indictments, 146,
    159, 161
  on Rose Mary Stretch, 4, 121–23
  on Watergate scandal, 2, 3, 4,
    9–10, 26, 34–35, 41, 48, 66, 70,
    86, 93–94, 108, 121–23, 146,
    164, 186, 200, 237
  on Watergate trial, 186, 200–201
  Wine-Banks and, 5, 68, 108,
    124–26, 202–4, 226

Railsback, Tom, 174
Rather, Dan, 108, 164
Redford, Robert, 209
Rehnquist, William H., 167
Rhodes, John, 179
Rhyne, Charles S., 110–11, 120,
    122, 137
Richardson, Elliot, 9, 22, 62, 71,
    135, 165
Rient, Peter, 18, 141
Road Map, 148–50, 156–57, 165
Robinson, Sugar Ray, 8
Rodino, Peter, 174
Roe v. Wade, 17
Rogers, Ann, 217
Rogers, Bernie, 213, 215, 217
Roosevelt, Franklin, 167
"Rose Mary Stretch," 4, 121–23,
    138
Roth, Philip, 176
Ruckelshaus, William, 62, 71
Rudd, Mark, 67
Ruff, Charles "Chuck," 8, 77, 80,
    208
Rumsfeld, Donald, 29
Russia, 225, 228

Ruth, Henry, 18, 73, 88, 93, 186,
    208

San Clemente, California, 42, 84,
    173, 180, 206
Sans Souci, 203–4
Saturday Night Massacre, 61–73,
    87, 231
Schlafly, Phyllis, 203
Scott, Hugh, 179
Secret Service, 39
  tape system and, 39–40, 75–77,
    115, 129–30
Senate, US, 22, 82, 175, 179
Senate Judiciary Committee, 87,
    111
Senate Watergate hearings, *see*
    Ervin Committee
sexism, 27, 86, 128, 213
  in the military, 213–14, 217, 227
  and other biases, 229
  Wine-Banks and, 27, 72, 77, 92,
    123–26, 184, 196–97, 222
Silverman, Sam, 8
Simon, Max, 101, 102
Sirica, John J., 1, 3, 21, 27, 29,
    36–38, 47–48, 51, 54, 68, 164,
    177
  courtroom style of, 51, 123–25,
    191–92, 196
  indictments against Watergate
    Seven, 156–61
  sexism of, 123–25, 196–97
  tapes hearings, 69–86, 93,
    107–33
  Watergate trial, 184–201, 204–5
"smoking gun" tape, 177–79, 191
South Korea, 215
Soviet Union, 11, 51
Stahl, Lesley, 108
Stans, Maurice, 32
St. Clair, James D., 168, 169, 173,
    175, 178

Steel, Joan E., 231
Stennis, John, 54–56
Stewart, Potter, 167
Story, Joseph, 151
Strachan, Gordon, 32, 147, 158,
    159, 161, 185
Students for a Democratic Society,
    67
Sullivan, John J., 131
Supreme Court, US, 16, 17, 18, 24,
    143, 151, 153, 166–67
    ruling on tapes, 166–74, 177, 225
Syria, 51

tapes, White House, 1–5, 39–49,
    145, 153, 157
    "accidentally erased" June 20,
        1972, tape, 1–5, 45, 79–81, 93,
        107–20, 121–33, 136–38, 173,
        236–37
    "cancer on the presidency"
        March 21, 1973, tape, 45,
        132–33, 135, 141, 158, 191
    Dean and, 45, 74–76, 132–33,
        158, 163–64, 188, 190–91, 234
    executive privilege argument,
        45, 46, 48, 168, 172
    FBI investigation of, 136–38
    House Judiciary Committee
        investigation and, 165–66
    machine system, 1–3, 79, 109,
        114–17, 120–23, 127–30,
        136–38
    missing, 74–81, 93
    in National Archives, 234,
        236–37
    Nixon's refusal to hand over,
        3–4, 46–51, 54–56, 69–70,
        138, 164–72, 225
    Secret Service and, 39–40,
        75–77, 115, 129–30
    sixty-four, 163–73
    "smoking gun" tape, 177–79, 191

"Stennis compromise," 54–56
subpoenas, 3, 46–49, 70, 109,
    118, 164–65, 169, 172,
    175
    Supreme Court ruling on,
        166–74, 177, 225
    tampered with, 128–31
    transcripts, 114–20, 122, 149,
        150, 164, 178–79, 182–83, 190,
        199, 236
    transferred from White House
        to court, 70, 73–75
    Watergate trial and, 188–91,
        198
    Woods and, 1–5, 45, 76–81, 93,
        107–20, 121–38, 183, 233–37
Teamsters Union, 15, 77, 80
television, 10, 63, 82, 85, 86, 153,
    215, 238
    fake news, 237–38
    impeachment proceedings, 150,
        173–74
    Nixon resignation, 179–80
    on Watergate scandal, 25, 31, 39,
        41, 108, 164, 173, 186, 238
    on Watergate trial, 186, 200
    Wine-Banks on, 202–4, 207, 215,
        226–27, 230
Texas, 89, 150, 181, 185
Thomas, Eugene, 227–28
Thornton, Ray, 174
Thurman, Max, 217–18
Time, 55
Tower, John G., 179
Travers, Mary, 220–21
Trump, Donald, 225–26
    danger of, 225, 238
    Nixon comparison, 225–26,
        237–38
    obstruction of justice, 226

Uher tape recorder, 1–3, 109, 115–23,
    127–30, 136–38

Ulasewicz, Anthony, 160
US Army, 212–13, 221
   sexism in, 213–14, 217, 226
   Wine-Banks as general counsel
      for, 212–21, 226, 227
US Court of Appeals for the
   District of Columbia Circuit,
   51, 69–70
US Court of Appeals for the
   Second Circuit, 18, 94
US District Court (Washington,
   DC), *see* Sirica, John J. *and*
   grand jury, Watergate
University of Illinois, Urbana-
   Champaign, 10, 106
use immunity, 43, 53

Veil, Simone, 222
Vietnam War, 28, 30, 51, 66–67,
   114, 195
   Nixon policy, 84, 85, 153
Volner, Ian, 7, 56–61
   marriage to Jill, 7, 13, 56–61,
      94–96, 100, 101, 106, 109–10,
      125, 149, 155, 162, 163, 208,
      210, 215–18, 231
Volunteers in Service to America
   (VISTA), 17
Vorenberg, James, 8, 11–13

Walters, Vernon, 178
Ward, Lloyd, 229
Warren, Gerald L., 171
Warren Commission, 90
Washington, George, 151
Washington Daily News, 10
Washington Post, 3, 20, 33–35,
   91, 97, 122, 146, 195, 203,
   206
Washington Star, 55, 204
Watergate break-in and cover-up,
   1, 3, 5–6, 9–11, 19–25, 26–30,
   114, 158–61, 187

burglary investigation and trial,
   20–22, 26, 27, 37, 54, 158, 161,
   191
Dean's role in, 40–46, 53–54,
   68, 74, 132–33, 158–61, 177,
   188–92
Ehrlichman's role in, 45, 112–13,
   117, 158–61, 164
Gemstone plan, 28–30
Haldeman's role in, 4, 40, 41,
   45, 93, 107, 112–18, 158–59,
   164, 173, 177–78, 187–88, 197,
   234, 237
hush money demands, 22,
   37, 40, 46, 132–33, 141–42,
   147–48, 158–60, 177–78, 188,
   191, 194, 198, 234–35
indictments, 138–55, 156–61,
   168–69, 180–82
investigation into, *see* Watergate
   investigation
Magruder's role in, 26–38,
   42–43, 159, 187, 192–94
Mitchell's role in, 28–32, 34, 74,
   76, 158–61, 187, 194, 195
Nixon's role in, 3–4, 32, 40,
   44–46, 107–20, 129–38, 141–42,
   145–50, 153–54, 174–75, 178,
   188–91, 232–37
planning of break-in, 29–30, 33
trial, *see* Watergate trial
Watergate Five, 185
Watergate investigation, 1–5
   "accidentally erased" June 20,
      1972, tape, 1–5, 45, 79–81, 93,
      107–20, 121–33, 136–38, 173,
      236–37
   copies of documents, 5, 52–53,
      63
   Cox as special prosecutor, 8–9,
      22–25, 35, 46–49, 53–56, 61
   Dean and, 40–46, 53–54, 68, 74,
      132–33, 158, 161, 177

grand jury indictments, 138–44, 145–55, 156–61, 168–69, 180–82

Jaworski as special prosecutor, 87–89, 111, 133, 136, 139–44, 154, 165–70, 180–82, 185

leaks, 34–35, 91

Magruder and, 26–38

obstruction charges, 3, 9, 21, 29, 37, 94, 111, 133, 141, 158, 175, 185, 189

public opinion on, 3, 50–51, 66, 143

Road Map, 148–50, 156–57, 165

Saturday Night Massacre, 62–77, 87, 231

"smoking gun" tape, 177–79, 191

subpoenas for tapes, 3, 46–49, 70, 109, 118, 164–65, 169, 172, 175

tapes hearings, 1–5, 69–86, 93, 107–20, 121–38

transfer of tapes from White House to court, 70, 73–75

trial team, 14–25

Wine-Banks joins, 7–13

Woods testimony, 1–5, 78–81, 107–26, 183, 196, 36

Watergate Seven, 147–48, 156–61, 163, 176, 177

Watergate Task Force, 9–13, 208

reunions, 231

team of lawyers, 9–13, 14–25

Wine-Banks joins, 7–13

Wine-Banks resigns, 208

See also specific lawyers

Watergate trial, 163, 166, 181, 182, 184–201

Dean's testimony, 188–92

defense case, 195–98

jury selection, 184–85, 186

Magruder's testimony, 192–94

Neal's summation, 198–99

Nixon's absence from, 191

preparation for, 163, 175–76, 182–83

prosecution case, 186–94

sentencing, 204–5

tapes and, 188–91, 198

verdicts, 199–200

Wein, Itzak, 103

Wertheim, Mitzi, 214

West Wing, 83, 130, 205

White, Byron, 167

White House, 1

leaks, 9

logs and diaries, 45–46, 140

Nixon leaves, 180

tapes, *see* tapes, White House

Wilson, John, 184, 189

Wine, Bert, 7, 13, 57, 101–6, 220

Wine, Robin, 60, 101, 102, 105

Wine, Stevie, 101, 102, 105, 171

Wine, Sylvia, 7, 13, 57, 101–6, 220

Wine-Banks, Jill

as ABA executive director, 227–28

activism of, 66–67

affair with Kurt, 97–100, 106, 110, 155, 162, 208–9, 210, 218, 220, 231

after Watergate, 202–11

as Army general counsel, 212–21, 226, 227

childhood of, 101–6, 219

at Columbia Law, 8, 10–11, 57–59, 67

courtroom style of, 1–5, 78–81, 94–95, 112–26, 183, 184, 195, 221

Cox and, 25, 53

divorce from Ian, 217–18, 227

home break-in and phone tapped, 5–6, 124, 126, 206

as Illinois deputy attorney general, 222–23

Wine-Banks (*cont'd*)
    Jaworski and, 88, 92, 111, 126,
        142, 144, 154, 170, 185
    Jewish heritage of, 57, 101–6, 229
    joins trial team, 7–13
    Justice Department job, 8, 11–13
    marriage to Ian, 7, 13, 56–61,
        94–96, 100, 101, 106, 109–10,
        125, 149, 155, 162, 163, 208,
        210, 215–18, 231
    marriage to Michael, 221,
        223–24, 228, 230, 231
    Maytag job, 229
    Motorola job, 228–29
    as MSNBC legal analyst, 226–27,
        230
    physical appearance of, 5, 7, 33,
        63, 68, 94, 105–6
    post-Watergate law career,
        206–11, 212–24, 227–30
    press and, 5, 68, 108, 124–26,
        202–4, 226
    resignation from Watergate task
        force, 208
    retirement of, 230
    Road Map, 148–50
    sexism and, 27, 72, 77, 92,
        123–26, 184, 196–97, 213, 222,
        227, 229
    on television, 202–4, 207, 215,
        226–27, 230
    Watergate investigation, *see*
        Watergate investigation
    Watergate trial, 184–201, 221
    Woods cross-examined by, 1–5,
        78–81, 107–26, 183, 196, 236

Wine Volner, Jill, *see* Wine-Banks,
    Jill
Winning Workplaces, 230
women lawyers, 150–54, 173, 207
    sexist attitudes toward, 27,
        72, 77, 86, 92, 123–26, 184,
        196–97, 213, 222, 227, 229
Women of Watergate, The
    (Edmondson and Cohen), 153
Women's Army Corps, 214
Wong, Alfred, 77
Woods, Joe, 84
Woods, Rose Mary, 1–6, 76–86,
    233–38
    abandoned by Nixon, 4–5, 122,
        233
    after Watergate, 205–6, 233
    demonstration of "accidental
        erasure," 4–5, 120–23
    lifestyle of, 84–85, 135, 205–6
    loyalty to Nixon, 81–86, 110,
        117–19, 122, 131, 138, 179,
        205–6, 233–36
    role in tapes controversy, 1–5,
        45, 76–81, 93, 107–20, 121–38,
        183, 233–37
    "Stretch," 4, 121–23, 138
    testimony in Watergate case,
        1–5, 78–81, 107–26, 183, 196,
        236
Woodward, Bob, 3, 10, 146, 209,
    177, 234
World War II, 11, 57, 82, 88, 97, 214
Wright, Charles Alan, 69–70

Ziegler, Ron, 131

ABOUT THE AUTHOR

Jill Wine-Banks is an MSNBC legal analyst, appearing regularly on the network's prime-time and daytime shows. She began her career as an organized crime prosecutor at the US Department of Justice, which led to her selection as one of three assistant special prosecutors in the trial of President Richard Nixon's top aides for obstruction of justice in the Watergate scandal. She has also served as general counsel of the US Army, solicitor general and deputy attorney general of the state of Illinois, and chief operating officer of the American Bar Association. In each case, she was the first woman to hold the position. Following her legal career, Jill was an international business executive at Motorola and Maytag, the head of career and technical education for Chicago Public Schools under Arne Duncan, and a frequent speaker. A graduate of the University of Illinois and Columbia Law School, she lives in Chicago.